C000245883

Palgrave Studies in the History of Childhood

Series Editors
George Rousseau
University of Oxford, UK

Laurence Brockliss
University of Oxford, UK

Aims of the Series

Palgrave Studies in the History of Childhood is the first of its kind to historicise childhood in the English-speaking world; at present no historical series on children/childhood exists, despite burgeoning areas within Child Studies. The series aims to act both as a forum for publishing works in the history of childhood and a mechanism for consolidating the identity and attraction of the new discipline.

Editorial Board:
Matthew Grenby (Newcastle)
Colin Heywood (Nottingham)
Heather Montgomery (Open)
Hugh Morrison (Otago)
Anja Müller (Siegen, Germany)
Sïan Pooley (Magdalen, Oxford)
Patrick Joseph Ryan (King's University College at Western University, Canada)
Lucy Underwood (Warwick)
Karen Vallgårda (Copenhagen)

More information about this series at
http://www.palgrave.com/gp/series/14586

Jennifer Crane

Child Protection in England, 1960–2000

Expertise, Experience, and Emotion

palgrave
macmillan

Jennifer Crane
University of Warwick
Coventry, UK

Palgrave Studies in the History of Childhood
ISBN 978-3-319-94717-4   ISBN 978-3-319-94718-1 (eBook)
https://doi.org/10.1007/978-3-319-94718-1

Library of Congress Control Number: 2018948678

© The Editor(s) (if applicable) and The Author(s) 2018. This book is an open access publication.
Open Access This book is licensed under the terms of the Creative Commons Attribution 4.0 International License (http://creativecommons.org/licenses/by/4.0/), which permits use, sharing, adaptation, distribution and reproduction in any medium or format, as long as you give appropriate credit to the original author(s) and the source, provide a link to the Creative Commons license and indicate if changes were made.
The images or other third party material in this book are included in the book's Creative Commons license, unless indicated otherwise in a credit line to the material. If material is not included in the book's Creative Commons license and your intended use is not permitted by statutory regulation or exceeds the permitted use, you will need to obtain permission directly from the copyright holder.
The use of general descriptive names, registered names, trademarks, service marks, etc. in this publication does not imply, even in the absence of a specific statement, that such names are exempt from the relevant protective laws and regulations and therefore free for general use.
The publisher, the authors and the editors are safe to assume that the advice and information in this book are believed to be true and accurate at the date of publication. Neither the publisher nor the authors or the editors give a warranty, express or implied, with respect to the material contained herein or for any errors or omissions that may have been made. The publisher remains neutral with regard to jurisdictional claims in published maps and institutional affiliations.

Cover illustration © imageBROKER / Alamy Stock Photo

This Palgrave Macmillan imprint is published by the registered company Springer Nature Switzerland AG
The registered company address is: Gewerbestrasse 11, 6330 Cham, Switzerland

Acknowledgements

I am incredibly grateful to a variety of groups and individuals whose mentorship, wisdom, and generosity has made this research possible.

I am very grateful to the Wellcome Trust for their Doctoral Studentship [grant number WT099346MA], without which I could not have done the PhD on which this research is based. The Wellcome Trust also jointly awarded Eve Colpus and I a small grant [200420/Z/15/Z] to convene a witness seminar about '30 Years of ChildLine' in June 2016. By working closely with Eve, and by meeting with contemporary witnesses, I was able to enhance my thinking about this topic. I am also grateful to the Wellcome Trust for providing the funding to make this book open access, and to the organisation's open access team, and the library team at the University of Warwick, for guiding me through the mechanics of this process. I have also always found the Humanities and Social Sciences team at Wellcome incredibly helpful, enthusiastic, and generous with their time, and appreciate the training opportunities and peer-support networks they facilitate.

I am very grateful to present and former colleagues at the Centre for the History of Medicine, University of Warwick, where I have undertaken my Masters, PhD, and first postdoctoral project in the lovely 'Cultural History of the NHS' team, led by Roberta Bivins and Mathew Thomson and funded by the Wellcome Trust [104837/Z/14/Z]. My PhD supervisor, Mathew Thomson, has always been a generous reader of my work and inspiring colleague. I have also been particularly grateful for insightful comments, career advice, and support from Centre colleagues Roberta Bivins, Hilary Marland, Angela Davis, Jane Hand, Tom Bray, Margaret

Charleroy, Rachel Bennett, Andrew Burchell, Flo Swann, and Kate Mahoney. In addition, I have benefited immensely from the hard work, organisational skills, wisdom, and good humour of our Centre administrators, Sheilagh Holmes and Tracy Horton.

More broadly—and outside of Warwick—a number of wonderful scholars have been generous enough to read drafts of my chapters, and I would like to thank Laura King, Eve Colpus, Grace Huxford, Hannah Elizabeth, Sophie Rees, Jono Taylor, and Phil King in particular. I am also grateful to the anonymous reviewers of this book, whose comments were challenging and enriching, and to Heather Montgomery, who provided generous feedback on the full final manuscript. My viva was also a useful and productive experience, for which I thank my examiners Pat Thane and Roberta Bivins. I am also grateful to Pat Thane for inviting me to join the European University Institute network, *The Quest for Welfare and Democracy: Voluntary Associations, Families and the State, 1880s to present*. Being a part of this network, and hearing from incredible scholars at their events, has really helped me to hone the arguments of this book.

Many archivists have been incredibly helpful while I conducted my research, notably at the Bodleian Library, British Film Institute, British Library, Children's Society, Hall-Carpenter Archives at the London School of Economics, Institute of Education, Kidscape, Liverpool University Special Collections and Archives, Modern Records Centre, National Archives, and Wellcome Library. I am always thankful for their wisdom and kindness. The editors at Palgrave Macmillan, Emily Russell and Carmel Kennedy, have also been very helpful, informative, and efficient throughout the publishing process. I am also grateful for the thought-provoking guidance and advice from Palgrave's History of Childhood series editors, Laurence Brockliss and George Rousseau.

Some ideas and discussions in this book were initially tested out and featured in two journal articles, in slightly different forms—"The bones tell a story the child is too young or too frightened to 'tell': The Battered Child Syndrome in Post-war Britain and America", *Social History of Medicine*, 28 (4) (2015): 767–788 and 'Painful Times: The Emergence and Campaigning of Parents Against Injustice in 1980s and 1990s Britain', *Twentieth Century British History*, 26 (3) (2015): 450–476. Both articles were published Open Access under a Creative Commons CC-BY article, thanks to the Wellcome Trust, and I have reproduced and reinterpreted some thinking and archival work from these articles in this book under the terms of that licence. I am grateful to *Social History of Medicine* and *Twentieth Century British History* for giving me the opportunity to publish this work as an early career researcher, and to the peer reviewers of these articles for their thought-provoking and generous comments.

I am as ever immeasurably grateful for the lifelong support and love from my husband, David Bowkett, and my parents, Steve and Hazel Crane.

Contents

CHAPTER 1

Introduction

In July 2014, then Home Secretary Theresa May established an Independent Inquiry into Child Abuse to 'consider whether public bodies—and other, non-state, institutions—have taken seriously their duty of care to protect children from sexual abuse'.[1] After the establishment of this inquiry, May emphasised the need to involve adults who had themselves been abused in childhood, reiterating her desire to gain the 'confidence of survivors who must be at the heart of this process'.[2] From the outset, voluntary groups working in this area voiced discontent. The National Association for People Abused in Childhood stated in November 2014 that the inquiry was 'a farce' and a 'dead duck' and highlighted that they had not been contacted until December 2014—months after the inquiry began to take shape.[3] Survivor groups were critical of the appointments of Baroness Elizabeth Butler-Sloss and subsequently Dame Fiona Woolf to chair the inquiry, and also argued that the inquiry should be granted statutory powers, so that it could seize documents and compel witnesses to provide evidence.[4] Such critique proved relatively influential. In February 2015, the inquiry was reconstituted on a statutory footing, and Butler-Sloss and Woolf both stepped down, to be replaced in March 2015 by Justice Lowell Goddard.[5] Resigning from the Inquiry, Woolf stated that 'It's about the victims—their voices absolutely have to be heard—if I don't command their confidence, then I need to get out of the way.'[6] Within the new statutory inquiry, led from August 2016 by Professor

© The Author(s) 2018

J. Crane, *Child Protection in England, 1960–2000*, Palgrave Studies in the History of Childhood,
https://doi.org/10.1007/978-3-319-94718-1_1

Alexis Jay, focus on survivor testimony remained central. The inquiry included a Victim and Survivors' Consultative Panel and 'The Truth Project', which allowed any adult abused in childhood to share their experiences by phone, email, post, online, or in person.[7]

The furore over the inquiry demonstrated that politicians have recently felt the need to seek out the opinions of people who may be personally affected by legislation. This example also indicates that voluntary organisations have emerged seeking to represent and empower people who have been affected by shared experience. Today these entwined phenomena—the public discussion of experiences, the interest of policy-makers in consultation, the emergence of representative voluntary groups—may appear relatively unremarkable. However, this book argues that these trends developed in tandem since the 1960s and indeed demonstrates that the ability of public groups and communities to represent themselves in media discussions and in policy has been hard won and contested, depending on the opening and closing down of media, political, and professional interest, and rarely guaranteed.

This is particularly the case in the field of child protection, social and political understandings of which have rapidly developed over the late twentieth century, with the testimonies of children, concerned parents, and survivors themselves increasingly made public. By examining the interplay between the politics of experience, expertise, and emotion in this area, this book demonstrates that lines between 'public' and 'expert' opinion have become blurred, notably by the campaigning of small voluntary organisations, often led by individuals with direct personal experience of the issues they campaign around. These groups have challenged traditionally placed 'experts', such as physicians, social workers, solicitors, and policy-makers, and have mediated and reshaped the concerns of new identity constituencies. In doing so, the groups relied on collaboration with media to express their viewpoints. They were not always able to change policy or practice. Nonetheless, they contributed to a moment in which experience and emotion were becoming more politically and publicly visible and, to an extent, more influential. The campaigning of these groups has not been studied before, yet it has been significant in shaping definitions of child protection, responsibility, harm, and experience, in terms defined by children, parents, and survivors. Through campaigning, children, parents, and survivors have become agents in, and subjects of, rather than objects of, social policy—directly involved in changing child protection policy and practice, often in emotional and experiential terms guided by personal life narratives.

Child Protection in England

In understanding the emergence of recent concerns about child abuse, it is useful to take a long historical view. Looking back over the past 150 years shows that there have been several other peaks of concern about child abuse and maltreatment, expressed in different terms. However, the experiences and emotions of children, parents, and survivors came more prominently and publicly to the fore from the 1960s. A key point in the modern history of child abuse was the emergence of concerns around 'cruelty to children' in North America and Western Europe in the 1870s and 1880s, which provided a significant label with which to criticise the maltreatment of children.[8] In Britain, the *Prevention of Cruelty to, and Protection of, Children Act* (1889) criminalised cruelty against children, which was defined as the behaviour of a guardian who 'wilfully ill-treats, neglects, abandons, or exposes such child ... in a manner likely to cause such child unnecessary suffering, or injury to its health'.[9] Harry Hendrick has written that this act created a 'new interventionist relationship between parents and the state', because for the first time police were allowed to enter family homes to arrest parents for ill-treatment.[10] Many significant voluntary organisations were also established in the Victorian era—the National Society for the Prevention of Cruelty to Children (NSPCC) (1884), Dr Barnardos' Homes (1866), the Church of England Central Society for Providing Homes for Waifs and Strays (1881), and the Children's Home (1869).[11] George Behlmer has persuasively argued that the NSPCC in particular constructed a 'new moral vision' in this period, in which the interests of the child were placed above those of the parent.[12]

Perpetrators of child sexual abuse were not always punished in the Victorian period, despite emergent concerns often framed around 'cruelty to children'. Drawing on the records of 1146 sexual assault cases tried in Yorkshire and Middlesex between 1830 and 1910, Louise Jackson has demonstrated that even when cases of sexual abuse were brought to the courts, usually as 'indecent assault', 31 per cent of defendants were acquitted, and punishments were often very lenient.[13] Jackson writes that court members 'found it very difficult to believe that a man who was a father could ever have committed acts of brutality'.[14] At the same time, she also argues that 'Judges and juries were of the opinion that sexual abuse by a father ... was a particularly serious offence.'[15] Linda Pollock has studied newspaper reports around court cases between 1785 and 1860 and similarly argues that parents who abused their offspring were seen as 'unnatural', 'horrific', and 'barbaric'.[16]

Adrian Bingham, Lucy Delap, Louise Jackson, and Louise Settle have persuasively argued that the 1920s was another 'time of high visibility and concern over child sexual abuse', brought forward by the campaigning of newly enfranchised female voters and female Members of Parliament.[17] The historians explain that the 1925 Departmental Committee on Sexual Offences Against Young People made numerous proposals in this context, calling for: the abolishment of 'reasonable belief' that a girl was over the age of 16 as a legal defence; the provision of a separate waiting room for young witnesses; and an institutional response exceeding 'ignorance, carelessness and indifference'.[18] Again, however, such concerns did not necessarily lead to change, and these measures were not broadly implemented.[19] In general, the Committee assumed that 'experts'—professionals, politicians, policy-makers, lobbyists—would speak on behalf of victims and survivors, rather than inviting them to provide direct testimony, although three mothers from Edinburgh whose children had been abused did testify, criticising the police and criminal justice system.[20]

Later in the interwar period, concerns about child abuse faded once again. The reasons for the falling away of concerns in this period were multiple: voluntary sector focus was on reconstruction; the woman's movement in part fractured following the granting of universal suffrage; and the NSPCC became less campaign-oriented following administrative changes.[21] These reasons for the diminishing of concerns foregrounded many of the significant elements that later revived public, media, and political interest in child protection from the mid-1960s until 2000. Professional interests, as in earlier periods, remained significant. Notably, the first chapter of this book examines how paediatricians and radiologists shaped early medical debates about 'the battered child syndrome' from the 1940s. These clinicians worked through international networks as concerns about child abuse developed across Western Europe, North America, Australia, and New Zealand in the late twentieth century.[22] Likewise, groups of parents and survivors mobilised both in Britain and in America over this period; mediating, criticising, and reshaping professional debate.[23] While paying brief attention to these international relationships, the book focuses primarily on how such debates were realised in distinctly British contexts, with a particular focus on England. In the English setting, cultural visions of family privacy and the 'stiff upper lip', as well as distinct contexts of state welfare provision, inflected discussion.[24]

As in the 1920s, the work of feminists was also significant in raising public and political awareness of child abuse in the late twentieth century, and the second-wave feminist movement drew public attention to family violence and established shelters to care for affected women and children. Notably, second-wave feminists also highlighted the significance of focusing on emotion and experience as forms of expertise, particularly by emphasising the importance of listening to women's stories and making the personal political. In the documentary *Scream Quietly or the Neighbours Will Hear* (1974), based on Erin Pizzey's ground breaking book, women housed at Chiswick Women's Aid refuge spoke openly about their experiences of abuse, their fears, the effects on their confidence, and the responses of their children.[25] Later accounts—for example, by Louise Armstrong—continued to explore and make public childhood experiences of abuse, and to encourage others to do the same.[26] While many second-wave feminists sought to entwine campaigning around violence against women and children, others acknowledged that social policy and media coverage typically treated these issues separately.[27] Nonetheless, while focusing on campaigning led by children, concerned parents, and survivors, this book also traces moments in which this campaigning interacted with feminist work, particularly in terms of criticising structural inequalities and professional hierarchies.

While professional and feminist voices remained important in post-1960s debates, the concern of the late twentieth century was also distinctive in two key ways, both of which are the focus of this book. First, this period was distinctive in the extent to which direct campaigning by children, parents, and survivors became important. The new focus on the experiences and emotions of those affected by child abuse extended beyond feminist activism alone, and indeed campaign groups in this area were established by a variety of families and individuals, many of whom had no connections with the feminist movement. Campaigners acted in collaboration and tension with the work of long-standing professions—relying on statutory agencies but also providing self-help groups, for example. Importantly, children, parents, and survivors both relied on and criticised the ability of professional categorisations to explain their personal experiences.[28] The term 'survivor'—which this book uses to echo contemporary accounts—has been adopted by voluntary groups. While such groups, echoing the psychiatric survivor movement, used the term to capture strength and resilience, they also argued that it did not capture the full complexity of lived experience.[29]

The ability of these voluntary groups to offer such critique and to construct new networks was entwined with the second key development of the post-1960s moment: the increasing interest of media outlets in representing the experiences and emotions of children, parents, and survivors. Newspapers have a long history of producing exposes around child protection, dating back to the report 'The Maiden Tribute of Modern Babylon' published in the *Pall Mall Gazette* in 1885.[30] Yet media interest in child protection reached new levels from 1960. Focus was often on specific cases, such as that of Maria Colwell, a seven-year-old who was beaten and starved to death by her stepfather in 1973, and the Cleveland scandal of 1987, in which two Middlesbrough doctors removed 121 children from their parents during routine paediatric check-ups, citing medical evidence of sexual abuse.[31] Media explorations became of great length and detail, presented in sensationalist terms, looking to make inner dynamics of family life or children's experiences public.

Child Protection in England thus focuses on activism by or on behalf of children, parents, and survivors, often enacted in collaboration with new media and through voluntary organisations. The book demonstrates that this activism has been influential in shaping public responses to child protection, and in mediating and reshaping the work of clinicians, social work, and policy—which have been central to previous historical accounts. This activism—taken 'from below'—has represented a broader form of challenge to long-standing professions, and to thinking about how and why expertise has been constructed and determined in late twentieth-century Britain. The period on which this book focuses, from 1960 until 2000, was one in which medical, social, and political conceptions of child protection shifted relatively rapidly. Broadly, over this period, conceptions of abuse shifted from being visualised as a 'medical' to a 'social problem'; from focus on the family home to 'stranger danger' and back to the family; and in terms of broadening in focus from the physical to the sexual to the emotional.[32] Accounts offered by children, parents, and survivors themselves, however, and increased attention paid to their emotions and experiences, shaped and added complexity to these changes. Children, parents, and survivors became 'expert' because of their ability to represent, channel, construct, and argue for the validity of experiential and emotional expertise—forms of knowledge which rapidly emerged and became public, and which are crucial to understanding the changing social, cultural, and political contexts of late twentieth-century Britain.

Expertise, Experience, Emotion

Three key concepts shaped the nature of concerns about child protection in the post-1960s context: expertise, experience, and emotion. This book is not a history of how people *felt* experiences or emotions over this period, no archives permit us to 'speak for' the people involved.[33] Instead, it is a history of the politics of experiences and emotions *as* expertise. The book assesses how increasing public and political spaces emerged in which personal experiences and emotions could be heard and indeed were expected to be performed in specific ways, bound by long-standing structural and professional hierarchies. As Joan Scott has argued, categories of experience and identity are not 'ahistorical' or 'fixed entities', but rather 'historical events in need of explanation'.[34] Looking at how ideas about experience and identity are produced, and the politics underlying this construction, can reveal the 'workings of the ideological system itself'.[35] As Stuart Hall tells us, 'identities are constructed within, not outside, discourse' and 'produced in specific historical and institutional sites within specific discursive formations and practices, by specific enunciative strategies'.[36]

This book therefore takes emotional, personal, political, and professional experience and expertise as ideas in flux, but whose interaction and importance to certain groups reveals shifting relations of power, authority, and hierarchy. Specifically, the primary interest of this book is in the interactions between expertise, experience, and emotion—how have these different concepts become visible and influential on the public stage over the late twentieth century? Which groups have been responsible for presenting and representing emotion and experience—small campaign groups or media, for example? To what extent has experience as a form of expertise displaced or been entwined with traditional sources of authority? This examination follows Selina Todd's call for historians to pay attention to the complex relationships between discourse and experience in post-war England. To understand the significance of social and political theories, and of debates in press and academia, we must also analyse who 'negotiated, modified and implemented' these ideas.[37]

In part, an expertise grounded in experience was not entirely new to the post-1960s moment. Angela Davis has argued that the belief that 'women learnt how to mother in the home' was prevalent in the middle decades of the twentieth century, drawn from psychoanalysis, sociology, and social learning theory.[38] The idea of experience as foregrounding expertise and authority was likely lived and discussed in daily life before this period.

What was new from the post-1960s moment, however, was the reframing of these ideas in individualist, public, and emotional terms: with individual people making personal and previously private experiences public and powerful. These changes were bound up with—and are significant for further tracing—a series of broader shifts in terms of identity, confession, and expertise. For Stuart Hall, the conditions of change in late modernity led to a 'fracturing' of identity. With the 'erosion' of the 'master identity' of class, and the development of New Social Movements, publics defined themselves in line with a series of new 'competing and dislocating identifications'.[39] Building on developments in the interwar period, from the mid-twentieth century a 'confessional culture' also emerged, visible in the popularity of agony aunts, the rise of memoirs, attendance at marriage guidance counselling, and increasing media coverage of family affairs.[40] While notions of expertise have shifted throughout time—for example, in relation to the emergence of the industrial society—Joe Moran has likewise discussed how new breeds of 'expert' emerged in the late twentieth-century period too. Not least, Margaret Thatcher's suspicion of public sector working drove a new focus on private sector expertise—for instance, as manifested by management consultants.[41]

There were hence a series of changes in the post-war period and from the 1960s specifically whereby discussions of experience and emotion became increasingly *visible*. Voluntary groups and individuals capitalised on and subverted media, political, and professional interest in experience and emotion, mobilising descriptions of these states to seek out change, as well as to form new social communities and identity groups. Looking at these processes, and particularly looking from the perspective of children, parents, survivors and voluntary groups, reveals broader structural and societal shifts in thinking about authority, identity, legitimacy over time. Of course, the work of children, parents, and survivors was to be coded, limited, and inflected by long-standing power structures. Looking at the limitations of these groups' influence, indeed, reveals how old concerns about class and gender continued to shape the new politics of experience.[42] Notably, and drawing on a long Western philosophical tradition in which women have been associated with 'emotion' and men with 'reason', gender framed the perception and portrayal of experiential and emotional expertise throughout the late twentieth century.[43] Chapter 2 traces how predominately male paediatric radiologists described their feelings of 'rage', 'disgust', and 'anger' about child abuse. For primarily female social workers operating at the same time, and for mothers campaigning through the 1970s, 1980s, and 1990s, media and personal accounts emphasised 'sadness', 'guilt', and 'fear'.

Thus, the ability of children, parents, and survivors to challenge overarching accounts of child protection has been limited not only by personal resource and professional attention, but also by a series of shifting—yet long-standing—cultural contexts and attitudes about *who* had the right to define their experiences and emotions in their own terms. These were debates about whose experiences were 'expert' and whose were not. Voluntary groups operating in this terse context analysed and criticised the construction of authority, power, and expertise. Parent campaign groups, studied in Chap. 6, advised mothers to tactically restrict their displays of emotion. Survivor groups meanwhile, described in Chap. 8, used powerful personal accounts of emotion and experience to demonstrate that abuse was an issue which affected all genders, classes, races, and ethnicities, and which was perpetrated in family, institutional, and community settings. These parent and survivor groups recognised, and sought to reframe, prevailing narratives about child protection and expertise.

In looking at the interactions between experience, emotion, and expertise, this book contends that personal emotion and experience, as mediated and represented by small voluntary organisations, became important and influential forms of expertise in the late twentieth century. Small organisations challenged, adopted, and subverted the work of long-standing professions in child protection, particularly in medicine, social work, and policy, and shaped the creation of policy, the form of the voluntary sector, and public and media understandings of child abuse, childhood, and family. Public challenges to professional expertise are evident in a variety of ways throughout this book—on the everyday level, by individual parents ignoring 'professional' advice about childcare, as well as in highly visible protests and demonstrations. Small voluntary groups have also challenged any division between 'professional' and experiential or emotional expertise: many leaders of such groups held multiple sources of authority, and they also encouraged practitioners to discuss their personal and family lives.

In this book, analysis of expertise, experience, and emotion will help to explain the post-1960s shift in discussions about child protection, whereby discussions became public, and different voices became privileged, when expressed in certain forms. This analysis will act as an example of how the nature of policy and politics shifted more generally in this era. In particular, the book examines how voluntary groups fundamentally challenged a conceptual and lived gap between expert and public thinking; a gap identified as a key post-war phenomenon by researchers in policy and sociology, as well as in contemporary media discourse around the public 'losing faith in experts'.[44] Voluntary groups, more than ever before, were the arbiters of experience, emotion, and expertise, and shaped a new late twentieth-century politics where experiential and emotional expertise held moral sway.

Voluntary Action and Public Participation

Following the work of, among others, Virginia Berridge, Alex Mold, Pat Thane, Tanya Evans, and Chris Moores, this book looks in depth at a series of case studies of small voluntary organisations in order to 'make sense' of this sector.[45] Many voluntary organisations traced in this book had less than ten members of staff and earned, through public donations, grants, and sometimes commercial work, in the tens, hundreds, or thousands of pounds each year. This marked each of these charities as significantly smaller than, for example, the Children's Society, NSPCC, and Action for Children, which raised millions of pounds and employed hundreds or thousands of members of staff over the same time period.[46] Notably, and despite their small size, the groups studied in this book attained significant influence in policy, public, and media debate, working with and challenging the work of long-standing professions, charities, and statutory agencies.

Each voluntary group studied in this book was different in terms of size, goal, and method, but each was constructed looking to provide services or representation for children, parents, or adults affected by abuse as children. There has been 'no one unified lobby group' that has called for change on behalf of children, parents, or survivors, but, rather, multiple local and national groups formed in specific ideological and cultural contexts over time and space.[47] Studying the array of groups in this book takes examination of voluntarism and voluntary organisations into new terrain. The book makes deep examination of how and when the subjects of policy have become involved in its creation and critique, and of the new challenges made to expertise by experience.

While the book studies a broad variety of groups and organisations, three coherent narratives are presented. The first is a reappraisal of the influences over child protection policy in the late twentieth century. Analyses led by academics of social work and media have provided rich exploration of how 'scandals' and 'moral panics' have driven policy and practice reform.[48] Scholars of social policy and history have charted the content of changing child protection policy, and discussed the myriad interactions between research evidence, policy change, and shifts in practice.[49] What have not yet been subjected to academic attention, however, are the forms of influence wielded by people themselves involved in these debates—children, concerned parents, and survivors. The influence of these individuals was limited, and indeed at times children and parents were unable to report abuse or to seek adequate redress from statutory services. Nonetheless, this book explores shifting moments in which small voluntary groups working in this area, and drawing on experiential and emotional expertise, did influence change, alongside and in collaboration and conflict with media and social policy-makers.

The second argument is that small voluntary organisations, sometimes with as few as ten members, could play a significant role in representing, shaping, and mediating discussions of experience, emotion, and expertise in late twentieth-century Britain. In part, these organisations held significant sway throughout the public sphere because of their collaborations with media.[50] The case studies that follow demonstrate how individual journalists built strong connections with particular voluntary sector leaders, and how media and voluntary groups used their highly public platforms in tandem, looking to reflect but also to shape popular morality. Using media materials in conjunction with the available archives from voluntary groups demonstrates that voluntary leaders were by no means naïve partners in working with newspapers and television. Rather, voluntary leaders drew on their own personal and professional skillsets to navigate media partnerships, and to advise their broader memberships about driving press agendas. Drawing on analysis by Peter Bailey about how respectability has been a 'choice of role', rather than a 'universal normative mode', the book examines how voluntary leaders displayed respectability, ordinariness, and gendered emotion to garner media attention.[51]

Child Protection in England's third contribution to the history of voluntarism is to assess how voluntary organisations have become key mediators of expertise, experience, and emotion. While forms of public participation and voluntary action have long histories, encompassing traditions of mutual aid, self-help, philanthropy, and early charitable trusts dating back to at least the sixteenth century, historians and sociologists have also identified distinct forms of activism which emerged in the post-war period.[52] From the 1960s and 1970s, fuelled by progressive Labour

Party legislation, groups of people who were previously criminalised, persecuted, or subject to philanthropic intervention 'began organising and speaking for themselves as never before', demanding a 'voice', 'equal rights', 'representation', and 'empowerment'.[53] Sociologists have also turned their attention towards these groups, developing New Social Movement theory in the 1980s and 1990s.[54]

Long-standing traditions of self-help remained important from 1945 also, for example, in playgroups, support groups for single mothers, and therapeutic communities for drug users.[55] Matthew Hilton, James McKay, Nicholas Crowson, and Jean-François Mouhot have described the emergence of large and highly professionalised 'non-governmental organisations (NGOs)' in the post-war period, which in part replaced the active membership of political parties, trade unions, and churches. Instead, members of the public often supported NGOs at 'arms-length', through donations.[56] Reflecting and facilitating the development of all of the above groups, political rhetoric around 'consultation', 'listening', and 'public involvement' also developed substantially in the late twentieth century.[57]

This book looks closely at a variety of voluntary organisations which have—to varying degrees—features of self-help, social movements, and NGOs, and which also emerged in a post-war and indeed post-1960s moment. Notably, the organisations which I study often acted 'professionally', conducting research and lobbying in a manner akin to large NGOs and professional unions, and yet also at the same time challenged long-standing professions and large-scale charities, seeking to directly address the issues of where expertise and power should lie in modern Britain. Further, these groups often held experiential knowledge, and many were formed by the communities they sought to represent. The book moves beyond categorisation and takes these groups on their own terms. In doing so, it demonstrates that divides between 'experiential' and 'professional' expertise were being challenged in late twentieth-century Britain. What is particularly notable about the voluntary organisations in this book is their small size. Representing experiential and emotional expertise was difficult—not all children, parents, or survivors wanted to discuss their experiences publicly. In this context, relatively small groups who could make claim to represent children, parents, and survivors became influential. Nonetheless, by the 1990s and 2000s, Chaps. 6 and 7 trace how professions and larger charities began to fight back against the development of experiential expertise, and to challenge the representativeness and utility of these small voluntary groups. The new politics of expertise, experience, and emotion has not yet been fully played out, and the media has—as we shall see—also shown growing interest in portraying divides between small voluntary groups, as well as their common agendas.

Histories of Childhood and Families

While histories of child welfare and health are often separate from those of child protection, this book seeks to ally the two fields.[58] Indeed, the issue of child protection has affected all children, parents, and families, not just those affected by abuse. Children's education has been changed by child protection classes; communities have reshaped children's curfews and the policing of individuals deemed 'suspicious'; parents have shaped their child-rearing styles and ambitions responsively. Importantly, the ability or inability of maltreated children to speak out cannot be separated from the broader social position of all children whose voices have not always been listened to in private or public. This book thus offers a history of childhood and family as well as a history of child protection. Moreover, it is a history of how public and private spaces have opened up over the late twentieth century for children and parents to discuss their experiences and emotions and, in doing so, to become 'expert'.

This history—a history of the politics of childhood—traces how the re-emergence of anxieties about child protection strengthened paternalist debate, for example among paediatric radiologists, and also the construction of a universalist model of childhood vulnerability, characterised around an ageless, classless, genderless 'child'. However, the book also traces the development of new spaces for children to defy professional and parental authority, and to themselves develop, exert, and challenge forms of expertise. In this thinking, the book uses a vision of childhood agency developed in new scholarship by Mona Gleason and Harry Hendrick. These scholars have developed a nuanced account of how children have acted as agents in dealing with their everyday lives, and indeed also of how their actions were at times exercised in partnership with adults, or in support of existing cultural and educational systems, as well as in overt resistance.[59] In taking such an approach to children's actions, this book challenges previous influential historical and sociological accounts which emphasise childhood powerlessness, and the significance of adult definitions of childhood in building nation states and shaping children's lives.[60]

Child Protection in England thus provides a useful addition to scholarship on childhood resistance and disobedience over time, emphasising that childhood expertise has been enacted, contested, and changed through everyday actions, for example by children using child protection education from school settings to defy and challenge their parents.[61] This type of everyday resistance is as important as visible types of disobedience—such as marches and strikes from school—and speaks to how overarching ideas about expertise and authority have shaped and reshaped daily life. Likewise, in the late twentieth century parents have manifested visible forms of political action, for instance, and as this book will trace, forming campaign groups, creating petitions, and becoming political advisors to governments, particularly in the New Labour administrations. However, parents have also exercised expertise in their daily lives, notably in terms of negotiating new child protection education programmes in the home, calling—and organising—parental helplines, and self-referring themselves to parenting classes. This book therefore considers a range of forms of 'political' action and activism performed and enacted by children, parents, and survivors in daily life and in political and public spaces. In doing so, the book demonstrates that children, parents, and survivors have adopted, appropriated, and rejected the shifting politics of child protection. More broadly, these actors have constructed, and worked within, new political spaces of late twentieth-century Britain—notably using and building new media interest in family life and new fora for public consultation by politicians. The political arena, and spaces for political action, have been broad, and have been mediated and shaped by small voluntary groups, often around experience.

In addition to thinking about the active political roles of children and parents, this book also seeks to trace the hopes placed on, and expertise manifested within, the family. Importantly, in terms of child protection the family is both a protective space—in which children have acted in partnership with parents and carers to change ideas of, or to learn about, child protection—and yet it is also a potentially dangerous arena. Over the late twentieth century, in the 1960s and subsequently again from the 1980s, family members were increasingly recognised as the primary source of violence against children. Social policy reflected these tensions: the *Children Acts* of 1948, 1975, and 1989 sought, in various ways, to: extend state welfare provisions, understand the interests of the child, maintain 'family life', and promote 'parental responsibility'.[62] In this context, debates about child protection became a particularly terse fora for conflicts about how family life was and should be lived. Questions about the policies and practices of child protection were used—as we see throughout this book—by conservative and progressive commentators alike seeking to further broader agendas relating to, for example, abortion, maternity leave, adoption, and moral visions of permissiveness and decline.

This book therefore adds to existing rich texts on histories of institutional abuse by focusing primarily on the politics of family life.[63] Indeed, uniquely this book emphasises that children, parents, and survivors were not only objects of child protection policy—used by policy-makers in broader debates about family life—but also subjects and agents. The lives of children, parents, and survivors were changed by child protection policy and, furthermore, campaigning for and by *families* actively intervened within political and media discussion. From the 1960s, Parents Anonymous groups were formed and made representations to Parliament looking to add complexity to visions of 'normal family life'. In the 1970s and 1980s, the New Right and Thatcher governments positioned the private sphere of the family as the primary organiser of social life, above the state, local government, and teaching and social work professions.[64] Campaign groups led by parents actively contested these visions, demanding further state resources and challenging individualist models of responsibility for child protection. Tracing such activism, this book demonstrates that 'the family' has not only been a proxy for political and moral anxieties in the late twentieth century, but that children, parents, survivors, and families have also challenged and changed ideas about family life and child protection.

Chapter Outline

This book traces both the re-emergence of concerns about child protection in Britain in the post-war period, and also the ways in which children, parents, and survivors shaped and mediated policy and practice in this area. Chapter 2 sets the scene for this examination. Exploring the 1940s, 1950s, and 1960s, the period in which child abuse came anew to public and political attention, it emphasises that children, parents, and survivors were rarely consulted or empowered in child protection discussion. Rather, paediatric radiologists, social psychologists, and the NSPCC dominated early debates. Debates were constructed transnationally—particularly between Britain and America—and looked to create policy *for* children, and which would categorise and understand the psychological motivations of parents. Debate was not unsympathetic towards children or parents, and indeed a level of paternalist concern about child welfare underlay later collaborative efforts between children, parents, psychologists, and charities.

Indeed, the remainder of the book explores in turn how children, parents, and survivors mobilised, in a variety of ways, looking to use their personal experiences to gain expertise, and to reshape public debates about child protection. Chapters 3 and 4 assess growing interest, particularly through the 1970s and 1980s, in consulting with children. Chapter 3 considers how public inquiries, charities, helplines, and media constructed new spaces to discuss and access children's experiences and emotions in public. Meanwhile, Chap. 4 analyses how small charities developed child protection education which, when enacted in schools and family homes, would empower children to act as experts, and to think critically about bodily autonomy, freedom, and consent. While children were to an extent made 'expert' by this work, adults remained mediators of child expertise. The structural barrier of age, often compounded by inequalities related to race, ethnicity, class, and gender, meant that not all children could share their experiences or expertise in public or private. While interest in experiential expertise—which could be inculcated, as well as accessed—thus grew over this period, these chapters therefore demonstrate clear limitations to this story.

Considering the same timeframe, Chaps. 5 and 6 address how and when parents sought to exert influence over child protection practice and policy. Chapter 5 analyses the significance of collective action by parents, which emerged from the 1960s in collaboration with NSPCC and in the establishment of individual self-help groups. These forms of collective action, as well as support groups established by and for parents falsely accused of abuse from the 1980s, added complexity to public policy conceptions of family life. Chapter 6 examines the partnerships formed between media and parent campaigners, and the gendered representations of mothers. In doing so, it emphasises a shift towards focus on individual parent campaigners as representatives, particularly under New Labour governments. Hence, these chapters begin to show the potential power which experiential and emotional expertise exerted in the late twentieth century. While showing how ideas of gender, in particular, limited the influence of parents, the chapters also argue that certain parent campaigners were able to critically navigate and reshape press and political interest.

Chapter 7 traces the realisation of experiential and emotional expertise in the 1990s and 2000s but also growing challenges which small representative voluntary groups began to face. The chapter discusses cases in which adults who had been affected by childhood abuse—survivors—increasingly discussed their childhood experiences, notably through letters to agony aunts, literature, and campaigning. Representatives from survivor groups criticised medical, social work, and legal professionals in complex ways which wove together historical and present analysis and which explored the interrelationships between childhood memories and adult experiences. While these groups were influential, their influence was also at times limited by political will, resources, and structural challenges. Further exploring developments visible in Chap. 6, this chapter also charts how professions and media began to challenge the moral authority of experiential experts in the 1990s and particularly from the 2000s, and to reassert the primacy and utility of evidence constructed by medicine, social work, policy, and law.

By taking a series of case studies from 1960 until 2000, *Child Protection in England* traces a shift in terms of media and public policy focus in child protection: from focus on consultation with clinicians, social workers, and established professions towards seeking out testimony from children, concerned parents and, in more recent years, survivors. The retrieval of experience became formally and informally ingrained in policy construction over the late twentieth century. Initially, in the 1960s and 1970s, the campaign groups studied in this book were consulted through select committees, or heard via media representation. From the 1980s and 1990s, the media remained important. However, successive governments and public inquiries also appointed voluntary leaders as individual experts.

While voluntary groups faced challenges relating to representativeness, tokenism, and the significance of experience, making children, parents, and survivors central actors in our histories provides rich insight into a new politics which emerged in late twentieth-century Britain. Definitions of child abuse and child protection were not only driven by media and social policy debate, but also by testimonies about experiences and emotions. Ideas about—and claims to represent—experience and emotion became publicly visible, bestowed expertise, and acted as disruptive forces between 1960 and 2000. Even very small voluntary groups were able to mobilise experiential and emotional expertise, to create and enter new political and media spaces, and to mount new challenges to professional authority. This analysis, therefore, places expertise, experience, and emotion as key themes in the history of modern Britain. It argues that historians can—and indeed must—trace the work conducted by individuals and families, often through small voluntary groups, to understand changing social, cultural, and political terrains. Finally—and as discussed in its conclusion—this book provides context for ongoing debates around historical child abuse: tracing shifting conceptions of child protection, and exploring the barriers faced by children, parents, and survivors in discussing and disclosing their experiences.

Notes

1. 'Written statement to Parliament: Child sexual abuse (Woolf Inquiry)', *Gov.uk*, 21 October 2014 <https://www.gov.uk/government/speeches/child-sexual-abuse-woolf-inquiry> (2 May 2015).
2. Sandra Laville, 'Child abuse survivors push Theresa May to save independent inquiry', *Guardian*, 14 January 2015 <http://www.theguardian.com/politics/2015/jan/14/child-abuse-survivors-theresa-may-inquiry>; Martyn Brown, 'Theresa May says sorry to victims for child abuse inquiry shambles', *Express*, 4 November 2014 <http://www.express.co.uk/news/uk/531088/Theresa-May-apology-child-abuse-victims-inquiry-shambles> (2 May 2015).
3. Jamie Doward and Daniel Boffey, 'Child abuse survivors tell Theresa May: inquiry must have full force of law', *Guardian*, 1 November 2014 <http://www.theguardian.com/society/2014/nov/01/child-abuse-theresa-may-inquiry-fiona-woolf> (2 May 2015); 'Abuse inquiry: Fiona Woolf is 'unsuitable' head, groups say', *BBC News*, 31 October 2014 <http://www.bbc.co.uk/news/uk-politics-29844612> (2 May 2015).
4. For full discussion of the series of events, see: Tim Jarrett, *The Independent Inquiry into Child Sexual Abuse and background*, House of Commons Library Briefing Paper, No. 07040, 11 August 2016.
5. 'Theresa May 'sorry' for two abuse inquiry resignations', *BBC News*, 3 November 2014 <http://www.bbc.co.uk/news/uk-29876263> (2 May 2015).
6. Dominic Casciana, 'Analysis: An inquiry doomed to fail?', *BBC News*, 31 October 2014 <http://www.bbc.co.uk/news/uk-29856114> (2 May 2015).
7. Jarrett, *The Independent Inquiry*, 10–12.
8. See: George Behlmer, *Child Abuse and Moral Reform in England, 1970–1908*, (California: Stanford University Press, 1982); Louise Jackson, *Child Sexual Abuse in Victorian England* (London: Routledge, 2000); Harry Hendrick, *Child Welfare: Historical Dimensions, Contemporary Debate* (Bristol: Policy Press, 2003), 23–40; Harry Ferguson, 'Cleveland in History: The Abused Child and Child Protection, 1880–1914', in Roger Cooter (ed.) *In the Name of the Child: Health and Welfare, 1880–1940* (London: Routledge, 1992), 146–173.
9. HM Government, *Prevention of Cruelty to, and Protection of, Children Act 1889* (London, 1889), 1.
10. Hendrick, *Child Welfare: Historical Dimensions, Contemporary Debate*, 28.
11. See: Behlmer, *Child Abuse and Moral Reform in England*; Terry Philpot, *NCH: Action for Children: The Story of Britain's Foremost Children's Charity* (Oxford: Lion Books, 1994); Winston Fletcher, *Keeping the Vision*

Alive: The Story of Barnardo's 1905–2005 (Essex: Barnardos, 2005); Dennis Burnier-Smith, *Thomas John Barnardo, His Life, Homes and Orphanages: A Short History* (Milton Keynes: AuthorHouseUK, 2010).

12. Behlmer, *Child Abuse and Moral Reform in England*, 16.
13. Jackson, *Child Sexual Abuse in Victorian England*, 18–23, 107.
14. Ibid., 126.
15. Ibid., 126.
16. Linda Pollock, *Forgotten Children: Parent-child relations from 1500 to 1900* (Cambridge: Cambridge University Press, 1983), 93.
17. Adrian Bingham, Lucy Delap, Louise Jackson and Louise Settle, 'Historical child sexual abuse in England and Wales: the role of historians', *History of Education*, 45 no, 4 (2016): 414, 427; Adrian Bingham, Lucy Delap, Louise Jackson, Louise Settle, 'These outrages are going on more than people know', *History & Policy*, 26 February 2015 <http://www.historyandpolicy.org/opinion-articles/articles/these-outrages-are-going-on-more-than-people-know> (6 June 2015). See also: Lucy Bland, *Banishing the Beast: Feminism, Sex and Morality* (2nd edition, London: Tauris Parke Paperbacks, 2001), 252–254.
18. Ibid.
19. Ibid.
20. Bingham, Delap, Jackson and Settle, 'Historical child sexual abuse in England and Wales', 421.
21. Parton, *The Politics of Child Protection*, 21.
22. Pierre E. Ferrier, 'Foreword—Proceedings of the 1976 International Congress on Child Abuse and Neglect—Geneva, W. H.O.—September 20–22', *Child Abuse & Neglect*, 1 (1977): iii–iv.
23. For discussion of parent advocacy groups mobilising against false accusations of abuse in the American context, see: Gary Alan Fine, 'Public Narration and Group Culture: Discerning Discourse in Social Movements', Hank Johnston and Bert Klandermans (eds) *Social Movements and Culture* (Minnesota: University of Minnesota Press, 1995), 138; Lela Costin, Howard Jacob Karger, and David Stoez, *The Politics of Child Abuse in America* (New York: Oxford University Press, 1996), 35. For discussion of survivor groups in the American context, and interviews with activists, see: Nancy Whittier, *The Politics of Child Sexual Abuse: Emotions, Social Movements and the State* (Oxford: Oxford University Press, 2009).
24. An interest in how child protection is shaped by the National Health Service and by social services, in contrast to the American systems, was expressed by Labour Member of Parliament Merlyn Rees in 1969. Rees suggested that the American doctor held a 'different contractual relationship with his patient', though he also emphasised that he did not have the full information available to understand and probe these national contextual differences (Hansard, House of Commons, Fifth Series, 25 July 1969, Vol. 787 col. 2315).

25. *Scream Quietly of the Neighbours Will Hear* (1974), dir. Michael Whyte, BFI Screen Online <https://player.bfi.org.uk/free/film/watch-scream-quietly-or-the-neighbours-will-hear-1974-online> (29 January 2018).
26. Louise Armstrong, *Kiss Daddy Goodnight: A Speak-Out on Incest* (New York: Simon & Schuster, 1978).
27. Positioning the fight against the sexual abuse of children as 'an integral part' of the feminist struggle: Romi Bowen and Angela Hamblin, 'Sexual Abuse of Children', *Spare Rib*, May 1981, Issue 106. Questioning the extent to which the causes of violence against women and children had been linked in media and political work: Jan Pahl, 'Preface', Alex Saunders, *"It hurts me too": Children's experiences of domestic violence and refuge life* (1995), iii; Maureen O'Hara, 'After Cleveland', *Spare Rib*, August 1989, Issue 204. Point also made by interviewer in: Maureen O'Hara, 'Marietta Higgs—In Her Own Words', *Spare Rib*, Issue 207, November 1989, 7.
28. For example, studies by ChildLine have demonstrated that children rarely used the definitions created by adults, such as the term 'domestic violence', but rather described abuse in their own ways. See: Carole Epstein and Gill Keep, 'What Children Tell ChildLine about Domestic Violence', in Alex Saunders, *"It hurts me too": Children's experiences of domestic violence and refuge life* (1995), 44.
29. Voluntary groups using this term in their titles include: Survivors Helping Each Other, Phoenix Survivors, Survivors Swindon, Survivors UK, and The Survivors Trust.

    See also: Jennifer Dunn, '"Victims" and "Survivors": Emerging Vocabularies of Motive for "Battered Women Who Stay', *Sociological Inquiry*, 75 (2005): 3; Michele Crossley and Nick Crossley, '"Patient" voices, social movements and the habitus; how psychiatric survivors "speak out"', *Social Science and Medicine*, 52 (2001): 1477–1489. Raising a critical challenge for the term 'survivor': Keenan, *Broken* (London: Hodder Paperbacks, 2008), back cover; 'Can you get over child abuse?', *Daily Mail*, 29 April 1998, 59.
30. Deborah Gorham, 'The "Maiden Tribute of Modern Babylon" Re-Examined: Child Prostitution and the Idea of Childhood in Late-Victorian England', *Victorian Studies*, 21 (1978): 353–379.
31. To read more on the Maria Colwell case from a social work and social policy perspective see: Nigel Parton, *The Politics of Child Abuse* (Basingstoke: Palgrave Macmillan, 1985), Chapter Four; Nigel Parton, 'The Natural History of Child Abuse: A Study in Social Problem Definition', *British Journal of Social Work*, 9 (1979): 431–451; Ian Butler and Mark Drakeford, *Scandal, Social Policy and Social Welfare* (Bristol: Policy Press, 2006), 76–102; Ian Butler and Mark Drakeford, *Social Work on Trial: The Colwell Inquiry and the State of Welfare* (Bristol: Policy Press, 2011).

For further academic descriptions of this case, see: Philip Jenkins, *Intimate Enemies: Moral Panics in Contemporary Great Britain* (New York: Aldine de Gruyter, 1992), 133–150; Harry Ferguson, 'Cleveland in History: The Abused Child and Child Protection', in Roger Cooter (ed.) *In the Name of the Child: Health and Welfare 1880–1940* (London: Routledge, 1992), 146–173; Mica Nava, 'Cleveland and the Press: Outrage and Anxiety in the Reporting of Child Sexual Abuse', *Feminist Review*, 28 (1988): 105. For two contrasting contemporary accounts see: Beatrix Campbell, *Unofficial Secrets: Child Sexual Abuse: The Cleveland Case* (London: Virago, 1988), Stuart Bell, *When Salem Came to the Boro: The True Story of the Cleveland Child Abuse Crisis* (London: Pan Books, 1988).

32. Many texts in this area have argued that the key transition in terms of changing definitions of 'child abuse' over this period was increased focus paid to sexual abuse from the 1980s, see, for example: Parton, *The Politics of Child Protection*, 24, 66–67; Jenkins, *Intimate Enemies*, xiii, 12–17, 101–107; Harry Hendrick, *Children, Childhood and English Society, 1880–1990* (Cambridge: Cambridge University Press, 1997), 60.
33. Carolyn Steedman, *Dust: The Archive and Cultural History* (Manchester: Manchester University Press, 2001).
34. Joan Scott, 'The Evidence of Experience', *Critical Inquiry*, 14 (1991), 792.
35. Ibid., 778, 791.
36. Stuart Hall, 'Who needs 'identity"?' P. du Gay, J Evans and P Redman (eds) *Identity: a reader* (London, 2000), 17.
37. Selina Todd, 'Family Welfare and Social Work in Post-War England, c. 1948–1970', *English Historical Review*, CXXIX (537) (2014): 364.
38. Angela Davis, 'Oh no, nothing, we didn't learn anything': sex education and the preparation of girls for motherhood, c. 1930–1970', *History of Education*, 37, no. 5 (2008): 663.
39. Stuart Hall, 'The Question of Cultural Identity' in Stuart Hall, David Held, Don Hubert and Kenneth Thompson (eds) *Modernity: An Introduction to Modern Societies* (Oxford: Wiley-Blackwell, 1995), 596–631.
40. Deborah Cohen, *Family Secrets: The Things We Tried to Hide* (London: Penguin, 2014); Martin Francis, 'Tears, Tantrums, and Bared Teeth: The Emotional Economy of Three Conservative Prime Ministers, 1951–1963', *Journal of British Studies*, 41 (2002): 354–387; Adrian Bingham, *Sex. Private Life, and the British Popular Press 1918–1978* (Oxford: Oxford University Press, 2009), 75–76. See also: Alexander Freund, '"Confessing Animals": Toward a Longue Duree History of the Oral History Interview', *The Oral History Review*, 41 (1) (2014): 1–26.

41. Raymond Williams, *Keywords: A vocabulary of culture and society* (2nd edition, New York: Fontana, 1983), 129; Joe Moran, 'The fall and rise of the expert', *Critical Quarterly*, 53 (2011), 19.
42. See: Bev Skeggs, *Formations of Class & Gender: Becoming Respectable* (London: SAGE Publications Ltd, 1997).
43. Leena Rossi and Tuija Aarnio, 'Feelings Matter: Historians' Emotions', *Historyka. Stuidia Metodologiczne*, 88 (2012): 172–3; Alison M. Jaggar, 'Love and Knowledge: Emotion in Feminist Methodology', *Inquiry*, 32 (1989): 163–164.
44. Yaron Ezrahi, *The Descent of Icarus: Science and the Transformation of Contemporary Democracy* (Boston, Massachusetts: Harvard University Press, 1990); Frank Fischer, *Democracy and Expertise: Reorienting Policy Inquiry* (Oxford: Oxford University Press, 2009); Anthony Giddens, *The Consequences of Modernity* (California: Stanford University Press, 1990).
45. Quote: Alex Mold, 'The Changing Role of NGOs in Britain: Voluntary Action and Illegal Drugs', in Nicholas Crowson, James McKay, and Matthew Hilton (eds) *NGOs in Contemporary Britain: Non-state Actors in Society and Politics since 1945* (Basingstoke: Palgrave Macmillan, 2009), 166. Successful examples of this approach, which have been particularly influential over my own work, are: Alex Mold and Virginia Berridge, *Voluntary Action and Illegal Drugs: Health and Society in Britain since the 1960s* (Basingstoke: Palgrave Macmillan, 2010); Pat Thane and Tanya Evans, *Sinners? Scroungers? Saints?: Unmarried Motherhood in Twentieth-Century England* (Oxford: Oxford University Press, 2012); Christopher Moores, 'Opposition to the Greenham Women's Peace Camps in 1980s Britain: RAGE Against the "Obscene"', *History Workshop Journal*, 78 (2014): 204–227.
46. Matthew Hilton, Nick Crowson, Jean-Francois Mouhot and James McKay, *A Historical Guide to NGOs in Britain: Charities, Civil Society and the Voluntary Sector since 1945* (Basingstoke: Palgrave Macmillan, 2012), 84, 127, 178.
47. Bingham, Delap, Jackson and Settle, 'Historical child sexual abuse in England and Wales', 428.
48. Presented as dominant academic interpretation in Ian Butler and Mark Drakeford, 'Booing or cheering? Ambiguity in the construction of victimhood in the case of Maria Colwell', *Crime, Media, Culture*, 4 (3) (2008), 368, which cites as examples: Peter Reder and Sylvia Duncan, 'From Colwell to Climbié: Inquiring into Fatal Child Abuse', in N. Stanley and J. Manthorpe (eds) *The Age of the Inquiry: Learning and Blaming in Health and Social Care* (London: Routledge, 2004), 92–115; Peter Reder, Sylvia Duncan and Moira Gray, *Beyond Blame—Child Abuse Tragedies Revisited* (London: Routledge, 1993); Brian Corby, *Child Abuse: Towards*

a Knowledge Base (2nd edn, Buckingham: Open University Press, 2000). See also: Butler and Drakeford, *Scandal, Social Policy and Social Welfare*; Butler and Drakeford, *Social Work on Trial*; Jenkins, *Intimate Enemies*.

49. Hendrick, *Historical Dimensions, Contemporary Debate*, 136–139; Harry Ferguson, *Protecting Children in Time: Child Abuse, Child Protection and the Consequences of Modernity* (Basingstoke: Palgrave Macmillan, 2004); Ray Jones, 'Children's Acts 1948–2008: the drivers for legislative change in England over 60 years', *Journal of Children's Services*, 4 (2009): 39–52; Nigel Parton, *The Politics of Child Protection: Contemporary Developments and Future Directions* (Basingstoke: Palgrave Macmillan, 2014).
50. Paul Pierson, *Dismantling the Welfare State? Reagan, Thatcher, and the Politics of Retrenchment* (Cambridge: Cambridge University Press, 1994), 158; Pat Thane and Tanya Evans, *Sinners? Scroungers? Saints?: Unmarried Motherhood in Twentieth-Century England* (Oxford: Oxford University Press, 2012), 136.
51. Peter Bailey, '"Will the real Bill Banks please stand up?": Towards a Role Analysis of mid-Victorian Working-Class Respectability', *Journal of Social History*, 12 (1979): 341–343. See also: Skeggs, *Formations of Class & Gender*.
52. For overviews of this history, see Pat Thane, 'The "Big Society" and the "Big State": Creative Tension or Crowding Out?', *Twentieth Century British History*, 23 (2012): 408–429; Justin Davis Smith, 'The voluntary tradition: Philanthropy and self-help in Britain 1500–1945', in Justin Davis Smith, Colin Rochester, and Rodney Hedley (eds), *An Introduction to the Voluntary Sector* (London: Routledge, 1994), 9–38.
53. Discussions of equality movements as related to older people, race, religion and belief, gypsies and travellers, gender, sexual orientation, and disability in the chapters of: Pat Thane (ed.), *Unequal Britain. Equalities in Britain since 1945* (London: Bloomsbury, 2010).

    In relation to sexuality movements, please see: Rebecca Jennings, '"The most uninhibited party they'd ever been to": The Postwar Encounter between Psychiatry and the British Lesbian, 1945–1971'. *Journal of British Studies*, 47 (2008): 883–904. On gay liberation, please see: Lucy Robinson, *Gay men and the left in post-war Britain: How the personal got political* (Manchester: Manchester University Press, 2007); Matthew Waites, Lesbian, Gay and Bisexual NGOs in Britain: Past, Present and Future', in Crowson, Hilton and McKay (eds), *NGOs in Contemporary Britain*, 95–112; Stephen Brooke, *Sexual politics: Sexuality, family planning and the British Left from the 1880s to the present day* (Oxford: Oxford University Press, 2011).

    On the Women's Liberation Movement: Sue Bruley, 'Consciousness-Raising in Clapham: Women's Liberation as "Lived Experience" in South London in the 1970s', *Women's History Review*, 22 (2013): 717–738;

Bridget Lockyer, 'An Irregular Period? Participation in the Bradford Women's Liberation Movement', *Women's History Review*, 22 (2013): 643–657; Sarah Browne, 'A Veritable Hotbed of Feminism: Women's Liberation in St Andrews, Scotland, c. 1968-c.1979', *Twentieth Century British History*, 23 (2012): 100–123; Sarah Browne, *The women's liberation movement in Scotland* (Manchester: Manchester University Press, 2014); Jeska Rees, 'A Look Back At Anger: the Women's Liberation Movement in 1978', *Women's History Review*, 19 (2010): 337–356; Sarah Crook, 'The women's liberation movement, activism and therapy at the grassroots, 1968–1985', *Women's History Review*, advance access online 16 March 2018.

54. Adam Lent, *British Social Movements since 1945: Sex, Colour, Peace and Power* (Basingstoke: Palgrave Macmillan, 2001); David Meyer and Sidney Tarrow (eds), *The Social Movement Society: Contentious Politics for a New Century* (Lanham, Maryland: Rowman & Littlefield, 1998); Sidney Tarrow, *Power in Movement: Social Movement and Contentious Politics* (Cambridge: Cambridge University Press, 1998); Nick Crossley, *Making Sense of Social Movements* (Buckingham, Philadelphia: Open University Press, 2002).
55. On therapeutic communities for drug users, please see: Alex Mold and Virginia Berridge, *Voluntary Action and Illegal Drugs: Health and Society in Britain since the 1960s* (Basingstoke: Palgrave Macmillan, 2010), 19–22, 26. On playgroups, please see: Angela Davis, *Pre-school childcare in England, 1939–2010* (Manchester: Manchester University Press, 2015), Chapter Four: Playgroups. Discussing self-help groups for multiple sclerosis patients, Malcolm Nicholas and George Lowis, 'The early history of the Multiple Sclerosis Society of Great Britain and Northern Ireland: A socio-historical study of lay/practitioner interaction in the context of a medical charity', *Medical History*, 46 (2002): 141–174.
56. Matthew Hilton, James McKay, Nicholas Crowson and Jean-Francois Mouhot, *The Politics of Expertise: How NGOs Shaped Modern Britain* (Oxford: Oxford University Press, 2013); Hilton, Crowson, Mouhot and McKay, *A Historical Guide to NGOs in Britain*; Matthew Hilton, James McKay, Nicholas Crowson, and Jean-Francois Mouhot, 'The Big Society: Civic participation and the state in modern Britain', *History & Policy*, 8 June 2010 <http://www.historyandpolicy.org/policy-papers/papers/the-big-society-civic-participation-and-the-state-in-modern-britain>; Matthew Hilton, 'Politics is Ordinary: Non-governmental Organizations and Political Participation in Contemporary Britain', *Twentieth Century British History*, 22 (2011): 230–268.
57. Much has been written about this with regards to the health care sector, for example: Alex Mold, 'Patient Groups and the Construction of the Patient-Consumer in Britain: An Historical Overview', *Journal of Social Policy*, 39 (2010): 510; Alex Mold, 'Making the Patient-Consumer in Margaret

Thatcher's Britain', *The Historical Journal* 54 (2011): 509–528; Alex Mold, *Making the patient-consumer: Patient organisations and health consumerism in Britain* (Manchester: Manchester University Press, 2015); Jennifer Crane, 'Why the History of Public Consultation Matters for Contemporary Health Policy', *Endeavour*, advance access 8 February 2018.

In terms of mental health, a shift on listening to patient voices is described in: Alison Faulkner, 'User involvement in twenty-first century mental health services: "This is our century"', in Charlie Brooker and Julie Repper (eds) *Mental Health: From Policy to Practice* (London: Churchill Livingstone, 2009), 14–26; Lynda Tait and Helen Lester, 'Encouraging user involvement in mental health services', *Advances in Psychiatric Treatment*, 11 (2005) 168–175; Michele Crossley and Nick Crossley, '"Patient" voices, social movements and the habitus; how psychiatric survivors "'speak out", *Social Science and Medicine*, 52 (2001): 1477–1489.

58. In doing so, it draws on the influence of Mathew Thomson's work, *Lost Freedom: The Landscape of the Child and the British Post-War Settlement* (Oxford: Oxford University Press, 2013), which describes how the emergence of concerns about paedophilia and sexual abuse in the 1970s played a role in heightening broader post-war anxieties about children's safety, and in shutting down 'the landscape of the child'.
59. Mona Gleason, 'Avoiding the agency trap: caveats for historians of children, youth, and education", *History of Education*, 45 no. 4 (2016): 446–459; Harry Hendrick, 'The Child as a Social Actor in Historical Sources: Problems of Identification and Interpretation', in Pia Christensen and Allison James (eds) *Research with Children: Perspectives and Practices* (London: Routledge, 2008), 46.
60. Cooter, *In the Name of the Child*; Viviana Zelizer, *Pricing the Priceless Child: The Changing Social Value of Children* (New York: Princeton University Press, 1985); Harry Hendrick, 'Children as Human Capital: Some Historical and Contemporary Perspectives on Social Investment', Draft paper presented at University of Warwick, 21 February 2012, 6; Phil Scraton, 'Whose "Childhood"? What "Crisis"?', in Chris Jenks (ed.), *Childhood: Critical Concepts in Sociology* (Abingdon: Routledge, 2005), 69; Nikolas Rose, *Governing the Soul: The Shaping of the Private Self* (London: Routledge: 1990), 121.
61. Stephen Humphries, *Hooligans or Rebels?: An Oral History of Working-Class Childhood and Youth 1889–1939* (Oxford: John Wiley & Sons, 1995); Linda Mahood, *Policing gender, class and family: Britain, 1850–1940* (London, 1995), 112–115. For the American context on these questions, please see: Michael Grossberg, 'Liberation and Caretaking: Fighting over Children's Rights in Postwar America', Paula Fass and Michael Grossberg (eds), *Reinventing Childhood After World War II* (Philadelphia, Pennsylvania, 2012), 19–37.

62. Selina Todd, *Harry Hendrick, Children, Childhood and English Society, 1880–1990* (Cambridge: Cambridge University Press, 1997), Chapter Four, Children and Social Policies.
63. See for example on abuse in religious institutions: Philip Jenkins, *Pedophiles and Priests: Anatomy of a Contemporary Crisis* (New York: Oxford University Press, 1996). See on abuse in institutional homes: Johanna Sköld and Shurlee Swain (eds), *Apologies and the Legacy of Abuse of Children in 'Care'* (Basingstoke: Palgrave Macmillan, 2015); Johanna Sköld, 'The truth about abuse? A comparative approach to inquiry narratives on historical institutional child abuse', *History of Education*, 4, no. 4 (2016): 42–509.
64. Jane Pilcher, 'Gillick and After: Children and Sex in the 1980s and 1990s', in Jane Pilcher and Stephen Wagg (eds), *Thatcher's Children? Politics, Childhood and Society in the 1980s and 1990s* (London: Routledge, 1996), 78; Andrew Gamble, *The Free Economy and the Strong State: The Politics of Thatcherism* (Basingstoke: Palgrave Macmillan, 1994), 14, 136, 200; Martin Durham, *Sex and Politics: The Family and Morality in the Thatcher Years* (Basingstoke: Palgrave Macmillan, 1991), 131–137; Martin Durham, 'The Thatcher Government and 'The Moral Right'', *Parliamentary Affairs*, 41 (1989): 58–71; Jennifer Somerville, 'The New Right and family politics', *Economy and Society*, 21 (1992): 93–128.

Open Access This chapter is licensed under the terms of the Creative Commons Attribution 4.0 International License (http://creativecommons.org/licenses/by/4.0/), which permits use, sharing, adaptation, distribution and reproduction in any medium or format, as long as you give appropriate credit to the original author(s) and the source, provide a link to the Creative Commons license and indicate if changes were made.

The images or other third party material in this chapter are included in the chapter's Creative Commons license, unless indicated otherwise in a credit line to the material. If material is not included in the chapter's Creative Commons license and your intended use is not permitted by statutory regulation or exceeds the permitted use, you will need to obtain permission directly from the copyright holder.

CHAPTER 2

The Battered Child Syndrome: Parents and Children as Objects of Medical Study

The roots of post-1960s concerns about child abuse lay in the 1940s and in particular in research conducted by paediatric radiologists in America and Britain. This chapter explores how such research named the 'battered child syndrome' and, in doing so, directed concern anew to physical violence against young infants. Clashes between and within medical professions shaped this dynamic transnational research context. In debates between radiology, paediatrics, ophthalmology, and dermatology, children and parents affected by abuse were primarily constituted as objects of study, and they were not directly engaged in discussion. Further, there was little analysis of the long-term effects of abuse.

Nonetheless, the roots of later influence for children and parents were visible in these early debates, and this chapter provides important framing for the post-1960s developments traced in this book, and for the rise of experiential and emotional forms of expertise. Notably, the NSPCC established an innovative new unit to research battered children, which also drew attention to the psychological characteristics of violent parents. Further, early clinical debates also expressed concerns about child wellbeing. While these studies and debates were framed in paternalist and heavily gendered terms, they also contributed to a moment in which new challenges were made to medical and social work expertise. By considering the inner lives of parents, and the effects of their emotions and experiences, clinicians and social workers began to discuss and reflect on their own

© The Author(s) 2018
J. Crane, *Child Protection in England, 1960–2000*, Palgrave Studies in the History of Childhood,
https://doi.org/10.1007/978-3-319-94718-1_2

sources of authority, and on the utility—or failures—of professional detachment. By reflecting on children's interests, furthermore, professional conceptions of the child remained characterised by vulnerability but also moved towards asking how children could be empowered and made expert.

The 'Battered Child Syndrome'[1]

America

To an extent, medical research drove the re-emergence of concerns around child protection in Britain and America in the post-war period. Descriptions of this time by historians and social policy theorists focus on the work of a series of pioneering male paediatric radiologists and the development of this profession.[2] Significant, and publishing sporadically from the mid-1940s until the mid-1950s, were John Caffey, Frederic Silverman, Paul Woolley, and William Evans, each of whom conducted research which utilised x-ray data to understand—and to make visible—the injuries of physically abused children.[3] These men were working at a time when radiology itself was relatively new, with x-rays only discovered in 1895 and then patchily adopted throughout Britain and America as a profession developed through the 1920s and 1930s, overcoming initial industrial injuries.[4]

The men's research began to draw attention to the idea that parents may have purposefully inflicted children's injuries, discussing parental violence for one of the first times in medical press. Caffey wrote that the fractures he observed 'appear to be of traumatic origin'.[5] Silverman argued that parents may 'permit trauma and be unaware of it, may recognize trauma but forget or be reluctant to admit it, or may deliberately injure the child and deny it'.[6] Woolley and Evans, conducting a retrospective study of children's hospital records, considered the 'aggressive, immature or emotionally ill' characters of certain parents and argued that medical assessment must pay attention.[7] These assertions were relatively tentative and made years apart, but nonetheless significant in connecting physical injury to violence, and in pushing for social assessment to become a medical responsibility.

Building on this small but important and growing body of literature, the paediatrician C. Henry Kempe was the first to explicitly detail and examine child battering at length in medical press.[8] A Jewish immigrant from Germany to America in 1939, Kempe became the youngest chairman of the Paediatrics Department at the University of Colorado at the age of 34 in

1956. In 1962, Kempe published an article, 'The Battered Child Syndrome', in the *Journal of the American Medical Association*; purposefully choosing the dramatic term 'battered child', he later commented, as a 'jazzy title, designed to get physicians' attention'.[9] The article's co-authors were a professor of paediatrics, Henry Silver; a professor of psychiatry, Brandt Steele; an assistant resident in obstetrics and gynaecology, William Drogemueller; and Frederic Silverman, the paediatric radiologist mentioned earlier. The authors described the 'battered child syndrome' as a 'clinical condition in young children', usually under three though possibly of 'any age', who had been subject to serious physical violence.[10] Emphasising that this was a 'frequent cause of permanent injury or death', the authors urged that physicians must consider this as a cause in children exhibiting symptoms such as fractures, soft tissue swellings, and skin bruising.[11]

The research of a small group drawn from paediatric radiology, paediatrics, psychiatry, obstetrics, and gynaecology was thus significant in bringing attention to an area that many clinicians had previously shied away from: violence against children, and in calling on physicians to assess parental explanations critically. This work relied heavily on the x-ray image. Discussing this, Kempe's initial article explained, 'To the informed physician, the bones tell a story the child is too young or too frightened to tell'.[12] In this account, the 'informed physician' was highly significant in terms of interpreting the x-ray image, but the image itself was also a key provider of data that had previously only been accessible by speaking to the child themselves. The x-ray image was to make the invisible visible. In doing so, this image would bring new attention to the child's physical injuries. Yet, it would also distract attention from children's individual testimonies, potentially replacing, rather than bolstering, interest in child voice. The x-ray image often revealed that children's bones were healing, demonstrating that without this internal examination, any external evidence of the child's injury may have been lost.

Given the significance of the x-ray image itself in discussing the battered child syndrome in America, technicians and members of radiological laboratory teams were key in this moment, producing the images that radiologists later interpreted and disseminated through publications. One of the earliest authors on x-rays and childhood violence—Caffey—acknowledged this while accepting an award in 1965, praising the 'faithful and skilful labors' of his laboratory team. In particular, Caffey accepted that his technician Edgar Watts and department supervisor Moira Shannon had saved him 'literally thousands of hours' with their work.[13] The medical research in this area was thus published by a small group of individuals, but conducted by, and raising awareness amongst, a broader community of technicians, assistants, and research laboratory staff. This is significant to acknowledge, because it spoke to a context in which concern about child protection was not only constructed by, or meaningful to, prestigious male paediatricians and radiologists. Indeed, this point demonstrates that both new technologies and auxiliary professions played a key role in re-awakening concerns about child abuse in the 1940s, 1950s, and 1960s.

Britain

Initial discussions around the battered child syndrome in America were the product of interactions between a maturing technology, the x-ray; a small professional community working primarily in radiology and paediatrics, supported by laboratory staff; and the explanations provided by parents and children themselves in daily interactions with clinicians. Through the published work in this field, as well as meetings at conferences, discussions around the syndrome were published in Britain during the mid-1960s, not long after the release of Kempe's initial article. Notably, in 1963, the orthopaedic surgeons D. Li Griffiths and F. J. Moynihan published an article in the *British Medical Journal* looking 'to give publicity to a syndrome which we think commoner than is usually believed'.[14] The article's characterisation of the syndrome was broadly in line with Kempe's original description, and offered three further case studies. Again, images from the x-ray were significant, with one showing healing fractures in seven ribs of a two-month-old baby, only made visible through this technology. Testifying to the challenges facing such work, Griffiths and Moynihan wrote that many doctors were 'reluctant to believe that such assaults on innocent babies are possible'.[15] Nonetheless, others wrote supportively to the *British Medical Journal*, suggesting that these cases may only be the 'tip of the iceberg', and lobbying for further research.[16]

The problem of battered children was conceptualised as a transnational or 'universal' one from its inception, and later consciously so at the International Congress on Child Abuse, held in Geneva in 1976.[17] Significantly, medical, social work, and charitable communities in Britain and America exchanged and co-constructed knowledge about this syndrome. Following a meeting with Kempe in Colorado in 1964, the Director of the NSPCC Arthur Morton became 'very keen that the society should be in the forefront of the work needed to counter what became known as the "battered baby syndrome"'.[18] Under Morton's guidance, the NSPCC founded the Battered Child Research Unit in 1966, aiming to 'create an informed body of opinion about the syndrome and to devise methods of treatment'.[19] Evidencing the significance of transatlantic relationships in this moment, the unit was established at 'Denver House' in tribute to Kempe's work in Denver, Colorado.[20]

While the NSPCC and British medical profession were initially 'conduits', 'exporting' American knowledge about the battered child syndrome, they came to be significant in constructing such knowledge also, as part of a broader transnational network united through, for example, work in the international journal *Child Abuse & Neglect*.[21] Morton and Kempe each spent time working within both America and Britain, and Steele—another author of the initial 'Battered Child' journal article—also held many discussions with the NSPCC.[22] These networks, then, evidence a transition of ideas between transatlantic medical communities, but also between medical and charitable ones.

While medical and charitable communities in Britain and America were discussing the 'battered child syndrome' by the mid-1960s, there was no singular definition of this term. Definitions were more clearly divided across professional lines than national ones. Broadly, clinicians agreed that the syndrome was a collection of symptoms and signs primarily apparent in young children under the age of three who were subjected to violence, usually at the hands of their parents.[23] Within this vague definition however, numerous medical specialists from various fields asserted the unique role of their own professions in providing the definitive characterisation. Radiologists argued that the battered child syndrome had distinct features which only x-rays could reveal.[24] M. J. Gilkes of the Sussex Eye Hospital highlighted the ocular conditions connected with the syndrome, claiming that in cases where the battered child was being diagnosed, specific appearances, visible only to trained ophthalmologists, would 'considerably increase one's suspicions'.[25] Suzanne Alexander, from the Institute of Dermatology in London, and surgeon A. P. Barabas likewise both emphasised their own professions' roles in differentiating between purposefully inflicted bruises and infants particularly prone to bruising due to the existence of an underlying condition (such as the Ehlers-Danlos syndrome).[26] Psychiatrists also became significant in the popular coverage of the battered child, and contemporary tabloid analysis speculated that psychiatrists may be able to undertake 'extensive brain checks' and to identify 'brain abnormalities' in violent parents.[27]

The initial development of the battered child syndrome was then not merely the emergence of child abuse as a 'medical problem', but rather was shaped by debates between several medical specialities, many of which, not least radiology, were becoming increasingly expensive in the 1960s due to the development of new technologies.[28] Early medical works on this topic included a clear focus on the character of violent parents, though in terms of understanding how best to identify such adults, rather than in thinking about how to treat them. Medical communities in Britain began to focus on this issue very quickly after those in America, in part because of the ease of transferring knowledge through international medical journals, but also reflective of the relatively small groups of researchers initially interested in this debate. Similar definitions emerged in Britain and America although, in subsequent years, Parliamentarians would suggest that the differences between the American health system and the National Health Service in Britain had shaped a different 'contractual relationship' between patient and doctor, and thus a separate model of moral duty around the battered child.[29] While the syndrome was said to potentially affect children of 'any age', a clear model of childhood vulnerability emerged, with a small group of researchers key in representing the interests of the helpless infant.

Recovering the Child[30]

Concerns about children's experiences and feelings were not absent from early medical discussions, though the characterisation of the battered child syndrome tended against consideration of children's own viewpoints in three key ways. First, the syndrome was typically restricted to apply to children under the age of three, in part given a hope that older children would be capable of themselves giving a reliable patient history.[31] Second, since this syndrome was initially characterised by radiologists, the diagnostic material used was an x-ray image: a monotone photograph which saw the inside of, and yet in a sense removed what was human from, its subject. With this diagnostic aid, the testimony of the interpreting physician was crucial, but accounts from the young children themselves were less necessary. Third, the construction of violence against children as a 'syndrome' put this issue firmly in the medical arena, as the responsibility of expert paediatricians to understand and manage.

At the same time, concerns about the child's social and emotional positions were never absent from early discussions of the syndrome. Notably, in defining the syndrome, clinicians recognised that a variety of forms of abuse often accompanied one another—that the physical abuse of the battered child would often be accompanied by emotional abuse and neglect, which must also be prevented and stopped.[32] Building on this recognition of the multivariate nature of many child protection cases, paediatricians, radiologists, and other clinicians recognised that they needed to work closely with a range of social agencies. Kempe's co-edited collection *The Battered Child* (1968) featured chapters written by a social worker, a welfare department worker, a lawyer, and a policeman, situated alongside those by a radiologist, a paediatrician, and a psychiatrist. The text explicitly highlighted the contributions made by 'many disciplines involved in helping the battered child and his parents'.[33] The battered child syndrome was thus not to be managed by clinicians alone, but rather by a range of social and clinical professionals. Such collaborative efforts were made even as social medicine itself shifted its focus towards individual responsibility and lifestyle issues.[34]

Focus was also moved from outside of professional spaces into community ones, with, for example, one letter to the *British Medical Journal* in 1964 calling for a shift in community attitudes whereby violence was no longer overlooked.[35] In making this type of case, clinicians acknowledged the limitations of their disciplines in child protection though, at the same time, the specific nature of these 'communities' was rarely addressed in medical publications. Challenging purely clinical explanations of the syndrome further, Caffey recognised that while radiologic signs may tell the radiologist with 'full confidence' that the child had 'suffered from mechanical injury', these visuals alone could not determine *who* had hurt a child.[36] These kinds of clinical arguments to an extent reflected a level of self-awareness from medical professionals concerned for child welfare, who were thinking about the social and emotional contexts of childhood and seeking inter-professional collaboration. However, the sense of concern about clinical accuracy also cannot be removed from a context in which, in the 1950s, 1960s, and 1970s, medical authority was encountering new challenges from malpractice suits, newspaper sensationalism, and an increased proliferation of alternative providers.[37]

Nonetheless, discussions of the battered child syndrome broke down certain clinical boundaries. Notably, radiologists, paediatricians, and other clinicians described these cases in highly emotional terms, again demonstrating a level of attentiveness to the interior lives of children and infants. Discussions in the *British Medical Journal* referred to 'our most helpless patients', and the 'evil' and 'distinctive nightmare quality' of battered child cases.[38] Expressing further concern about the inner lives of the child, Caffey, addressing the American Pediatric Society in 1965, emphasised how many of his 'thousands of small patients' were 'exhausted by disease and frightened by the seeming horrors of radiographic examination'.[39] When narrating their own responses to these cases, and in professional discussion, clinicians thus near immediately felt compelled to discuss their own emotions as well as their professional credentials.

As a letter from Kempe to a friend, later published by his daughter, claimed, he was in part driven to his work by an academic agenda of 'intellectual honesty' and 'rage' at the misplaced diagnoses children were given. He was also however, he stated, motivated by concern for the abused child, his siblings, and his parents.[40] Such evocative uses of language, and expressions of emotion as motivators for research, were not common in contemporary medical journals.[41] Not only did these statements break down cultural tropes of detached clinical authority, they also demonstrated that the re-emergent anxieties about child abuse in the mid-twentieth century would be embedded, even from an early stage, with concerns about the emotions and experiences of children and professionals. The expectation that clinicians, social workers, and policy-makers would also discuss their family lives, and that they would perform experiential and emotional expertise, developed significantly in later decades, as this book will trace.

Anticipating later tensions in these debates, one piece in the *British Medical Journal* in 1964 stated that the 'emotions aroused by these cases' may incite the 'quixotic desire for retribution' and a 'fervour to protect possibly innocent relatives'.[42] Indeed, while interest in thinking about the social and emotional connotations of child protection developed from the 1960s, medical communities in Britain and America also rejected the idea of parental violence. Touring America, giving speeches about this syndrome in hospitals and universities, Kempe's wife Ruth, herself a significant paediatrician who co-authored his later work, received mixed responses. She later reported that while half of those she met responded with, 'Thank you so much for confirming what I've suspected, and for educating us', the other half argued, 'I don't know where you get your information, I've been in practice for years and have never seen any evidence of child abuse.'[43] In the British context, likewise, an editorial in the *British Medical Journal* recognised that 'medical men' were 'naturally unwilling to become involved in criminal proceedings', but argued nonetheless that it was 'clearly' their 'duty'.[44] This careful framing suggested an ongoing expectation of professional resistance, and an early moment in which ideas about child protection were being tied to theories of duty, responsibility, and morality. Interest in children's emotional and social lives underlay early understandings of the battered child syndrome, but these interests were not universally accepted.

Studying the Parent

In the initial medical descriptions of the battered child, parents tended to be a side feature. Kempe's initial 'Battered Child' article acknowledged that there was 'meager' research around the parents of battered children, despite the fact that they were the primary perpetrators of violence.[45] From the time that this article was published in 1962, however, numerous social and psychological surveys emerged in Britain seeking to further understand violent parents. One of the earlier studies in this area was by the NSPCC's Battered Child Research Unit and was entitled, *78 Battered Children*. Published in September 1969, the study was co-authored by Angela E. Skinner, an associate at the Institute of Medical Social Work, and Raymond Castle, a social worker. The research assessed 45 battered boys and 33 battered girls aiming to establish the demographics and social and psychological characteristics of the families involved.[46] Skinner and Castle compiled their sample retrospectively, by asking all NSPCC-employed social workers to provide their case records about under-fours who had warranted medical attention due to physical injury between July 1967 and June 1968.[47] Of the parents who had hurt their children, the report identified 33 were male, 42 female, and 3 acting in collaboration. Battering parents in the sample were often relatively young, with the mean age of 22–25. The study argued that battering had a strong correlation with 'character disorders', with parents either 'habitually aggressive' or suffering from 'impoverished personalities' that left them unable to 'sustain nurturing relationships'.[48] Notably, in this work the violent parent shifted from a side-consideration of medical studies, focused on 'objective' signs such as x-ray imagery, to the centre of psychological and social examination.

Interest in the psychological and social contexts of violent parents continued apace in the late 1960s and the 1970s, led by the NSPCC and also by independent psychiatrists. Two separate key themes emerged in this research—tensions about whether such parents were part of a 'social problem group' and, relatedly, about whether the parents had themselves been subject to violence in childhood. In terms of the first theme, numerous psychological studies emphasised that violent parents did not typically belong in any one demographic group, and that nor were they defined by social class, ethnicity, gender, or education.[49] At the same time, clinical and media discussions of these parents echoed historic discussions of 'social problem groups' or 'problem families' which have reappeared in various forms since at least the Victorian period.[50] Indeed, letters to the *British Medical Journal* in 1966 and 1967 explicitly characterised battering parents within a 'large group of social problem families', and as often 'already known to their general practitioners, health visitors, and various social agencies as having many problems'.[51]

This representation—of families afflicted by low levels of personal responsibility, poor social environments, and inadequate skills of home management—was taken up enthusiastically by tabloid press discussing battered children. In April 1965, the *Daily Mail* discussed battered babies as a 'major social disease'; making clear the competing visions of child protection as a social and a medical problem in this moment.[52] The article quoted an unnamed 'London psychiatrist', who reportedly told the paper that battering parents were not drawn predominantly from 'the lower-paid section of the community, nor are they unintelligent'.[53] Further, the article asserted, such parents may be 'well-dressed', with a baby who appears 'healthy, despite his bruised face and limbs'.[54] Nonetheless, and in highly coded language, the article also quoted the psychiatrist's statement that battering families were those 'living in isolation, without friends, without grandparents to help care for children, with economic difficulties, who are overworked and overtired'.[55] While overtly denying that they perceived a class basis in battered child-cases, tabloid press and clinicians alike were explicitly—and not subtly—placing their discussions within a significant historical trajectory of stigmatising and paternalist debate.

The second key theme in early research about battering parents was an assumption that they had been subjected to violence themselves during their own childhoods. This assumption emerged from the very inception of discussions about the battered child syndrome: Kempe's original article emphasised that there was 'some suggestion that the attacking parent was subjected to similar abuse', and that this may be 'one of the most important factors' in these cases.[56] The NSPCC, likewise important in early debates about the syndrome, confidently stated in a review article that there was 'general agreement' in relevant literature that violent parents 'were themselves the victims of physical/emotional abuse or neglect'.[57]

This idea of violence as cyclical extended beyond these intense research communities alone. In Parliament in 1969, Labour Member Joan Lestor, a former nursery school teacher, argued that there was 'one single matter' through the battered child cases—that the parents involved may have had 'grossly unhappy and grossly deprived childhood[s]'.[58] In the same year, Home Secretary James Callaghan expressed an aim to 'prevent the deprived and delinquent children of today from becoming the deprived, inadequate, unstable, or criminal citizens of tomorrow'.[59] As was suggested by Lestor's language of unhappiness, thinking about cycles of violence was sometimes used sympathetically, looking to explain the inexplicable behaviours of parents. In one of Kempe's case studies, for example, he explained that a mother repeated a pattern of violence from her own childhood, despite her 'very strong conscious wishes to be a kind, good mother'.[60] Discussing the battered child further, paediatricians and representatives of the UK Home Office argued in the late 1960s that best interests of the child and the rehabilitation of parents were 'not contradictory aims' but rather 'joint ones'. These spokespeople argued that the majority of parents could stop injuring their children, with professional intervention, and that many parents felt 'exasperated' by their children's behaviours at certain times.[61]

While offering a sympathetic approach to parents, therefore, discussions about the battered child did not lead to debate about how best to support all survivors of abuse. Early discussions about the battered child syndrome contained threads of interest in parental experience, but these were analysed through the interlinked lenses of social problem groups and cyclical violence, and used to justify paternalist professional intervention. Psychological, political, and charitable interest turned quickly to the inner lives of parents involved in child protection cases; however, parents were unable to guide such debate. These clinical and political visions of parenting emerged as part of a broader focus on preventative casework and family maintenance in the 1950s and 1960s.[62] While children, parents, and survivors did not actively influence mid-twentieth-century discussions, these discussions did contain early interest in the experiences and emotions of families. This interest became significant over the late 1960s, 1970s, and particularly in the 1980s, as the rest of this book demonstrates. Indeed, this initial construction of child protection was quickly challenged, broadened, and, to an extent, overturned. Notably, the next two chapters trace rising concerns about children's experiences and emotions. In these debates, the initial sympathetic approach to parents and to family maintenance became controversial.

Conclusion

Drawing on research from the 1940s and 1950s, from the early 1960s a shift occurred in British society within which academic, medical, charitable, and social work communities increasingly discussed the mistreatment of children in published works. While a shift took place over these years, the pace of change should not be overstated. By 1970, many practising medics and social workers continued to deny or ignore the existence of parental violence. Writing for the *British Medical Journal* in 1970, the paediatrician Bruno Gans described the case of a five-month-old infant repeatedly admitted into a southeast London Hospital with injuries in his hand. Despite x-ray evidence that a needle had been embedded in the child's heel, and the fact that the child's sibling had recently died in another hospital, Gans reported that his suggestions that this child may manifest the battered child syndrome were met with horror. When suggesting the diagnosis to his ward sister, Gans wrote, 'she was appalled at my even thinking of such a possibility'.[63] In 1969, relatedly, the NSPCC's *78 Battered Children* survey emphasised that social workers and clinicians alike struggled to believe that parents could or would hurt their children.[64] The report also emphasised that some social workers pushed parents towards alternative explanations of childhood injury. In one reported case, a social worker suggested 'all kinds of accidents' may have caused a child's injuries and 'even suggested the dog', but the parent 'would have none'.[65]

Thus, a change took place in the mid-twentieth century in terms of medical and social work discussions of abuse, and yet this was not instantaneous nor was it entirely 'new'. Nonetheless, some attitudinal shifts did take place, often motivated by research. In the early 1960s, the paper by Kempe, Silver, Steele, Drogemueller, and Silverman was highly significant. In later years, Kempe was nominated for Nobel Peace Prize for his contribution to children's safety, and the American Medical Association recognised this paper as one of the sixty most important published medical manuscripts of the twentieth century.[66] From the late 1960s, the NSPCC's Battered Child Research Unit became significant in conducting research around the syndrome, and seeking to characterise and understand families. Work exchanged amongst transnational communities of radiologists, paediatricians, social workers, and charities in Britain and North America thus sought to direct further resources to the study of battered children which, from early discussions, became conversations about physical, emotional, and neglectful forms of maltreatment more broadly.

The growing awareness of child abuse in this period was complex. There was no simple shift in the management of violent families from public health doctors to social workers, or from the medical to the social.[67] Rather, medical concerns about child protection were always inflected by social anxieties, developed alongside the strengthening of social medicine in the 1940s and 1950s, and shaped by clinical collaboration with social work agencies. Paediatric radiologists and other clinicians expressed their concerns about abuse in emotional language. Collaboration between social and medical actors did not yet extend to including children, parents, or survivors in debate. Indeed, much research was framed in paternalist and stigmatising terms, and research was often driven by a primary fixation on family maintenance. Nonetheless, these shifts in thinking about the inner lives of children and parents did, at the same time, set the stage for the developing significance of experiential and emotional expertise.

Notes

1. Parts of the following section were first explored and used in my article, Jennifer Crane, '"The Bones Tell a Story the Child Is Too Young or Too Frightened to Tell": The Battered Child Syndrome in Britain and America', *Social History of Medicine*, 28 no. 4 (2015): 767–788. Select points and ideas are reused here in line with the article's open access status, as it was published under a Creative Commons CC-BY license.
2. Nigel Parton, 'A Natural History of Child Abuse: A Study in Social Problem Definition', *British Journal of Social Work*, 9 (1979), 436; Harry Ferguson, *Protecting Children in Time: Child Abuse, Child Protection and the Consequences of Modernity* (Basingstoke: Palgrave Macmillan, 2004), 4, 80, 89, 104, 108–109; Harry Hendrick, *Child Welfare: Historical Dimensions, Contemporary Debate* (Bristol: The Policy Press, 2003), 161–163; Harry Hendrick, *Child Welfare: England 1872–1989* (London: Routledge, 1994), 225.
3. See Crane, "The bones tell a story the child is too young or too frightened to tell": 767–788.
4. For personal recollections on the early development of x-ray departments in various regions see: Henry Crooks, 'A Life History with X-Rays', *The Invisible Light: The Radiology History and Heritage Charitable Trust*, 13

(May 2000): 11–38, the Chesney Twins, 'We Remember…', *The Invisible Light: The Radiology History and Heritage Charitable Trust*, 16 (2001): 6–13, Mavis V. Reynolds, '50 Years on—What it was like to be a radiography student in 1946', *The Invisible Light: The Radiology History and Heritage Charitable Trust*, 17 (2002): 8–10, Rita Mason, 'A Family Affair', *The Invisible Light: The Radiology History and Heritage Charitable Trust*, 18 (2002): 16–27. Adrian M. K. Thomas, 'The development of radiology from the discovery of x-rays in 1895', *The Invisible Light: The Journal of the British Society for the History of Radiology*, 23 (November 2005): 14.

5. Reprinted in: John Caffey, 'The Classic: Multiple Fractures in the Long Bones of Infants Suffering from Chronic Subdural Haematoma', *Clinical Orthopaedics and Related Research*, 469 (2011): 757.
6. Fred Silverman, 'The Roentgen Manifestations of Unrecognised Skeletal Trauma in Infants', *American Journal of Roentgenology*, 69 (1953): 424.
7. Paul V. Woolley and William A. Evans, 'Significance of Skeletal Lesions in Infants Resembling those of Traumatic Origin', *Journal of the American Medical Association*, 158 (1955): 541.
8. C. H. Kempe, Frederic N. Silverman, Brandt F. Steele, William Droegemuller, Henry K. Silver, 'The Battered Child Syndrome', *Child Abuse and Neglect*, 9 (1985): 143, originally published in *Journal of the American Medical Association*, 181 (1962): 17–24.
9. Kempe et al., 'The Battered Child Syndrome', pp. 143–154; Annie Kempe, *A Good Knight for Children: C. Henry Kempe's Quest to Protect the Abused Child* (e-book, 2007), 69%.
10. Kempe et al., 'The Battered Child Syndrome': 143–144.
11. Ibid., 143.
12. Ibid., 144.
13. John Caffey, 'Significance of the history in the diagnosis of traumatic injury to children', *The Journal of Pediatrics*, 67, no. 5 (1965): 1009.
14. D. Li. Griffiths and F. J. Moynihan, 'Multiple Epiphysial Injuries in Babies ('Battered Baby' Syndrome)', *British Medical Journal*, 21 December 1963: 1558–1561.
15. Ibid., 1558–1561.
16. Anthony Vickers, 'Battered Babies', *British Medical Journal*, 4th January 1964, 60, Arthur Morton, 'Battered Baby' Syndrome', *British Medical Journal*, 18 January 1964, 178.
17. Pierre E. Ferrier, 'Foreword—Proceedings of the 1976 International Congress on Child Abuse and Neglect—Geneva, W. H.O.—September 20–22', *Child Abuse & Neglect*, 1 (1977), iv.
18. John Low, 'Obituary: The Reverend Arthur Morton', *The Independent*, 4th April 1996, available online at <http://www.independent.co.uk/news/people/obituary--the-rev-arthur-morton-1303186.html>.

19. Edwina Baher, Clare Hyman, Carolyn Jones, Ronald Jones, Anna Kerr, Ruth Mitchell, *At Risk: An Account of the Work of the Battered Child Research Department, NSPCC* (London and Boston: Routledge & Kegan Paul, 1976), vii; Arthur Morton, 'Foreword', in Angela Skinner and Raymond Castle (eds) *78 Battered Children: A Retrospective Study* (Hoddesdon: Thomas Knight and Co, 1969).
20. Phillip Jenkins, *Intimate Enemies: Moral Panics in Contemporary Great Britain*, (New York: Aldine de Gruyter, 1992): 104; Parton, 'A Natural History of Child Abuse': 439.
21. Jenkins, *Intimate Enemies*, 104, Hacking, *The Social Construction of What?* (Cambridge, MA: Harvard University Press, 1999), 148.
22. Betty Jerman, 'You seen a clean pinny. The bruises are underneath', *The Times*, 8 January 1967, 10; Low, 'Obituary: The Reverend Arthur Morton'; Arthur Morton, 'Introduction', Skinner and Castle, *78 Battered Children*.
23. Memorandum of the British Paediatric Association Special Standing Committee on Accidents in Childhood, 'The Battered Baby', *British Medical Journal*, 1 (1966): 601, as cited in Arthur F. Hughes, 'The Battered Baby Syndrome—a Multi-disciplinary Problem', *Case Conference*, 14, no. 8 (December 1967): 305.
24. See for example Bruno Gans, 'Unnecessary X-Rays?', *British Medical Journal*, 28 February 1970: 564; John Caffey, 'Significance of the history in the diagnosis of traumatic injury to children', *The Journal of Pediatrics*, 67, no. 5 (1965): 1012.
25. M. J. Gilkes and Trevor P. Mann, 'Fundi of Battered Babies', *The Lancet*, 26 August 1967: 468–469.
26. Suzanne Alexander, '"Battered Baby" Syndrome', *British Medical Journal*, 9 May 1964: 1255; A. P. Barabas, 'Battered Baby or Ehlers-Danlos Syndrome?', *The Lancet*, 4 March 1967: 511.
27. Keith Colling, 'Battered babies "face new dangers"', *Daily Mail*, 2 April 1973: 11.
28. Adrian M. K. Thomas and Arpan K. Banejee, *The History of Radiology* (Oxford, e-book, 2013), 78%.
29. Hansard, House of Commons, Fifth Series, 25 July 1969, Vol. 787 cc. 2315.
30. Parts of the following section were first explored and used in my article, Crane, '"The bones tell a story the child is too young or too frightened to tell": 767–788. Select quotes and ideas are reused here in line with the article's open access status, as it was published under a Creative Commons CC-BY license.

31. Caffey, 'Significance of the history': 1013; Hughes, 'The Battered Baby Syndrome': 305.
32. This was particularly recognised from the later 1970s, see: Ruth S. Kempe and C. Henry Kempe, *Child Abuse* (Cambridge, Massachusetts: Harvard University Press, 1978), 12–13.
33. Ray E. Helfer and C. Henry Kempe, 'Introduction', in Ray E. Helfer and C. Henry Kempe (eds) *The Battered Child* (Chicago: University of Chicago Press, 1968).
34. Shaun Murphy, 'The Early Days of the MRC Social Medicine Research Unit', *Social History of Medicine*, 12, no. 3 (1999): 389–406.
35. Eric Turner, '"Battered Baby" Syndrome', *British Medical Journal*, 1 February 1964: 308.
36. Caffey, 'Significance of the history': 1012.
37. Edward Shorter, 'The History of the Doctor–Patient Relationship', in W. F. Bynum and Roy Porter, eds, *Companion Encyclopedia of the History of Medicine, volume 2* (New York, London: Routledge, 2001), 794–795; Allan M. Brandt and Martha Gardner, 'The Golden Age of Medicine?', in Roger Cooter and John Pickstone, eds, *Companion to Medicine in the Twentieth Century* (London: Routledge, 2003), 21–38. Mike Saks explores the rise of a 'counter culture' against 'orthodox medicine', symbolised by trends in litigation and self-help, and rising public interest in alternative medicine and holistic health care in 'Medicine and the Counter Culture', in Cooter and Pickstone, *Companion to Medicine in the Twentieth Century*, 113–123.
38. Griffiths and Moynihan, 'Multiple Epiphysial Injuries in Babies': 1558–1561; 'Cruelty to Children', *British Medical Journal*, 21 December 1963: 1544; E. E. Sumpter, 'Battered Baby Syndrome', *British Medical Journal*, 26 March 1966: 800–801.
39. Caffey, 'Significance of the history': 1009.
40. As quoted in Kempe, *A Good Knight for Children*, 66–67%.
41. This assumption—about the absence of emotion in contemporary medical publications—will be tested and challenged by the work of the Wellcome Trust Senior Investigator Award on 'Surgery and Emotion', led by Dr Michael Brown at the University of Roehampton. This research group provides regular updates on their work through their website, http://www.surgeryandemotion.com/.
42. Eric Turner, '"Battered Baby" Syndrome', *British Medical Journal*, 1 February 1964: 308.
43. Kempe, *A Good Knight for Children*, 71%.
44. 'Cruelty to Children', p. 1544.
45. Kempe et al., 'The Battered Child', 145.
46. Skinner and Castle, *78 Battered Children*, 1.
47. Ibid., 4.

48. Ibid., 15–16, 20.
49. B. F. Steele and C. B. Pollock, 'A psychiatric study of parents who abuse infants and small children', P. F. Helfer and C. H. Kempe (eds), *The Battered Child*; C. H. Kempe, 'The battered child and the hospital', *Hospital Practice*, 4 (1969): 44–57 as cited in Selwyn M. Smith, 'The Battered Child Syndrome—Some Research Aspects', *The Bulletin of the American Academy of Psychiatry and the Law*, 4, no. 3 (1976): 235.
50. See: John Welshman, *Underclass: a history of the excluded since 1880* (2nd edition, London: Bloomsbury, 2013); John Welshman, 'Troubles and the family: changes and continuities since 1943', *Social Policy and Society*, 16 (1) (2017): 109–117; John Welshman, *From Transmitted Deprivation to Social Exclusion: Policy, Poverty, and Parenting* (Bristol: Policy Press, 2007); Michael Lambert, *"Problem families" and the post-war welfare state in the North West of England, 1943–74* (PhD thesis, Lancaster University, 2017).
51. Simon Yudkin, 'Battered Baby Syndrome', *British Medical Journal*, 16 April 1966, 980; G. M. Fleming, 'Cruelty to Children', *British Medical Journal*, 13 May 1967, 422.
52. Hugh McLeave, 'What makes these parents so cruel', *Daily Mail*, 22 April 1965, 10.
53. Ibid., 10.
54. Ibid., 10.
55. Ibid., 10.
56. Kempe et al., 'The Battered Child Syndrome', 145.
57. Baher et al., *At Risk*, 65.
58. Hansard, House of Commons, fifth series, 25 July 1969, vol. 787, col. 2309.
59. Callaghan quote: Hansard, House of Commons, fifth series, 11 March 1969, vol. 779, col. 1176.
60. Kempe et al., The Battered Child Syndrome', 145.
61. Simon Yudkin, 'Battered Baby Syndrome', *British Medical Journal*, 16 April 1966, 981; G. M. Fleming, 'Cruelty to Children', *British Medical Journal*, 13 May 1967, 422. See also: Kempe and Kempe, *Child Abuse*, 8, 10.
62. Call for a sympathetic approach in: Skinner and Castle, *78 Battered Children*, 20. An emphasis on prevention is clear within the Annual Reports of Barnardos and the Children's Society: Liverpool University Special Collections and Archives, Barnardos Archives, D239 A3/1/98, Annual Report 1963, 12; Children's Society Archives, Annual Reports, AR85.0063.44 *Annual Report for 1966*, 4; Children's Society Archives, Annual Reports, AR85.0063.454, *Annual Report for 1967*, 3. For discussion of social policy of this period which focused on prevention and family maintenance see: Harry Hendrick, *Children, Childhood and English Society 1880–1990* (Cambridge: Cambridge University Press, 1997), 56–57.

63. Gans, 'Battered Babies', 1286–1287.
64. Skinner and Castle, *78 Battered Children*, 7.
65. Ibid., 19.
66. Kempe, *A Good Knight for Children*, 71%.
67. See discussion of this shift, and of when exactly it occurred, in: Pat Starkey, 'The Medical Officer, the Social Worker, and the Problem Family, 1943 to 1968: The Case of Family Service Units', *Social History of Medicine*, 11, no. 3 (1998): 421–441.

Open Access This chapter is licensed under the terms of the Creative Commons Attribution 4.0 International License (http://creativecommons.org/licenses/by/4.0/), which permits use, sharing, adaptation, distribution and reproduction in any medium or format, as long as you give appropriate credit to the original author(s) and the source, provide a link to the Creative Commons license and indicate if changes were made.

The images or other third party material in this chapter are included in the chapter's Creative Commons license, unless indicated otherwise in a credit line to the material. If material is not included in the chapter's Creative Commons license and your intended use is not permitted by statutory regulation or exceeds the permitted use, you will need to obtain permission directly from the copyright holder.

CHAPTER 3

Hearing Children's Experiences in Public

This chapter explores how interest in children's experiences and emotions emerged and developed from the early 1970s to the early 1990s. In particular, it looks at how public policy, often through the work of charities, sought to understand, bring to light, consider, mediate, and assess children's self-expressions and representations of their inner worlds. This chapter demonstrates that, to an extent, these decades were characterised by increasing interest in children's experiences from psychologists, psychiatrists, and children's charities such as the NSPCC and ChildLine. At the same time, adult definitions of children's experiences were never clear-cut or uncontentious. Not all children had equal opportunities to contribute to public inquiries or to use voluntary services and, significantly, the idea of the child's interests, intimately bound up with experience, could also be deployed by adults in pursuit of specific agendas. This chapter is not therefore an examination of what children's experiences and emotions were in the late twentieth century. Indeed, in part what this chapter argues is that children's experiences cannot be—and have never been—accessed without significant mediation and reconstruction. Looking to reconstruct precisely what children said in such recent child protection cases would be particularly problematic, given the confidential nature of many children's testimonies to legal and social work inquiries.

What this chapter does offer, however, is analysis of the changing public and political spaces in which children's experiences and emotions were

© The Author(s) 2018
J. Crane, *Child Protection in England, 1960–2000*, Palgrave Studies in the History of Childhood,
https://doi.org/10.1007/978-3-319-94718-1_3

sought out and made public in the 1970s, 1980s, and 1990s, and in which adult ideas of these abstract conceptions—'child experiences' and 'child emotions'—became significant in shaping social policies, public inquiries, and voluntary work. Such established interest in child experience and emotion was a new phenomenon to these decades and marked a significant development from the paternalistic interests in child wellbeing discussed in Chap. 2, which were entwined with a vision of childhood vulnerability and powerlessness. Nonetheless, read alongside Chap. 4, this chapter demonstrates how children faced particular challenges in accessing and utilising a broader expertise grounded in experience and emotion, which was adopted by parents and survivors, as hierarchies between adults and children proved difficult to disassemble.

Where Was the Child? The Maria Colwell Case

Looking closely at the landmark case of Maria Colwell—and comparing this at the end of this chapter to the significant Cleveland case—demonstrates the extent to which public policy interest in children's experiences increased over the 1970s and 1980s. Maria Colwell was the fifth child of Raymond and Pauline Colwell, born in 1965 in Brighton. Her father died when she was a baby, and she was placed into the care of her aunt and uncle, the Coopers, while her siblings remained with their mother. On remarrying to William Kepple in July 1970, Pauline became 'determined' to regain custody of Maria.[1] In October 1971, social services returned Maria to her mother.[2] In the ensuing months, Maria was subject to severe physical and emotional mistreatment at the hands of her new stepfather and neglect by her mother. Maria was regularly locked into her bedroom, whilst Pauline Kepple's other children were given sweets and ice cream.[3] On the night of 6 January 1973, when Maria was just seven years old, William Kepple beat her until she died. The public inquiry conducted months later noted that it was impossible to ascertain the precise circumstances surrounding the days preceding Maria's death, particularly given the conflicting and confused evidence provided by William and Pauline Kepple.[4]

William Kepple was sentenced to eight years in prison for manslaughter (later reduced to four years).[5] In the ensuing months the residents of Whitehawk Council estate, where Maria had lived, the *Brighton Argus* newspaper, and the local Conservative Member of Parliament, Andrew Bowden, campaigned for a government inquiry into the supervision of

Maria by local authorities and other agencies. In May 1973, following a meeting with Bowden, this request was granted by the Conservative Secretary of State for Social Services, Keith Joseph.[6] With no precedent for such an inquiry, it took the form of a quasi-judicial hearing, meaning that witnesses appeared voluntarily and were open to cross-examination by both defence and prosecution.[7] Following a preliminary hearing on 24 August 1973, there were 41 days of public hearings between 9 October and 7 December 1973, where the inquiry heard 70 witnesses, received 13 written submissions, and examined 99 documents.[8] The inquiry gained widespread media coverage and public attention, and was significant in bringing awareness of child protection issues to social and political arenas. The format set by the inquiry also established a compositional pattern replicated in following inquiries over the next quarter of a century.[9]

Professional conflict and failure was the primary focus of the public inquiry and media coverage around this case. The inquiry report discussed poor communication between Maria's school, social services, the NSPCC, housing departments, police, and local communities.[10] Maria's social worker, an inspector from the NSPCC, and Maria's family doctor came under scrutiny for missing concerns raised by Maria's neighbours and schools.[11] The castigation of these individuals was framed primarily in terms of 'responsibility' rather than 'blame', particularly in the minority report provided by committee member and social worker Olive Stevenson.[12] While the majority report criticised those who allowed Maria's mother to regain custody, Stevenson emphasised the difficulties for social workers of having to make decisions under time pressure and with limited resources.[13] Stevenson supported the decision of the social worker to allow Maria to return to her mother, arguing that she could not have foreseen Maria's death.[14] This position found sympathy in contemporary newspaper coverage of the case, much of which replicated the British Association of Social Workers' (BASW) post-inquiry statement that their profession was 'on the edge of a precipice'. Notably, the BASW statement also criticised the 'dilution of child care expertise' following the consolidation of disparate social work departments into one generic 'social services' in 1970.[15]

In addition to underlining the role of 'experts', the Colwell report and subsequent newspaper coverage also paid much attention to 'society'. Society was in part conceptualised vaguely and in terms which suggested focus on professional relations: the public inquiry concluded by stating that 'the system' had failed to 'absorb individual errors' and it was society, which had created this system, on which the 'ultimate blame must rest' for Maria's death.[16] At the same time, ideas about communities and specifically working-class communities were also embedded in discussions of the social. The inquiry report's conclusion suggested that the 'highly emotional and angry reaction of the public in this case may indicate society's troubled conscience', suggesting a vision of broader public responsibility for child protection.[17] Attention was paid to how several neighbours had sought to bring concerns about Maria's treatment to statutory and voluntary agencies. Meanwhile, the report also reproduced warnings from 'several agencies involved in the inquiry' that the neighbours' evidence should be treated with caution as the Kepples were 'social "misfits"' in a 'somewhat superior council house area' and as many neighbours were related and 'anti-Kepple'.[18]

Concurrent media coverage praised residents of the Whitehawk estate for their attempts to report Maria's case and for their lobbying for a public inquiry. The *Sunday Times* described the 'people of Maresfield Road' as 'ordinary, respectable people' who 'tried to warn officials'.[19] Notably, responsibility for child protection was placed not only on individuals or on family units at this time. Responsibility was also situated in specific neighbourhoods, with particular pressure for council estate residents to perform 'ordinary respectability'.[20] Ingrained within this account, and within this stated vision of classlessness, was deep interest in linking the morality of working-class people with examination of their homes and personal appearances. While media described the residents of Maresfield Road as 'respectable', police reports referred to Mrs Kepple as 'low class and lacking in intelligence'.[21] The involved social worker portrayed the Kepple household as 'poorly furnished and managed; clothing adequate; rather dirty', while the Cooper house by contrast was deemed 'reasonably clean and well kept though somewhat cramped'.[22] The public inquiry chairman, Thomas Field-Fisher, likewise asked each witness whether the Kepples were a 'problem' family.[23] In the debates surrounding this inquiry, ordinariness and respectability thus became tropes to aspire to. Nonetheless, long-standing frameworks of class—the problem family and indeed visions of 'intelligence'—also remained significant in inflecting professional analyses, as in the work of the 1960s about the battered child.[24] These frameworks mediated and controlled how, and the extent to which, communities could report child protection concerns, and constructed a hierarchical relationship between families and professionals, where families were analysed, assessed, and judged.

While focus was shifted to society, community, and family, to an extent the children involved in the Maria Colwell inquiry were represented as passive agents. In this period, media narratives were representing children as a symbol for broader adult anxieties, for example around 'tug of love' adoption cases between biological and adoptive families.[25] Maria Colwell in particular became symbolic of a broader need for legislative change in child protection, as exemplified by calls in the House of Commons and newspapers to answer 'how many more Marias are there'?[26] Concurrently however, the public inquiry report also represented an early attempt to understand the perspectives of young children. The report argued that 'even very small children possess sometimes a remarkable acuity as to the implications of both situations and conversations which adults ignore at their peril'.[27] Indeed, the report found that statutory agencies had had interest in Maria's interior life and her emotions—social workers and teachers had observed how Maria became upset during visits from her mother before she was rehomed, and that this may have marked her first 'fears for her security and happy home at the Coopers'.[28] In addition, the report noted that previous case discussions around Maria had discussed the potential for her 'stress and trauma'.[29]

While practitioners had demonstrated interest in Maria's emotional life, knowledge of this had been primarily derived from observation, not consultation. Practitioners interacting with Maria drew their conclusions by observing her performed emotional states—whether Maria was 'happy', 'outgoing', or 'subdued' was gleaned from observation of her physical behaviours, for example, repeatedly running away from visits with her biological mother, and showing 'strenuous' resistance by 'kicking and screaming'.[30] Further validating the idea that observation was seen as a key means to access children's inner worlds in the mid-1970s, the social worker involved told the inquiry that she had had to make 'an intelligent guess as to Maria's true feelings'.[31] Testimonies from Maria herself were not featured in the majority report from the public inquiry, though they were discussed in Stevenson's minority report.[32]

The Colwell public inquiry report hence provided evidence of professional interest in accessing children's emotions and experiences, primarily through observation rather than expression. However, the discussions of this report also demonstrated that these testimonies were not yet central to the decisions made in case conferences nor to public inquiry analysis. Commenting on the case, child psychologist and Director of the National Children's Bureau Mia Kellmer Pringle argued that it demonstrated that 'professional opinion' may still 'weight the scales' in favour of adults over children, and that children's voices must be heard independently of adults.[33] While social and political attention had turned further to focus on children's welfare, the child was also a symbol for the negotiation of broader professional and 'community' tensions, and not always a direct participant within decision-making about their own lives.

Children's Experiences: Rhetoric or Practice?

Following interest from the early 1970s in listening to the 'thoughts, beliefs, experiences and reactions' of adults who used social work services, practitioners' concerns about 'listening', 'hearing', 'believing' in, and 'validating' the 'experiences' of children developed from the 1980s and in the 1990s.[34] Different interpretations of 'experience' underpinned this work. In part, to listen to children's experiences was to interview children, capture their testimonies, and disseminate edited versions of these publicly. This was the approach, for example, of a 1979 collection by the clinical psychologist Valerie Yule on 'the origins of violence'. Yule described her collection as presenting stories and poems 'told by children who could not write them'.[35] While Yule's interviewees were primarily from the industrial inner suburbs of Melbourne, Australia, her book was published in London and prefaced by words from a former physician at the Hospital for Sick Children, Great Ormond Street.[36] The images and words produced explained how children saw violence in their own terms with, for instance, one eight-year-old describing domestic violence faced by her mother: 'She -uh-her-the man going kill her/Then the ambblelan will come.'[37] In this collection, the reproduction of children's misspellings and pronunciations was positioned as evidencing a direct representation of their testimonies, and as revealing the connections that children were making between the violence in their domestic spaces and the responses of the statutory or voluntary sectors.

In *Life and Love and Everything: Children's Questions Answered by Claire Rayner* (1993), popular agony aunt Clare Rayner interpreted children's experiences in a related fashion. Rayner extended her agony aunt service—further subject to analysis in Chap. 7—towards children, again replicating and in this case answering their concerns. The letters from children reprinted included a variety of queries about social life and wellbeing, with discussions of violence introduced as part of these broader worlds. In one letter, a child called Meena asked what to do 'when my mum is all ways [sic] smacking me on my bottom because I don't listen to her'. While the specific dynamics of this violence were unclear, Rayner responded by encouraging Meena to speak with her mother and to 'make a plan'.[38] Rayner also suggested that if a deal was not made, Meena ask her father or grandmother to intervene and to establish what was fair.[39] In a sense then, popular culture and literary works were disseminating children's experiences. To represent experience was perceived as to replicate children's writings or words, including the direct reproduction of their dialectic and misspellings. The case studies from Yule and Rayner demonstrated the ways in which this interest in childhood experiences was to be mediated and curated by adults, and also suggested a shift in terms of children's accounts being marketed as 'entertainment' in popular book collections. Such collections discussed violence within broad discussions of child and adult lives, marking an entwinement between therapy and entertainment in culture also visible in the popularity of the agony aunt phenomena and in later 'reality' television coverage of marital and family life.

In addition to such mediated published accounts, the self-representation of children, discussing their own experiences, was also becoming important in a series of new legal, political, and medical spaces: in courtrooms, through voting, in doctors' surgeries, and at self-help groups. In 1969, medical confidentiality was granted to those aged 16 and older and the age of majority was reduced from 21 to 18. The *Criminal Justice Acts* of 1988 and 1991 allowed child witnesses to testify in court.[40] The *Children Act* of 1975 stated that courts and adoption agencies must seek 'so far as practicable' to 'ascertain the wishes and feelings of the child regarding the decision'.[41] The same period saw doctors beginning to consider children as active consumers of the healthcare system, for example, as the House of Lords rejected Victoria Gillick's challenge to whether doctors could prescribe contraceptives to children under the age of 16 without parental consent. The legal judgement in this case paid testimony to the idea that a child could reach a 'sufficient understanding and intelligence to be capable of making up his own mind'.[42] Hearing children's experiences by creating pathways through which children could represent themselves in public, in law, in education, and in medicine became increasingly important. By the 2000s, children's testimonies were sought out—at least in theory—through school councils, peer counselling in schools, by a children's commissioner, and in young people's forums for medical Royal Colleges.[43] New private fora were also being created in the 1980s for children to hold open conversations with professionals, for example in the self-help groups for children who had been abused organised at Great Ormond Street Hospital.[44]

These diverse trends all reflected a sense in which stated interests in children's experiences were enacted in various public and private spaces. While recourse to child experience was not merely a rhetorical strategy, significant disagreement remained about how, where, and when to best access it. In terms of child protection, psychologists disagreed about whether interrogative questions should be leading, to encourage children to speak about their experiences, or 'neutral', and around whether using anatomically accurate dolls would help children to discuss abuse or confuse their testimony.[45] Contemporary research from sociology and social work emphasised that structurally disadvantaged children were the least likely to be able to be heard in these new spaces.[46] Social anthropologists, notably Judith Ennew, also argued that child protection concerns should be taken broadly, in terms of prostitution, poverty, family, and the social relations of power.[47] These debates demonstrated the ways in which professional communities sought to negotiate new interest in children's inner lives, and the challenges of ensuring that all children's experiences could be heard.

Significantly, concerns about children's emotions were central in interpretations of child experience, acting as a perceived marker for whether children's experiences had been accessed successfully. Notably, this was in contrast to earlier accounts of the 1960s and 1970s, studied in Chap. 2, in which policy and practitioner focus centred on the emotions of the parents and clinicians involved in child protection cases. In part, the new interest in child emotional life was driven by psychologists and educators in child protection, who emphasised that analysis of children's emotions would enable people to identify if they were being abused, spotting if they seemed 'depressed and low in spirits' or had a 'fear of a particular individual'.[48] At the same time, children and parents themselves, relying on and contributing to increased interest from researchers, were also drawing attention towards the significance of emotion. In a publication from 1995, interviewers working for the Women's Aid Federation of England provided accounts of domestic violence in children's own terms, which expressed guilt, confusion, anger, powerlessness, bitterness, and rejection.[49] Children reported a struggle to express their feelings, for example testifying that, 'I used to smile so that people wouldn't know'.[50] Parents likewise, psychologists reported, were calling for increased training and information about how to protect children from their own emotions and from those of strangers.[51]

Interest in children's experiences therefore was in a sense developing in the 1980s and 1990s, in part reliant on interest from researchers and psychologists but, at the same time, also guided by discussions with certain children themselves, who provided testimony and drew attention to their emotions. Personal testimonies demonstrated that children used physical and behavioural performances to mask and represent specific emotional states. The published accounts which emerged presented a contrasting model to earlier accounts of the 'battered child' as too young or vulnerable to express their own experiences, though nonetheless the narration of children's emotions remained curated by adults.

Adult Interpretations of Child Experience

With the construction of child experience emerging as powerful, the claim to be listening to, creating spaces for, or representing children's voices could function to promote or conceal specific adult agendas. To take just one example—writing the introduction for an edited collection, *The Maltreatment of Children*, published in 1978, psychiatrist Myre Sim sought to speak *in* the voice of a child.[52] Writing that 'we are all very small and helpless', Sim argued that 'society' had raised funds, passed legislation, sponsored research, and changed training, but that these measures had not made a substantial difference, either in terms of the outcome of child protection cases or by placing further social emphasis on children's lived experiences. While this demonstrated interest in expressing and representing children's views, children themselves did not contribute to this collection, and indeed they were represented as 'all very small and helpless'.[53]

In part, Sim utilised this space, which was curated by and directed at professionals, to demand a professional-level rethink of professional action. Sim argued that there was too little urgency in child protection work, and that fundraising, legislation, training, and research had made little difference.[54] While calling professionals 'well-intentioned' and 'some of the kindest and most concerned people', Sim also labelled them 'incompetent' and 'touchy'.[55] His article did not only challenge professional practice in general, but specifically questioned a 'slavish devotion' to psychologist John Bowlby's views on attachment theory.[56] Further demonstrative of the politicised potential of using descriptions of childhood experience, Sim also used this piece to challenge abortion policies, criticising the pro-choice movement and arguing that 'most battered babies are not unwanted; many are over-wanted'.[57] This piece therefore was a provocative one, framed by a specific political viewpoint. While intending to address child protection practitioners, rather than to reconstruct or report on children's own viewpoints, Myre simulated child voice as a powerful tool.

By the mid-1980s to early-1990s, an active critique of how adults may utilise children's testimony about their own experiences emerged, particularly in discussions around satanic ritual abuse. Concern about satanic ritual abuse emerged in America and later in Britain and Western Europe from the 1980s, with accusations that networks and cults were abusing children as part of satanic rituals involving murder, cannibalism, animal sacrifice, and torture. In Britain, analysis of alleged cases in Rochdale, Nottingham, and the Orkney Islands saw controversy about whether the satanic elements of these organised abuse cases were 'moral panics' or 'real', and about the roles of media, child protection professionals, evangelicals, and children and adults themselves in raising and shaping concerns.[58] In professional reflection on these cases, a key question became about how children's accurate accounts could be accessed and understood—framed by media in terms of separating 'fact from fantasy', and about the extent to which 'video nasties', media representations, and the interview styles of practitioners shaped children's narratives.[59]

The Department of Health funded the anthropologist Jean La Fontaine to produce a report on these cases, *The Extent and Nature of Organised and Ritual Abuse* (1994). Investigating 84 cases of organised child abuse containing allegations of ritual or satanic components, the report found no evidence that abuse had been conducted as part of a satanic ritual, and only three cases that showed any evidence of ritual.[60] In this report, and in a subsequent book discussing the case, *Speak of the Devil* (1998), La Fontaine argued that 'adult constructions' had shaped children's accounts, and also that 'different professionals'—foster parents, social workers, police, psychiatrists, and charities—used 'children's sayings and behaviour ... as evidence for particular conclusions'.[61]

In part, La Fontaine argued, the assumption that 'telling' was key for children, the 'first step ... on the road to a normal life', motivated adults to try and push children to provide answers, or to see children's silences as suspicious during interviews.[62] La Fontaine argued that fixation on satanic abuse specifically was a cultural phenomenon and served to distract from work with damaged or disadvantaged children.[63] La Fontaine's report was not without its critics, notably survivor support groups, and child psychologists who argued that they had worked with children who had experienced satanic abuse and survivor support groups.[64] Valerie Sinason, a child psychotherapist at the Tavistock Clinic in London, was significant in providing an intentional 'counterpart' to La Fontaine's work. Sinason released a collection, *Treating Survivors of Satanist Abuse* (1994), a few weeks before the publication of La Fontaine's report, and it contained contributions by psychotherapists, psychiatrists, social workers, counsellors, and journalists.[65] Media framing around this publication challenged what type of 'evidence' La Fontaine wanted, and her omission of not speaking to adult survivors.[66]

Significantly, these contested and controversial debates drew professional and public attention to the complexity of accessing child experience, and to questions about how existing power dynamics between children and adults would shape its manifestations. The debates demonstrated that interest in children's opinions, beliefs, and voices would be judged, mediated, and interpreted through broader adult debates, notably in the media as well as by and between psychologists and sociologists. They also suggested an extent to which the turn towards thinking about children's inner worlds, and towards taking their emotions and experiences seriously, would be met by moralising and anxieties about the authenticity of children's accounts, and about the 'fantasies' or 'fevered imagination[s]' uncovered.[67] While clear power dynamics were significant here, the issue of power—as relating to age, class, gender, race, and ethnicity—rarely became central in debates about how to construct and narrate child experience. This absence persisted even as the mid-1980s public inquiries into the deaths of Jasmine Beckford and Tyra Henry challenged how effectively statutory agencies served and investigated black and minority ethnic families.[68] The focus on children's experiences thus opened up a new space in which children were recognised as capable of holding expertise which would, for example, be crucial for criminal cases. At the same time, children remained relatively powerless in terms of governing how and when their voices were heard, and child experience was typically discussed in abstract terms.

Helplines[69]

One key medium for the expression of children's experiences from the mid-1980s was the helpline. In relation to child protection, this medium was first used through the Incest Crisis Line from 1982, the National Children's Home 'Touchline' for sexually abused children, which opened in Yorkshire in 1986, and with the inception of ChildLine in 1986.[70] ChildLine was launched after Esther Rantzen, the presenter of the contemporary consumer affairs programme *That's Life!*, approached British Broadcasting Corporation (BBC) Controller Michael Grade having read newspaper coverage of the death of a toddler.[71] In Spring 1986, *That's Life!* appealed for responses to a survey about child abuse. Three thousand adults replied, 90 per cent of whom were women. Of all respondents, 90 per cent recounted experience of sexual abuse perpetrated in nine of ten cases by a member of their own family. The programme also opened a helpline for 48 hours, run by social workers who spoke to around one hundred children about sexual abuse. Following this, the special programme *Childwatch* was aired on 30 October 1986 to launch ChildLine, which also received premises and a telephone number from British Telecom (BT). The institution of ChildLine was thus deeply shaped by media influence from its inception, and found influential early support from the BBC and BT.

Testimonies about experience were central to the early foundation of ChildLine, featured heavily on *Childwatch* alongside 'expert' testimony and also in newspaper coverage around the new charity which republished survey responses. *The Times* reprinted testimony from a 13-year-old that she walked home slowly from school, hoping to be 'mugged, raped or run over', as she knew that these things would not be 'as bad' as what waited for her at home.[72] The newspaper also reprinted a report from a woman who was abused as a child, who would be left in a freezing cold and dark attic and who recalled how 'frightened' she was.[73] Rantzen told *The Times* that these testimonies left her 'shocked' but mostly 'angry'.[74] While Rantzen felt that national polls had given 'the cold statistics' about the prevalence of abuse, she emphasised that the *Childwatch* survey had shown 'what it feels like to be abused as a child and how it affects the rest of your life'.[75] Notably, the producers of *Childwatch*, Ritchie Cogan and Sarah Caplin, also recognised the significance of a global context, particularly in terms of proving the validity of, and need for, this new approach. Writing for the *Observer*, Cogan and Caplin emphasised that Holland had a parallel service, Kindertelefoon, established in 1979, while Sweden and America also had similar organisations.[76]

From the inception of this phone line therefore, its significance was couched in terms of being shaped by, and enabling the spread of, children's testimonies—internationally, as well as nationally. Thinking about inner feelings was presented as fuelling mobilising emotions within the group's founders. Emotions embedded in qualitative testimonies were motivators to action, shaped and supported by quantitative research that vindicated the broader significance of such narratives. Criticism of

Childwatch was likewise couched in terms of warning against the dangers of such emotional affect. For example, the *Daily Mail* questioned whether the show 'whips people up into a state of agitation', causing 'too much' emotion which, the newspaper contended, may then mean that children were taken unnecessarily from their parents.[77]

For children nonetheless, ChildLine positioned the sharing of emotion and experience as a positive phenomenon, both for individual therapeutic purposes but also in terms of forming a sense of ownership over ChildLine itself as a virtual space. On an individual level, children's ownership was promoted by the medium of this organisation—the phone line—which meant that children could avoid eye contact and guide the duration and timing of their encounters. ChildLine also had a confidentiality policy from its inception, only making referrals to statutory agencies if the child consented, unless their life was under threat. In ChildLine's *Annual Report* of 1994, Rantzen emphasised that the organisation only referred a 'tiny fraction' of all calls to social services, because their counsellors job was rather to 'listen, to comfort and to help children to work through their pain'.[78] This tended to involve directing children to speak with an adult they trusted, rather than approaching statutory services directly.[79] The length of time of the call was important too—children could speak with counsellors for as long or as short a period as they wished.[80] The notion of local voice was highly significant within the helpline model, and ChildLine established regional counselling centres across the UK, in addition to their London headquarters, to enable children to speak to counsellors from nearby areas. The organisation's leaders suggested that children would benefit from speaking to people with a familiar accent and with understandings of children's regional subcultures.[81] The inflections and tones of the voices heard were thus conceptualised as important, alongside the new nature of listening to experiences and emotion. Throughout this organisation, interest in the physicality of voice was blended with concern about childhood openness and sharing.

Volunteers met the invitation for children to discuss their concerns. Annual reports described how volunteer counsellors were 'carefully selected and trained', and that many had previously worked with children as, for example, teachers, nurses, and social workers, while valued equally were 'fathers, mothers, students, retired people, actors, bank clerks'.[82] This statement again promoted a model of 'ordinariness', whereby 'relatable' and 'respectable' individuals in communities would volunteer through ChildLine to enact child protection work. The key qualification presented was that counsellors 'love children and enjoy listening to them'.[83] Indeed, ChildLine emphasised that visitors were impressed by its 'professionalism', though also that it was founded because of abstract ideals—'commitment, compassion and love of children'.[84] The dual focus on emphasising professionalism and compassion emerged as the voluntary sector more broadly professionalised, amidst pressure to reform institutional children's services, but also with the politicisation of debates about what, exactly, 'children's experiences' were. By using and promoting the empathy and compassion of volunteers, ChildLine presented a positive model of society and of community life, whereby many people from many professions were willing and able to make a time commitment to help children. Simultaneously, the organisation's work also drew attention to abuse, violence, and childhood unhappiness within communities, families, and institutions.

While adult volunteers were key, from its inception ChildLine's leaders sought to emphasise that the organisation was not theirs, but rather 'took root in the minds of children and young people as their line … the place that children and young people identify as their own'.[85] This notion was to an extent validated within children's use of the line to discuss, at first sexual and physical abuse, primarily within the home, but later a range of issues around bullying, unhappiness, emotional problems, self-harm, eating disorders, and physical and mental health.[86] Following this range of defined issues, ChildLine's definitions of 'abuse' were shaped by children themselves in terms of, Rantzen told *Newsround*, 'anything that troubles a child really', or anything which made a child feel 'pain', 'uncomfortable', or 'unhappy'.[87] Contemporary testimony collected in 2016 by the *One Show*, for the 30th anniversary of ChildLine, reflected the ongoing significance of these narratives of child ownership and listening, with adults testifying that as children the organisation had 'listened [to them] when no one else did', and been '[t]here to listen'.[88] While adult volunteers were positioned as important, children were expected—or invited—to feel a sense of ownership over this virtual space. Nonetheless, ChildLine faced contemporary critique for enabling children to express testimonies in their own terms. *The Times* journalist Barbara Amiel challenged ChildLine's definition of abuse as 'too broad', potentially including 'little girls afraid of the dark and little boys with school nerves'.[89] The idea of girls and boys as 'little' again presented a model of vulnerability and powerlessness, and of children whose fears—school or darkness—were not always significant. By the 1980s, therefore, children's emotions and experiences *could* be made public, but they were not always taken seriously, nor used to influence change.

ChildLine thus occupied an important place in discussions of child protection in mid-1980s Britain. Its focus on testimony and also on providing children's services over the phone, while in accord with broader legal, medical, and social interest in children's experiences, also put ChildLine in to tension with existing child protection charities and state agencies. Looking retrospectively in 2016 to the foundation moment of ChildLine, Shaun Woodward, its former Deputy Chair, and Anne Houston, a former director in Scotland, reflected back that existing 'experts' expressed concern that the organisation represented 'well-intentioned meddling by amateurs', while ChildLine felt able to 'challenge traditional agencies'.[90] These concerns, while recorded retrospectively, were echoed in contemporary newspaper coverage, suggesting that 'experts' had 'reservations' about the organisation—about whether it was necessary and also conversely about whether it would uncover needs which social services could not meet.[91] Reflecting challenges for female leaders in the voluntary sector at this moment, contemporary newspaper coverage also discussed an 'image war' between the organisation's leaders, Valerie Howarth, director of ChildLine, and Esther Rantzen, the founder.[92]

These 'expert' tensions represented broader disagreements about whether the priorities of child protection work should be led by journalists and media, increasing public awareness and lobbying government, or by ongoing intervention and campaigning from statutory agencies and charities. ChildLine would mediate between these lines. The charity drew support from the BBC and BT, but also met with criticism from tabloids. ChildLine received funding and support from successive governments, though at times the charity's leaders were also critical of statutory services. Howarth positioned ChildLine as operating within a 'tapestry of services for children', but it was also a disruptive force, challenging existing relationships between voluntary and statutory agencies, media, governments, and public.[93]

To an extent, children were also to be trained by ChildLine in later years to meet one another's needs: the ChildLine in Partnership with Schools programme, founded in 1996, enabled psychologists to teach children to help one another.[94] At the same time, psychologists also told children to 'be aware of the limits of their own expertise', and to refer serious problems to teachers.[95] Nonetheless, the idea that ChildLine should address children directly was taken up in Parliament. In 1989, members questioned Home Office regulations assuming that parents should be responsible for educating children about child protection, citing calls to ChildLine as evidence that these adults may be the perpetrators of abuse.[96] The interest in communicating child protection directly to children is addressed in the following chapter of this book, demonstrating how interest in understanding, recording, and inculcating children's expertise emerged hand-in-hand in the mid-1980s. In the case of ChildLine, addressing children directly to an extent bypassed broader debates about the role of communities and families in child protection: about what 'communities' and 'families' were, how they had changed in late modernity, and whether they were acting as protective or dangerous spaces for children.

Thus, the renewed interest in seeking out children's experiences was met by a range of actors, in part continuing existing hierarchies—for example, between teachers and students—but also testing out relations anew, for example between voluntary sector and state and between parent and child, in a disruptive moment met with concern about making 'private parenting concerns' public.[97] Interest in child experience was not only a political construct utilised to mask broader agendas, but also lived in the voluntary sector through conscious efforts to enable children to speak in their own time, in their own terms, to volunteers. ChildLine's work was reliant on the media—the service was launched by the BBC and featured heavily in national newspapers. While the *Daily Mail* questioned whether child protection was becoming 'show-biz', this also marked a significant transformation in terms of the public discussion and exposition of children's testimonies.[98] From the mid-1980s and by the 1990s, as subsequent chapters demonstrate, media interest in the experiences and emotions of children, parents, and survivors developed further still.

Children in Public Policy

ChildLine sought to mobilise children's testimonies politically, and thus to make them powerful in public policy. This aim was conceptualised by ChildLine's leaders not merely as an extension of their work, but as a moral and social duty. The organisation's *Annual Report* of 1994 emphasised that with 'listening' came a responsibility for ChildLine to 'give children a voice', and to use their 'unique access' to 'children's views and experience' to inform 'decision-makers'—notably based on contact with around 80,000 children and young people per year in the early 1990s.[99]

This vision of moral duty, borne from the service's unique work, reshaped the working lives of volunteers. From inception, ChildLine volunteers took physical notes of each child's call, later writing them into full case notes and entering them into computers.[100] This had therapeutic focus—enabling different counsellors to advise the same children; legal purpose—with the children's permission, the notes could be used as evidence in court cases; and political power.[101] While records were drawn from a sample and completed as a record of a phone call, rather than representing a direct recording of the child's comments, these summarised notes became central to ChildLine's published studies around, for example, bullying, child abuse, and racism.[102]

Looking at a case study reveals the ways in which ChildLine sought to turn children's testimonies into a political resource, a source of critique, and a mode of childhood empowerment. In a chapter of "*It Hurts Me Too*": *Children's Experiences of Domestic Violence and Refuge Life* (1995), ChildLine workers Carole Epstein and Gill Keep sought to 'highlight the predicament' of children affected by domestic violence by 'conveying their own thoughts and words'.[103] Epstein and Keep emphasised that the organisation held a 'rich source of information' drawn from 'direct communication with large numbers of children who give us their accounts, views and feelings about their predicament'.[104] Between June 1993 and May 1994, ChildLine had spoken to 1554 children about domestic violence, and the chapter analysed a sample of 126 calls. Within the sample, the majority of children were between 11 and 15 years old, and 91 per cent of callers were female—above the overall ratio of girls to boys calling ChildLine at that time, which was four to one.[105] The majority of children—110—described violence against their mother perpetrated by her partner.[106]

From this sample, Epstein and Keep drew clear messages: that children rarely used the term 'domestic violence', that violence nonetheless had typically been occurring for a long time, and that children struggled to make sense of this.[107] Children's emotions were a key focus in this chapter, which discussed how children often empathised with their mothers' feelings and felt 'angry' and 'hurt' but also 'disappointment' and 'intense frustration' when their mother did nothing, or took her partner's side.[108] The chapter expressed concern about the connections between these emotions and the physical states of children, suggesting that this emotional stress may cause abdominal complaints, asthma, ulcers, arthritis, and enuresis.[109] Children's emotions were framed around vulnerability, with discussion of them feeling anxious, confused, alarmed, fearful, alert, scared, frightened, distraught, sad, helpless, betrayed, ashamed, and powerless.[110] These expressed emotions were said to demonstrate that children were 'helpless', not 'strong' or 'powerful'. Thus, this lived testimony, and indeed the specific framing of this testimony, demonstrated the challenges in this moment of making children 'expert'. Their testimonies would be listened to and disseminated but, as in earlier debates about battered children, discussion was still framed around how adults had a moral duty to ensure that children were 'looked after, nurtured, protected'.[111]

Recognising conflicting thinking about how to use their insights, and a level of tension between ChildLine's roles as lobbyist and counsellor, Epstein and Keep argued that the counselling was 'child-led', and that volunteers would not ask children questions that would *only* be useful for information purposes. Nonetheless, the organisation was able to utilise their counselling calls to reshape political debate. Drawing on information from their calls, ChildLine provided statistics and case studies to prominent public inquiries, for example into the Cleveland affair and the deaths of Jasmine Beckford, Kimberly Carlile, Victoria Climbie, and Baby P. Childline also provided data to brief Parliamentarians on legislation including the *Criminal Justice Acts* (1988 and 1991), *Children Act* (1989), and *Sex Offenders Act* (1997). ChildLine evidence also fed into voluntary and educational contexts: contributing for example to National Children's Home research on children who abused other children and to educational discussions of bullying, as an analysis of ChildLine's calls, *Bullying—The Child's View* (1991), was circulated to all schools.[112] ChildLine's routes into policy, therefore, were multiple: through national and local, political, educational, and voluntary settings, and in reactive response to crises, as well as in the proactive formulation of legislation. Notably, Parliamentarians and journalists alike framed the role of ChildLine around its capacity to channel and to represent children's experiences. Discussing ChildLine statistics in 1987, indeed, Labour Member of Parliament Llin Golding linked this data to her ability to 'speak on behalf of young children'.[113] This statement represented a series of significant and transformative beliefs, which came to the fore in the 1980s: that children's testimonies were important, and would potentially shape political debate, and that ChildLine had a unique ability, derived from phone counselling, to mediate between children's lives and political change.

The NSPCC was likewise seeking to translate children's experiences in to policy at this time. In 1988, the Society produced a campaign entitled

'Putting Children First', asking children about how they perceived their lives and conducting a survey including questions such as, 'What is the most difficult part of being a child?'[114] In response, children expressed their frustrations about structural hierarchy, answering, for example, 'not having a say in anything, especially in what happens to you', 'adults don't always understand what you are talking about', and 'not being trusted by adults'.[115] In 1994, the NSPCC commissioned the sociologists Ian Butler and Howard Williamson to conduct a further survey, looking to 'listen and learn from what children have to say to us' and to reshape children's services accordingly.[116] Butler and Williamson interviewed 190 young people aged between 6 and 17, consciously looking to overrepresent children from the care system (46) and from minority ethnic backgrounds (74) in their sample, arguing that the 'experiences' of these children were 'especially important to hear'.[117] Interest in empowering children was clear from the design of the study, and children were allowed to stop the taped interview at any time, and to decide whether they would prefer to be interviewed individually or in a group.[118] The research was presented to children as 'an opportunity for their voice to be heard; if they wished to use their voice, the NSPCC, through the research was listening'.[119] Children were able to pursue any line of thought, though researchers would, after listening carefully, look to redirect the 'main thrust' of the inquiry towards the project's key themes.[120]

Overall, the final study argued that children's accounts must be considered in their own terms and 'not dismissed or devalued because they do not conform to some existing classifications of child abuse'.[121] Indeed, Butler and Williamson argued that 'less objectively awful events'—an adult construction—may have 'a more lasting impact' on young people than 'more awful' ones.[122] Discussing a 17-year-old whose mother was killed by her father, they emphasised that she found what was 'actually worse' than the death itself was that no one told her where her mother was buried, and indeed 'nobody even tried'.[123] Ideas about 'objectivity', guided by adults, remained in these surveys. At the same time, they demonstrated widespread interest from significant charities in translating children's testimonies into change at the institutional and social policy levels. Recognising that such changes would be made by adults, Butler and Williamson's report questioned, 'can adults listen and learn from what is being said?'[124]

A variety of organisations were hence looking to access, develop, reshape, and mobilise constructions of children's experiences from the mid-1980s, and to bring them to bear on their own internal organisational structures as well as on a national policy level. Not all children's voices were heard equally, but nonetheless the stated interest in experience extended beyond rhetoric alone, and was matched by voluntary efforts to access children's testimonies and to make them powerful—and indeed 'expert'—in public policy.

Cleveland: A Case Study

Analysing the public inquiry into the Cleveland case in 1987, conducted 14 years after the Colwell inquiry, demonstrates how—and to what extent—public policy and professional interest in children's experiences developed across the 1970s and 1980s. In Cleveland, England, in the first half of 1987, 121 children were removed from their families under suspicion of child sexual abuse.[125] Many cases were referred by two local paediatricians, Dr Geoffrey Wyatt and Dr Marietta Higgs, who relied in part on a controversial physical assessment of abuse, the reflex anal dilation test. As the number of referred cases rose, investigations were prompted by police and social services. Civic and social spaces were disrupted by this case: as the foster homes in Cleveland were full, children slept in the accident and emergency ward of Middlesbrough General Hospital, reportedly, contemporary newspapers stated, with their parents staying nearby on camp beds.[126] In July 1987, the Secretary of State for Social Services established a statutory public inquiry around this case, led by Justice Elizabeth Butler-Sloss. The subsequent public inquiry report criticised the lack of attention paid to children, writing that 'attention was largely focussed upon the adults, both parents and professionals, and their interpretation of the children involved.... The voices of the children were not heard.'[127] The inquiry did not invite children to give evidence, to 'shield' them from the 'enormous burden' of speaking either in the private sessions, with approximately 50 people, or the public sessions.[128]

Nonetheless, and consciously looking to 'redress this imbalance', the inquiry asked the Official Solicitor to represent the children, to meet with them, and to record their views.[129] Of the 165 children examined by the paediatricians at Middlesbrough General Hospital between January and July 1987, 51 were over eight years old, and 32 of these met with the Official Solicitor—again reflecting an assumption, present in the 1960s debates, that younger children would not be able to express their own accounts.[130] One chapter of the inquiry report sought to explain the 'impressions and perceptions' of the children spoken to. The testimonies described the broad effects which the inquiry had on the children, including the discomfort of their physical examination, the loneliness of waiting in hospital, and a case of subsequent bullying at school, by a child who was called 'child abuse kid' by her peers because she was featured in a newspaper.[131] The chapter discussed the cases of children who had had positive encounters with various child protection professionals, as well as negative ones. For example, one eight-year-old girl, who had been abused by a man outside of her family, saw doctors and nurses who were 'nice'; while a 16-year-old reported liking her social worker, and being glad to be in care, though she 'could not stand the police'.[132] Summarising the findings from this report and the meetings with the children, the Official Solicitor stated that the children felt a range of emotions: 'misunderstanding, mistrust, discomfort, anger, fear, praise, gratitude and sheer relief'.[133]

The report overall emphasised that listening to the child was 'essential' to investigate an allegation of abuse.[134] Demonstrating the shift made over time, one expert witness, child psychologist Dr Arnon Bentovim, testified that until 'a few years ago', the practice was 'to disbelieve the child', rather than 'taking it [their allegation] seriously' and investigating it 'properly and thoroughly'.[135] The focus on consulting with children, and on making children's testimonies central, was thus a new feature of public inquiries towards the late 1980s, acting in significant contrast to earlier inquiry reports such as that around the Maria Colwell case. Social workers and other statutory agencies had long been concerned about child welfare. Newly, however, policy and press would consider, criticise, and respond to prominent child protection cases in terms framed by children's own accounts. Policy and press continued to analyse co-operation and conflict between statutory agencies and the voluntary sector, but children's testimonies became central metrics with which to judge professional 'competency'.

There was not a full or instantaneous change. Butler-Sloss emphasised in the report that 'not every detail' of the child's story should be 'taken literally', signalling an extent to which children's accounts were still questioned, and accessed and expressed through mediators.[136] The public inquiry report also referred to the focus on adults' voices as, 'perhaps inevitable'.[137] Further, while the report signalled a shift in how children's experiences were being approached, media coverage around the Cleveland case maintained many parallels with that around the Colwell case. Such coverage, particularly from tabloid newspapers, continued to focus on professional tension and to describe children in powerless terms, in line with the 'fetishistic glorification of the "innate innocence" of childhood' described by Jenny Kitzinger.[138]

One *Daily Mail* article from July 1987, for example, argued that the children involved in this case had, 'lost their innocence and that is priceless', and presented a vision of 'empty bedrooms where dolls and toy guns are gathering dust ... houses with no children'.[139] This article also discussed a 'secret battle' between doctors, social workers, and police. Positioning consultants, social workers, and 'bureaucrats' as 'well meaning, well qualified, and articulate', parents were also represented as relatively powerless in the face of professional authority, and described as 'confused', 'often tongue-tied when first faced with officialdom' and with 'a deep respect bordering on awe for the medical profession'.[140] The idea of acting as a 'voice for the children' was also used defensively within media coverage, for example by the husband of an involved paediatrician looking to defend his wife's decisions.[141]

Again, the construct of children's experiences had growing power—in this case, realised in terms of the growing interest of public inquiries in employing expert mediators to talk with children. Nonetheless, visions of childhood experience remained underdefined, and at times were used as a proxy for broader professional conflicts. An article in *Spare Rib* in August 1987 further emphasised that a focus on broader questions of class, power, and gender were lacking from analysis of the Cleveland case.[142] The focus on children's experiences could function to challenge structural oppression—giving children a platform to criticise inequality or professional ineptitude. However, it could also further a focus on looking to the individual to resolve child protection issues, or on constructing an abstract vision of 'childhood experience' detached from structural inequalities.

Conclusion

This chapter demonstrates the significance of thinking about children's experiences in the 1970s, 1980s, and 1990s. Interest in children's inner worlds emerged from specific circles of charity, psychology, psychiatry, and policy, but also significantly influenced the media reporting and conduct of the Cleveland public inquiry by 1987. In part, this period offered a conception of childhood as fragile and vulnerable, potentially unable to take up these new avenues of consultation and influence. Such accounts expressed an ongoing vision of childhood, even among children's charities, as a stage 'in waiting', with children ready to grow in to 'caring adults'. This representation of the child as vulnerable and innocent was in part grounded on recognition of structural inequality relating to age. This representation also sought to contest previous psychological and cultural visions of childhood agency as complicity, visible in the 'Lolita' trope.[143] Nonetheless, emphasis on vulnerability constructed a distinction between the 'knowing' child, who was stigmatised, and the innocent one.[144]

Thinking about children's experiences did not entirely overcome biases in terms of who was listened to and when—it is important to analyse which children's experiences were being accessed, appropriated, and disseminated on the public stage, when the records become available to study this. Nonetheless, this historical moment represented active and engaged attempts by psychologists and children's charities to understand childhood interiority, and to make it powerful. These groups operated in a specific cultural and political moment of the 1980s, drawing on ideas of experiential expertise and childhood representation in medicine and law, and looking to represent knowledge as empowering and to present children as complex and emotional. Again reflective of the mid-1980s moment, much innovation came from the voluntary sector, and particularly from small organisations less impeded by central government management. Children's charities were key mediators of children's experiences, and they worked with successive governments, reshaping the objects of their inquiry and providing services, but also against them, briefing journalists and directly challenging policy. The networks through which charities and government were working together were reliant on the work of individuals—for example, Esther Rantzen and Shaun Woodward worked in both policy and charitable circles, transferring knowledge and expertise.

Interest in the politics of childhood experience and emotion provides a useful addition to scholarship around children's rights, helping us to unpick the extent to which ideas about rights imposed from above were also shaped by a broader responsive context around listening to and engaging with children, and reconstructing them as thinking, reflexive subjects. In this context, the last decades of the twentieth century were not only characterised by conflicts between the state and the voluntary sector, nor by growing disagreement between social, medical, and psychological services. To make this analysis is to miss the campaigning of a small but significant group of psychologists, psychiatrists, and children's charities attempting to access children's experiences, in a variety of ways, across this period. Adults would access and disseminate children's experiences and would offer solutions which required children to adopt adult behaviours—for example, writing to agony aunts or using helpline therapy. Nonetheless, children also sought out such help and learnt at times to express their experiences and emotions through the available channels and to offer critical accounts. The next chapter assesses attempts to make children themselves 'expert', and explores the extent to which interest in child experience, emotion, and expertise were reflective of a mid-1980s 'moment' or continuations of a series of longer-term social trajectories.

Notes

1. 'Mother was "determined" to get child back', *The Times*, 24 November 1973, 3. See also: Modern Records Centre, University of Warwick (hereafter MRC), MSS.318/BASW/C/68, *Report of the Committee of Inquiry into the Care and Supervision Provided in Relation to Maria Colwell* (hereafter *Colwell Report*), May–October 1974.
2. Ian Butler and Mark Drakeford, *Social Work on Trial: The Colwell Inquiry and the State of Welfare* (Bristol: Policy Press, 2011), 78 emphasises that 'if one is to judge by the tone of the court report ... they did so with considerably greater reluctance than has been reported elsewhere'.
3. MRC, *Colwell Report*, 68.
4. Ibid., 8–69.
5. Far more severe sentences have been given for similar crimes since this case. For example, the parents and guardians convicted as responsible for the murders of Tyra Henry (1985) Kimberley Carlile (1985), Leanne White (1992), and Victoria Climbie (2001) were all jailed for life.
6. MRC, *Colwell Report*, 6.
7. Dave Merrick, *Social Work and Child Abuse* (London: Routledge, 1996), 181 highlights a 'long and continuing tradition' of changing the format and ceremony of public inquiries into child care according to the particular case—some are public, some private, some internal, some external, some instigated by local authority, some by secretary of state for social services.
8. MRC, *Colwell Report*, 6.
9. Ian Butler and Mark Drakeford, *Scandal, Social Policy and Social Welfare: How British Public Policy is Made* (Basingstoke: Palgrave Macmillan, 2003), 88.
10. MRC, *Colwell Report*, 70–102.
11. Ibid., 63–64.
12. Ibid., 2, 106–140.
13. Ibid., 106.
14. Ibid., 3.
15. MRC, BASW, Correspondence and Papers 1976–1980, MSS 378/BASW/2/486, Press Cuttings, 'Maria Colwell—It Could Happen Again', *Northern Echo*, 9 September 1974; 'Maria Case 'Not the Last',

Sheffield Morning Telegraph, 6 September 1974; 'There Could Be Another "Maria" Tragedy Warn County Social Workers', *Leicester Mercury*, 7 September 1974; '"More Contact" Call in Avon', *Bristol Evening Post*, 5 September 1974; '"Maria" Plea in City', *Nottingham Evening Post*, 7 September 1974; Mrs J. Thorburn, 'Maria Colwell—and the Rates', *Eastern Evening News*, 10 September 1974; 'Threat of More Maria Tragedies', *Northamptonshire Evening Telegraph*, 10 September 1974; MRC, BASW, Correspondence and Papers 1976–1980; MSS 378/BASW/2/486, Press Cuttings, 'Tragic Lesson that has Shamed a Nation', *Western Daily Press*, 5 September 1974.

16. *Report of the Committee of Inquiry into the Care and Supervision Provided by Local Authorities and Other Agencies in Relation to Maria Colwell and the Co-ordination Between Them* (London: Her Majesty's Stationary Office, 1974), 86. Point echoed in: MRC, BASW, Correspondence and Papers 1976–1980, MSS 378/BASW/2/486, Press Cuttings, 'The Errors that Led to Maria's Death', *Glasgow Herald*, 5 September 1974; MRC, BASW, Correspondence and Papers 1976–1980, MSS 378/BASW/2/486, Press Cuttings, 'Tragic Lesson that Has Shamed a Nation', *Western Daily Press*, 5 September 1974.
17. *Report of the Committee of Inquiry*, 86.
18. Ibid., 34.
19. 'Battered Maria: Neighbours "Tried to Warn Official"', *Sunday Times*, 21 October 1973, as cited in Ian Butler and Mark Drakeford, 'Booing or cheering? Ambiguity in the construction of victimhood in the case of Maria Colwell', *Crime, Media, Culture*, 4, no. 3 (2008): 375.
20. For discussions of ordinariness, see: Florence Sutcliffe-Braithwaite, 'Discourses of "class" in Britain in "New Times"', *Contemporary British History*, 31, no. 2 (2017): 294–317. For a useful discussion of respectability, see: Peter Bailey, "Will the real Bill Banks please stand up?': Towards a Role Analysis of mid-Victorian Working-Class Respectability', *Journal of Social History*, 12 (1979): 341–343.
21. Ibid., 376.
22. *Report of the Committee of Inquiry*, 18.
23. Butler and Drakeford, 'Booing or cheering?': 381.
24. Sutcliffe-Braithwaite, 'Discourses of 'class": 294–317.
25. Butler and Drakeford, *Scandal, Social Policy and Social Welfare*, 85–87.
26. 'How many more Marias are there?', *Daily Mail*, 7 November 1973, 37; David Cross, 'MP's adoption shock', *Daily Mail*, 21 June 1975, 9.
27. *Report of the Committee of Inquiry*, 16.
28. Ibid., 16, 111–120.
29. Ibid., 19.
30. Ibid., 24–25.
31. Ibid., 27.

32. Ibid., 98, 104–105.
33. Mia Kellmer Pringle, 'Every day, two children…', *Observer*, 25 August 1974, 18.
34. In terms of paying attention to the perspectives of social work clients, see: John Eric Mayer and Noel Timms, *The Client Speaks: Working Class Impressions of Casework* (London: Routledge and Kegan Paul, 1970); Eric Sainsbury, *Social Work with Families: Perceptions of Social Casework Among Clients of a Family Service Unit* (London: Routledge and Kegan Paul, 1975); *Peter Philmore, Families Speaking: a study of Fifty-One Families' Views of Social Work* (London: Family Service Units, 1980). In terms of interest in the perspective of the child at this moment see, for example: Harry Blagg, John A. Hughes, Corinne Wattam (eds) *Child sexual abuse: listening, hearing and validating the experiences of children* (Harlow: Longman, 1989).
35. Valerie Yule, *What happens to children: the origins of violence, a collection of stories told by children who could not write them* (London: Angus & Robertson: 1979), 'Introduction'.
36. Ibid., 'Foreword'.
37. Ibid., 46.
38. Claire Rayner, *Life and Love and Everything: Children's Questions Answered* (London: Kyle Cathie Limited, 1993), no page references. See also: Claire Rayner, *When I Grow Up: Children's views of the adult world* (London: Genesis Productions Ltd, 1986).
39. Rayner, *Life and Love and Everything*, no page references.
40. HM Government, *Criminal Justice Act 1988* (London: Her Majesty's Stationary Office, 1988); HM Government, *Criminal Justice Act 1991* (London: Her Majesty's Stationary Office, 1991); Amanda Elizabeth Wade, 'The Child Witness and the Criminal Justice Process: A Case Study in Law Reform, unpublished thesis, March 1997, 1–10.
41. HM Government, *Children Act 1975* (London: Her Majesty's Stationary Office, 1975), 1–3.
42. As quoted in Harry Hendrick, *Children, Childhood and English Society 1880–1990* (Cambridge: Cambridge University Press, 1997), 98.
43. As pointed out by: Mary MacLeod, in '30 Years of ChildLine (1986–2016)', Witness seminar, held 1 June 2016 at the BT Tower, London, held at Modern Records Centre, Coventry, 22.
44. 'Support at the end of the line', *The Times*, 30 October 1986, 17.
45. Frances Gibb, 'Call to widen new-style video questioning in cases of child abuse', *The Times*, 28 November 1986, 7.
46. As cited in, Alex Saunders, *"It hurts me too": Children's experiences of domestic violence and refuge life* (1995), 37.
47. Judith Ennew, *The Sexual Exploitation of Children* (Basingstoke: Palgrave Macmillan, 1986).

48. Oralee Wachter and Dr Andrew Stanway, *No More Secrets for Me: Helping to Safeguard Your Child Against Sexual Abuse* (London: Penguin Books, 1986), 11.
49. Saunders, *"It hurts me too"*, 8.
50. Ibid., 8.
51. Helen Franks, 'A world of secrets', *Guardian*, 5 July 1989, 21.
52. Myre Sim, 'Introduction—a child speaks', Selwyn M. Smith (ed.) The Maltreatment of Children (Lancaster: MTP Press, 1978), 1.
53. Sim, 'Introduction—a child speaks', 1.
54. Ibid., 1.
55. Ibid., 2.
56. Ibid., 2.
57. Ibid., 4–5.
58. Multiple accounts of these cases have emerged. Philip Jenkins has described these cases in detail in the framework of 'moral panic' in Philip Jenkins, *Intimate Enemies: Moral Panics in Contemporary Great Britain* (New York: Aldine de Gruyter, 1992), 154–194. Jean La Fontaine provided several anthropological contemporary accounts: Jean La Fontaine, *Speak of the Devil: Tales of Satanic Abuse in Contemporary England* (Cambridge: Cambridge University Press, 1998), and for the Department of Health: Jean La Fontaine, *The Extent and Nature of Organised and Ritual Abuse* (London: Her Majesty's Stationary Office, 1994). Another article worth reading on this account was an interview by Jean La Fontaine by Celia Kitzinger: 'Satanic disabuser', *Times Higher Education*, 25 August 1995. A contrasting contemporary account by psychologists claiming to have treated ritual abuse survivors is: Valerie Sinason (ed.), *Treating Survivors of Satanist Abuse* (London: Routledge, 1994). Looking to move 'beyond disbelief', and to analyse why and how 'validity' was 'accorded to some kinds of life-stories and not others', how some people were constructed as 'reliable witnesses of their own lives' while others were 'discredited': Sara Scott, *The Politics and Experience of Ritual Abuse: Beyond Disbelief* (Buckingham: Open University Press, 2001), 1.
59. Discussion of separating 'fact from fantasy' in terms of recommendations from Health Minister Virginia Bottomley: 'Shake-up follows Satan scandal', *Daily Mail*, 11 March 1991, 9. Discussing the role of video nasties in these cases: John Woodcock, 'Video nasties named in child abuse probe', *Daily Mail*, 14 September 1990, 2.
60. La Fontaine, *The Extent and Nature of Organised and Ritual Abuse.*
61. La Fontaine, *Speak of the Devil*, 119–120.
62. Ibid., 124.
63. La Fontaine, *The Extent and Nature of Organised and Ritual Abuse.*
64. See: Sinason, *Treating Survivors of Satanist Abuse.* The Ritual Abuse Information Network is mentioned in the following article: David

Brindle, 'Therapists reject Bottomley claim that new report "explodes myth"', *Guardian*, 3 June 1994, 2.

65. Describing the piece as a 'counterpart': Catherine Bennett, 'Satanic Verses' *Guardian*, 10 September 1994, 12–20. Edited collection is: Sinason, *Treating Survivors of Satanist Abuse.*
66. See: Bennett, 'Satanic Verses' 12–20.
67. Discussion of 'fevered imagination' was in court case at Rochdale described in: Stephen Oldfield and Andrew London, 'Tears as judge releases snatched children', *Daily Mail*, 8 March 1991, 1. Discussion of 'fantasy' in a Manchester court case, described in: Andrew Loudon, 'Lessons to be learned over satanic abuse questioning', *Daily Mail*, 19 December 1990, 9.
68. See discussion in Ravinder Barn, '"Race", Ethnicity and Child Welfare: A Fine Balancing Act', *British Journal of Social Work*, 37 (2007): 1425–1434.
69. This research about ChildLine was enriched through collaboration with Dr Eve Colpus (University of Southampton), as we worked together to convene a witness seminar in 2016 reflecting on '30 Years of ChildLine'. This project was funded by a Wellcome Trust grant, number 200420/Z/15/Z.
70. Jill Sherman, 'Sex-threat children get Sos touchline', *The Times*, 28 October 1986, 5; Harriet Lane, 'He wants to kill his father… But he's already dead. So Richard Johnson took revenge in writing', *The Observer*, 5 September 1999, 4; 'News in brief', *The Times*, 1 December 1979, 3.
71. Esther Ranzten, in '30 Years of ChildLine (1986–2016)', 7.
72. 'Support at the end of the line', 17.
73. Ibid., 17.
74. Ibid., 17.
75. Quote from Rantzen on Childwatch as cited in: Stuart Bell, 'Childwatch: Is this the most dangerous show on TV?', *Daily Mail*, 6.
76. Ritchie Cogan and Sarah Caplin, 'Phone-ins work', *The Observer*, 26 October 1986, 56.
77. Mary Kenny, 'The serious doubts about Childwatch', *Daily Mail*, 29 November 1986, 6.
78. Bodleian Library (hereafter Bod), P.C06240, ChildLine Annual Reports 1991–1994, *Annual Report 1994*, 'Chairman's report', Esther Rantzen, 3.
79. Bod, *Annual Report 1994*, 'How ChildLine works', 7.
80. Ibid., 7.
81. Ibid., 6.
82. Ibid., 4.
83. Ibid., 4.
84. Ibid., 4.

85. Hereward Harrison, 'Childline—the first twelve years', *British Medical Journal*, 82 (2000), 283.
86. See contemporary description of calls in: BL, *Annual Report 1994*, 'Facts and figures', 18; BL, *Annual Report 1992*, 'The Children who Call ChildLine', 5.
87. As cited in: Barbara Amiel, 'Teaching children to complain', *The Times*, 5 November 1986, 15.
88. Testimonies shared by Esther Ranzten, in '30 Years of ChildLine (1986–2016)', 10–11.
89. Barbara Amiel, 'Teaching children to complain', *The Times*, 5 November 1986, 15.
90. Quotes from: Anne Houston, in '30 Years of ChildLine (1986–2016)', 26–27. Also discussed by: Shaun Woodward, in '30 Years of ChildLine (1986–2016)', 18.
91. Peter Hildrew, 'Danger: crossed wires on the crisis line', *Guardian*, 28 November 1986, 23; 'Support at the end of the line', 17; Jill Sherman, 'Childline shake-up as pressure grows', *The Times*, 9 January 1987, 3.
92. Victoria McKee, 'Out of the fire, into the firing line', *The Times*, 2 September 1987, 15.
93. Bod, *Annual Report 1994*, 'Chief executive's report', Valerie Howarth, 5.
94. Helen Hague, 'ChildLine aims for 700 schools', *Times Educational Supplement*, 30 January 1998.
95. Ibid.
96. Hansard, House of Commons, Sixth Series, 20 December 1989, vol. 164, col. 438.
97. Amiel, 'Teaching children to complain', 15.
98. Kenny, 'The serious doubts about Childwatch', 6; Bell, 'Childwatch: Is this the most dangerous show on TV?', 6.
99. Bod, *Annual Report 1993*, 'A year for children', 2. Baroness Valerie Howarth, Chief Executive of ChildLine from 1986 to 2001, reflected back in 2016 that listening had 'never been enough', and that ChildLine then 'told the nation about just what was happening to children' Valerie Howarth, in '30 Years of ChildLine (1986–2016)', 14.
100. Bod, *Annual Report 1993*, 'How ChildLine works', 4.
101. Ibid., 4.
102. Mary MacLeod, in '30 Years of ChildLine (1986–2016)', 20; see also Mary MacLeod, Sally Morris and Valerie Howarth, *Why me?: Children talking to ChildLine about bullying* (London: ChildLine, 1996); ChildLine, *Children and racism* (London: ChildLine, 1996).
103. Carole Epstein and Gill Keep, 'What Children Tell ChildLine about Domestic Violence', in Saunders, *"It hurts me too"*, 43.

104. Ibid., 44.
105. Ibid., 44.
106. Ibid., 45.
107. Ibid., 44–47.
108. Ibid., 51.
109. Saunders, *"It hurts me too"*, 10; Epstein and Keep, 'What Children Tell ChildLine', 48–49.
110. Epstein and Keep, 'What Children Tell ChildLine', 44–48.
111. Ibid., 50.
112. Bod, *Annual Report 1992*, 'Executive Director's Report', Valerie Howarth, 4.
113. Hansard, House of Commons, sixth series, 31 March 1987, vol. 113, col. 951.
114. National Society for the Prevention of Cruelty to Children, *Putting Children First: An NSPCC Guide* (London: NSPCC, 1988), 3, 7.
115. Bod, NSPCC, Miscellaneous Publications, *Putting Children First: An NSPCC Guide* (London: 1988), 7.
116. Ian Butler and Howard Williamson, *Children speak: children, trauma and social work* (Harlow: Longman, 1994).
117. Ibid., 26.
118. Ibid., 25–26.
119. Ibid., 25.
120. Ibid., 25.
121. Ibid., 50.
122. Ibid., 51.
123. Ibid., 52.
124. Ibid., x.
125. For further academic descriptions of this case see: Jenkins, *Intimate Enemies*, 133–150; Harry Ferguson, 'Cleveland in History: The Abused Child and Child Protection', in Roger Cooter (ed.) *In the Name of the Child: Health and Welfare 1880–1940* (London, 1992), 146–173; Mica Nava, 'Cleveland and the Press: Outrage and Anxiety in the Reporting of Child Sexual Abuse', *Feminist Review*, 28 (1988): 105. For two contrasting contemporary accounts, see: Beatrix Campbell, *Unofficial Secrets: Child Sexual Abuse: The Cleveland Case* (London: Virago, 1988), Stuart Bell, *When Salem Came to the Boro, the true story of the Cleveland Child Abuse Crisis* (London: Pan Books, 1988).
126. Roger Scott and John Woodcock, 'The Doctor in Child Abuse Storm', *Daily Mail*, 24 June 1987, 1.
127. Elizabeth Butler-Sloss, *Report of the Inquiry into Child Abuse in Cleveland 1987*, Cm 412 (London: Her Majesty's Stationary Office, 1988), 25.
128. Ibid., 25.
129. Ibid., 25.

130. Ibid., 25.
131. Ibid., 25–35.
132. Ibid., 34–35.
133. Ibid., 25.
134. Ibid., 204.
135. Ibid., 204.
136. Ibid., 204.
137. Ibid., 25.
138. In terms of analyses of representations of childhood in media, see: Jenny Kitzinger, 'Who Are You Kidding? Children, Power, and the Struggle Against Sexual Abuse', in Allison James (ed.) *Constructing and Recconstructing Childhood: Contemporary Issues in the Sociological Study of Childhood* (London: Psychology Press, 1997), 164. See also: Jenny Kitzinger, 'Defending Innocence: Ideologies of Childhood', *Feminist Review*, 28 (Spring, 1988): 77–87. For analysis of the media coverage around this case described as variously as: an attack by vindictive professionals on the nuclear family; a sign of the over-extended state; or demonstrative of the patriarchal family, see, Nava, 'Cleveland and the Press': 103–121.
139. Roger Scott, 'Facts of the secret battle between the doctors, social workers and the police', *Daily Mail*, 13 July 1987, 18.
140. Ibid., 18.
141. Scott and Woodcock, 'The Doctor in Child Abuse Storm', 1.
142. Susan Ardill, 'King Herod Comes to Salem', *Spare Rib*, August 1987, Issue 181.
143. Kitzinger, 'Defending Innocence': 79.
144. Ibid., 80.

Open Access This chapter is licensed under the terms of the Creative Commons Attribution 4.0 International License (http://creativecommons.org/licenses/by/4.0/), which permits use, sharing, adaptation, distribution and reproduction in any medium or format, as long as you give appropriate credit to the original author(s) and the source, provide a link to the Creative Commons license and indicate if changes were made.

The images or other third party material in this chapter are included in the chapter's Creative Commons license, unless indicated otherwise in a credit line to the material. If material is not included in the chapter's Creative Commons license and your intended use is not permitted by statutory regulation or exceeds the permitted use, you will need to obtain permission directly from the copyright holder.

CHAPTER 4

Inculcating Child Expertise in Schools and Homes

This chapter continues arguments from Chap. 3 in terms of how new spaces opened up for children to be 'expert' in the 1970s, 1980s, and 1990s, and in terms of how the voluntary sector played a significant role in soliciting, mediating, and presenting children's experiences and emotions. While the previous chapter focused on public policy spaces in which children would be able to speak—notably through the mediated forum of public inquiries—this chapter considers how, through voluntary sector intervention, fora emerged in the classroom and the family home. While the previous chapter focused on children who had faced abuse, this chapter considers the attempts of charities, teachers, and parents to engage with *all* children, looking to prevent abuse from happening. This shaped a significant difference: notions of childhood vulnerability and powerlessness, key in adult categories of the previous chapter, became less present here. Significantly also, while Chap. 3 assessed interest in accessing children's experiences, and in taking them as expert, this chapter argues that charities also played a significant role in looking to inculcate expertise in children. Children were thus constructed in this time as both expert and as potentially expert.

The family home and the school, the key areas of investigation in this chapter, were permeable spaces; each shaped children's everyday lives, but necessitated that children perform different versions of self—private and public, family and peer.[1] Despite the differences in these spaces, child

© The Author(s) 2018

J. Crane, *Child Protection in England, 1960–2000*, Palgrave Studies in the History of Childhood,
https://doi.org/10.1007/978-3-319-94718-1_4

protection education sought to offer similar messages in both, disseminating similar films and television shorts, manuals, and fiction. These materials are the primary focus of this chapter. The materials were produced by the Central Office of Information, commercial businesses and, significantly, by small organisations in the voluntary sector. Key amongst these was Kidscape, whose materials recur throughout this chapter. Founded in 1986, Kidscape was a relatively small children's charity—with less than ten staff for much of its lifetime—however also one which amassed significant influence in policy, family homes, and teacher training.[2]

Importantly, the storybooks and films in this chapter are not read in terms of how parents, carers, or children behaved in the past. Rather, they are analysed as reflections of the shifting spaces in which children were able to act, behave, and indeed learn to feel.[3] These materials provide evidence 'of manual-writing behavior and values' and access to powerful adult constructions of childhood agency, entitlement, sexuality, experience, and emotion.[4] By taking these commerical and everyday objects seriously, the chapter traces how a public, professional, and voluntary vision of childhood 'expertise' emerged in the mid-1980s and was—perhaps surprisingly—able to bypass the broader moral and sexual politics of this decade. At the same time, this chapter demonstrates that long-standing hierarchies between adults and children were not fundamentally disrupted by new visions of childhood experience, expertise, and emotion. While the following two chapters argue that relationships between parents and professions were fundamentally changed in the mid-1980s, interactions between children and adults proved harder to reform.

Child Protection Education

In America, amidst heightened public and political concerns about child abuse from the mid-1960s, charities and researchers created educational storybooks directed at teenagers and children.[5] Despite much transnational interchange in terms of child protection research, this specific cultural and literary practice did not transfer to Britain until the 1980s. Indeed, even from the late-1970s, researchers in Britain expressed cynicism about whether such texts were needed or specific to the American context. Following a conference in London in 1978, including speeches by Ruth and Henry Kempe, the executive director of the National Advisory Centre for the Battered Child, Roy Castle, remained cautious about believing that child sexual abuse also occurred in British family homes. He told the *Daily*

Mail that he had 'taken note of the concern expressed in America', but that his group would be carefully researching and finding local reports before determining 'whether Britain has the same kind of problem'.[6] This statement expressed the significance vested in research by this centre but also a level of belief that British homes may be unaffected by abuse, or that this may be an 'imported problem'.[7]

Scholars of history and social policy have already paid attention to the significance of the mid-1980s as a time in which policy-makers, press, and publics became increasingly concerned about child sexual abuse, which emerged as '*the* child protection issue', to the exclusion of media focus on physical and emotional abuse and neglect.[8] What has not yet been subject to academic analysis, however, is the role of small children's charities in terms of shaping these developing concerns. Kidscape emerged in this heated period. The charity was started when the American educational psychologist Michele Elliott mortgaged her London flat to fund a pilot project from 1984 to 1986.[9] Working with 14 primary schools in London attended by 4000 students, Elliott provided workshops for parents, teachers, and children. These workshops discussed strategies through which children could protect themselves, focused on ideas of bodily autonomy, the rights to say no, and warning against keeping secrets. Indicative of the success of this approach, and how it chimed with this moment, Elliott received thousands of enquiries whilst conducting her pilot programme and decided to establish Kidscape in 1985.[10]

The inception of child protection education was separate from, but linked to, broader trends in sex education over the late twentieth century. In schools, sex education had developed significantly earlier than child protection education, in the early twentieth century as part of hygiene teaching.[11] In the immediate post-war period, the Ministry of Health lobbied for sex education to become a key component of public health. While the Department of Education initially resisted this, concerned about political implications, sex education was included in public health education from the 1970s and 1980s.[12] While sex education developed in schools, and with new materials produced for homes, formal child protection education, provided by commercial or state sectors, did not emerge until the mid-1980s.[13] Testifying to this, when the feminist theorist Jane Cousins Mills started researching her sex education book *Make It Happy* in 1978, she found that none of the sex educators, child psychologists, parents, or doctors she consulted raised the subject of child sexual abuse.[14] Notably however, and indicative of the distance between lived experience and political expectations at this time, the teenagers who Cousins Mills spoke with discussed sex education and sexual abuse in tandem.[15] Indeed, formal child protection education was preceded by informal community enactment, for example through personal warnings about specific individuals.

Before formal child protection education emerged, a significant moral politics was surrounding sex education. From the 1960s, 'pro-family' and morally conservative groups, such as the Responsible Society and the National Viewers and Listeners Association, argued that sex education was fuelling a breakdown in family life and the corruption of childhood.[16] Controversial sex education films tested the boundaries of this moral politics. To take one example, the film *Growing Up* (1971) featured video footage of naked people having sex (rather than drawings) for the first time in the English-speaking world out of the pornographic context. The film also lobbied for the age of consent to be lowered.[17] In the 1980s likewise, sex education films challenged social stigma by teaching about HIV and AIDS. Progressive sex education advocates of this decade argued that such education could improve children's individual self-expression and empowerment, and would not confuse or distress them.[18]

Child protection education emerged in this context. Like much sex education, it offered a vision whereby children would become empowered experts through the consumption of information. Unlike sex education, child protection education to an extent managed to bypass the sexual politics of the 1980s, and notably to avoid contentious debates around sex education and the 'promotion' of homosexuality.[19] While sex education was often 'sub-contracted' to voluntary organisations, such as the Family Planning Association, significantly smaller charities—such as Kidscape—were key providers of child protection education.[20] While child protection education had its critics, as this chapter will go on to demonstrate, it did not attract the broader levels of moral ire that faced sex educationalists. This was despite the fact that child protection education was to be offered to children from infancy—whereas sex education would often only be offered when children reached puberty.[21] Broadly, child protection education became subject to cross-party consensus as a 'positive' phenomenon, and as an 'appropriate' response through which to enable individual children to protect themselves from abuse. This was to an extent an individualistic vision, placing responsibility for child protection on to children themselves, but also one which sought to conceptualise children as having the potential to hold expertise, and which relied in part on state, carer, and community action.

Education Through Fiction

Detailed examination of Kidscape's storybooks makes clear the vision of childhood which underpinned the organisation's work: one of childhood as capable, powerful, and mutually supportive. Two key pillars of the Kidscape programme—bodily autonomy and the right to say no—focused on engendering individual expertise into children. The fiction books, however, also presented models whereby children already held this form of expertise, and were highly capable of enacting such principles. In one of the Kidscape storybooks, focused on the *Willow Street Kids*, children called Amy and Gill noticed that their friend, Julia, was upset. By speaking with Julia, they realised that her uncle was abusing her, and gave her the confidence to report this to her mother.[22] Gill explicitly stated, 'I think kids can help each other sometimes, don't you?'[23] In another example from the book a child, Deidre, received phone calls from a prank caller who said 'rude things'.[24] Following advice from her older sister, Deidre blew a whistle down the phone, and the man did not call again. Deidre repeated this advice from her sister to another friend.[25] In this engaging vision of childhood, children were able to resolve their own problems through peer support. The books sought to inculcate a form of empowered childhood expertise, but also emphasised that children already held such potential.

Another key pillar of the Kidscape programme was about warning against keeping secrets. This tenet relied on a wider context of adult responsibility. In the fiction books, if children did choose to disclose their problems to an adult, a positive vision of their reactions emerged. Children in the *Willow Street Kids* stories received help from their mothers and their fathers equally, as well as from members of their extended families and teachers. One teacher in the *Willow Street Kids* series—Mrs Simpson—stated that 'personal safety was one of the most important lessons' for her students.[26] Fathers, mothers, and other relatives in the stories were all supportive of child protection education, and highly sensitive when children disclosed cases of abuse.[27] When Julia told her mother that her uncle was abusing her, her mother emphasised that this was not Julia's fault, she was not angry, and that her only wish was that she could have stopped this sooner.[28] Julia's father added that the family would work together to make decisions in the days to come, and that they would ensure that Julia was safe.[29]

The representation of parents as trustworthy was significant. This was created in a context where research increasingly identified family members as the primary perpetrators of abuse. At the same time, this representation was also produced as sex education initiatives had to defend themselves from the critique of family values campaigners.[30] Notably, the representation of fathers and mothers as both supporting children was in contrast to other educational materials produced in the 1980s, which focused predominately on mothers.[31] Child protection education in this moment thus could provide a more radical representation than sex education, because of the perceived moral worth of child protection. At the same time, child protection education also sought to draw a series of balances: offering a complex representation of family life but also mitigating broader right-wing anxieties; representing children's individual empowerment but also describing a context of adult support.

These books offered a significant new contribution into debates around child protection in mid-1980s Britain. Children were represented as holding the potential to be expert, which they could realise through the consumption of consumer texts. Notably, children in the books would seek out adult help in their own time, and on their own terms, to an extent redressing power imbalances within the family. While these books focused on child protection, they also offered broad messages relevant to children's daily interactions with classmates at school and with relatives. In this way, child protection work was conceptualised as a reflection of the social position of children more broadly: a connection that earlier debates did not always make. At the same time, to an extent the focus on individual, rather than structural, factors in child protection cases continued, given the individualist focus on 'consent' and children's empowerment, for example through peer support. While broader debates about sexual attitudes shifted from focus on 'public morality' towards individual attitudes and behaviours, Kidscape materials addressed individual children, families, and communities in tandem.[32]

Representing 'Truth'?

Kidscape's response to these tensions—between individualism and family support, and between representing family life and defending 'the family'—was to emphasise that their stories were 'true'. The prefaces to the organisation's storybooks often insisted that the stories within were 'all true', and 'told by children whom they have happened to'.[33] This interest in authenticity—and in describing experiences as stories—was also visible in their books' plotlines. For example, contemporary research supported the idea that children tended to rely on one another for peer support: a survey by ChildLine published in 1996 found that over 30 per cent of the 2500 people between 11 and 16 questioned would be most likely to confide in another young person first if they had a problem.[34] Looking to represent a broad demographic range of children, the books also portrayed, through illustration and text, children of different ethnicities, races, and genders, again acting in contrast to the 'invisible norm' of parenting manuals of this period towards discussing the white, male, and middle-class child.[35] Interest in challenging structural inequalities was key to Kidscape's broader work, and Elliott criticised the disproportionate media coverage given to middle-class children, for instance.[36]

Such work marked both an interest in addressing all children as expert, or potentially expert, and also a new level of concern about representing children's experiences in an 'authentic' way, representing stories which were judged as 'true' because they came from children themselves. These interests had broader resonances across children's literature and the voluntary sector. The idea of informing children about complex issues through literature, for example, was also present in the Children's Society 1986 book *Bruce's Story*, about fostering and adoption.[37] Broader concerns about representation and authenticity in children's literature were visible in new texts such as John Rowe Townsend's *Gumble's Yard* (1961), and in the critique and practice of children's book editor and author Leila Berg.[38] The work of Kidscape was thus drawing on broader trends, and was not an isolated phenomenon. At the same time, it offered something new in child protection education. Crucially, the organisation turned interest in children's experiences, visible in Chap. 3, into concrete advice about how children could be heard and empowered as expert on an everyday level. The idea of representing experience in an authentic or 'true' fashion was a means to connect with children, but also a mode through which to defuse broad tensions about the moral politics of child protection education.

While navigating the moral politics of sex education, Kidscape's approach was not without contemporary critics. Carrie Herbert, a child protection consultant, questioned whether the books fully represented the challenges for children of saying 'no' to adults.[39] Herbert emphasised that many adults continued to struggle to refuse people in authority. Further, she argued, this individualistic advice could leave children experiencing feelings of 'guilt and failure' if their abuse continued.[40] More broadly, through the 1970s, 1980s, and 1990s, feminist critics raised similar questions about how women and children could enact resistance in a patriarchal society.[41] Would the experiential and emotional expertise of children, once encouraged by storybooks, ever be taken seriously? Thus, doubts remained about whether children would be able to apply their new expertise in practice, and about potential gaps between theoretical models and lived experiences of childhood expertise.

These problems were not fully resolved or discussed in texts of this period, not least because of the significant burden placed on the voluntary sector, and on relatively small organisations such as Kidscape, to provide answers. This reliance on the voluntary sector in education was not entirely new, but nonetheless left small groups holding powerful positions in shaping child protection, and, further, in constructing a vision of childhood expertise that developed outside of the sexual politics of the 1980s. Significantly, this vision of childhood challenged an earlier conception, visible in the early-to-mid-twentieth century, and guiding much work in Chap. 2, of children as deeply innocent yet corruptible.[42] Instead, Kidscape texts presented children as simultaneously expert and potentially expert, empowered and ready to be empowered by the consumption of fiction.

Child Protection Films

This vision of childhood was also visible in short films about child protection. Charities, governments, and companies first produced child protection films in the 1970s, and the use of this medium was popularised from the 1980s in America, Canada, and Britain, with growing awareness that children were the 'most voracious viewers' of television.[43] In Britain, the Central Office of Information made some of the earliest films of this nature, creating six films about childhood safety in 1973. The one-minute films centred on Charley the cartoon cat and dealt with topical concerns of the day—matches, drowning, hot stoves, hot water, leaving the house, and strangers. Symbolic of how the earliest child protection films operated, these materials addressed children as passive actors, using simple messages. In *Charley—Strangers* a narrator, a small boy, accompanied Charley on a trip to the park. An older man approached and asked if the companions would like to see some puppies. While the narrator leapt at this opportunity, Charley reminded him that his mother said he should not 'go off' with people he did not know.[44] On telling his mother how he avoided this situation, the boy received an apple.[45] In this film, the primary threat was a mysterious, shadowy, stranger, whose features were not illustrated. *Charley—Strangers* thus exemplified the 1970s conception of

'Stranger Danger'; the idea that the key threats to children were easily identifiable strangers.[46] The best thing for children to do was to run away from such strangers, and to report them to parents.

Children were not addressed as completely powerless in this narrative, and indeed the filmmakers made some efforts to make their materials appealing to younger viewers, using a cartoon and employing Kenny Everett, a popular broadcaster, to voice the piece. There is evidence to suggest that the Charley films remained influential in popular memory. In 1991, dance act The Prodigy used Charley's mews in their debut single, 'Charly'.[47] In 2006, a poll conducted by *BBC News* of nearly 25,000 readers found that the Charley cartoons were the 'Nation's Favourite Public Information Film'.[48] While potentially well liked and well remembered, however, the Charley films were not necessarily effective at teaching children about child protection. Indeed, in 1987, internal correspondence at the Central Office of Information suggested that children remembered the film's key messages, and that they remembered the cartoon cat, but that they did not remember to enact these strategies in practice.[49] Again, a concern about the ability of children to absorb expertise through cultural or consumer mediums developed.

Based on engagement with children themselves, small contemporary children's charities offered further evidence that these films were not necessarily informative. In 1984, Kidscape interviewed 500 children between the ages of five and eight. Nine out of ten of these children knew that they should never go home with a stranger, but could not identify or define what a stranger looked like.[50] Children believed that strangers were always ugly, wore masks, smelt bad, had beards, and wore dark glasses.[51] Six out of ten children said that a woman could not be a stranger and eight out of ten that the interviewer, who they had never met before, was not a stranger because she 'didn't look like one'.[52] In press, Elliott offered further criticism of these films as unnecessarily one-directional. Writing for the *Times Educational Supplement* in 1986, she wrote that films should introduce children to this sensitive and important area in an 'interactive' way, ideally through discussion with an adult.[53]

This critique echoed that made by psychologists about road safety programmes in the 1940s and 1950s—that children did not remember lists of instructions, should be engaged, and could be critical of the patronising tone of the films.[54] Notably however, while there were continuities in debates around children's safety, there was also change. Policy-makers of the 1940s and 1950s chose to interpret the 'lesson' of road safety research to show that no kerb drill could be effective, and thus that they should clear children off the streets.[55] In the 1980s, film-makers began to focus on how public information films could further engage children, partially by working in partnership with children's charities. Following their earlier critique, Kidscape went on to work closely with a television puppet show called 'Cosmo and Dibs', part of the BBC schools television series, aimed at the under-fives, and aired between 1981 and 1992.[56]

The Cosmo and Dibs programmes featured four-minute sketches where human presenters worked at a market stall with brightly coloured, animal-like puppets, and conversed about topical issues. In 1987, Elliott advised the BBC while they produced five special episodes on the theme of 'Keeping Safe'. In the episode 'Harry's Cousin', the presenter Harry saw the puppet Cosmo tell his address to a stranger.[57] Harry warned Cosmo that while it was 'very nice to be friendly', children must be careful as well, because some people were not 'kind or nice'. Harry reassured Cosmo that saying no, for example if someone wanted to touch or stroke him, or if he did not feel safe, was not rude.[58] In the programme 'Observation', the puppets practised describing a stranger who had stolen a candlestick from their market stall. In 'Secret', Cosmo asked Dibs to keep a secret, that he has broken a jug, but ultimately learnt that it was better to tell others the truth.

These episodes disseminated key lessons inherent in the Kidscape programme: never keep secrets, you can say no, and you have bodily autonomy. Rather than presenting a unilateral monologue, the sketches replicated an interactive conversation between adult and child, portraying Cosmo gaining access to increasing levels of information through dialogue with Harry. Another strategy of engagement was the use of children's television characters who were already popular. The show also presented complexity. In one episode, a man approached the stall, and was regarded as suspicious, but ultimately was revealed as Harry's cousin. This reflected the idea that, in life, children would need to be cautious, because it was difficult to tell who dangerous people were. Echoing broader Kidscape materials, these films addressed children as intelligent and informed. Reflecting this, in 1987 the *Times Educational Supplement* gave the producers 'full marks' for suggesting that children needed 'an active sense of self worth'.[59] The newspaper suggested that self-worth and child protection should be taught at the same time as numeracy, as a necessary part of childhood development.

At a similar time, those working in state departments, as well as in children's charities, began to address children as active subjects in child protection films. In 1987, a spokesperson from the Department for Health and Social Security told a conference on child protection that one of the most effective preventive measures against child sexual abuse could be 'to give children strategies to protect themselves'.[60] In the same year, the Central Office of Information released a campaign called 'Children Say No', a series of 60-second television fillers.[61] One featured children singing a song which insisted, for example, that, 'If a grown-up tries to trick us we say No. No. No'. Children also sung that they would respond 'no', even if offered a sweet or a treat, because the 'best defence' was to 'act with common sense'.[62] The song's refrain of 'common sense defence' was akin to Kidscape's 'good sense defence' programme, again suggestive that this charity wielded some influence. By producing a song, the Central Office of Information sought to make their message simple and to engage children who could memorise the tune and repeat it.

This interest in children's 'self-worth' and engagement with television materials was all part of a moment in which, in these limited mediums, children were re-conceptualised as holding the potential to develop expertise. This vision of childhood stretched further than in materials produced by Kidscape, but was by no means universally adopted. Indeed, concurrently politicians were also discussing whether and how children's ability to watch film and video should be restricted in the 'video nasties' debates.[63] In discussions around road safety as late as 1990, advice offered to parents in Leeds argued that children of 'all ages' were 'immature, impulsive, unpredictable, lacking in skill and experience' and that, 'even at 15 he or she is still a child'.[64] Local and issue-related variation remained, with the Leeds example notably rejecting the idea that children could hold different levels of expertise at each developmental stage. Nonetheless, in terms of child protection specifically, and in part because of the influence of small children's charities, a significant vision of childhood emerged, in which children could be equipped with practical expertise from infancy. This vision was in part individualist—the individual child would be the key respondent to child protection concerns—yet it also relied on dissemination of key materials by parents and teachers.

Gatekeepers: The Home

While new books and films addressed an empowered child, adults continued to manage the purchase, consumption, and use of these products, notably governing the ages at which children would access these messages. Recognising the authority of the parent and teacher, indeed, Kidscape aimed their products broadly at the 'under-fives', 'six- to eleven-year olds', and 'twelve-to-sixteen year olds', but also advised that adults may determine when children were 'ready' for each text. Adults would decide, likewise, when children may read the books in their daily lives, and who with—whether on their own or with parents, teachers, grandparents, or other adults.[65] This demonstrates that concerns about child protection did not always function to disrupt established relations between parents and children; they sometimes reinforced them. Relevant adults, in contact with children on an everyday level, would be responsible for drawing the boundaries of children's developmental stages.

Reflecting the significance of adults as purchasers and consumers, as well as gatekeepers of acceptable materials for children, reviews of these products placed adult testimony as key to establishing their worth. In 1985, *The Times* asked a psychiatrist, a general practitioner, a social worker, and a teacher to review five of the 'more serious' child protection films. While preferring films said to offer clear delivery and minimal gimmicks, notably all panellists critiqued this 'crude' tool for dissemination.[66] Preceding the first edition of the *Willow Street Kids*, likewise, were endorsements from a member of social services, a NSPCC team leader, and two child psychiatrists. The quotations presented testified that 'there is nothing frightening or disturbing in it', it is 'very tactful' and 'not at all threatening', and that the personal safety theme 'develops very appropriately throughout the book'.[67] Here, quotations from individuals with traditional sources of expertise—from social work, psychiatry, and the long-standing children's charity the NSPCC—defined the boundaries of appropriate child protection education in the home.

One of the key perceived barriers to the consumption of these products was around their use of language. To ameliorate this, the Kidscape books described genitals as 'the parts covered by bathing suits' or 'private parts', based on Elliott's concern, also echoed by parental rights groups of the period, that discussing the penis, vagina, or sex in relation to abuse may conflate the concepts in children's minds.[68] *The Times* reported in 1985 that the film company Oxford Polytechnic had cut what they called a 'penis song' from their programme *Strong kids, safe kids*. This decision reflected concerns that parents would not give children permission to watch the films, and anxieties about children's responses.[69] The choice of words in these products was thus governed both by ideas about the understandings and sensitivities of children and of adults. Notably, contemporary debate posited a distinction between children who had faced abuse and those who had not, with publishers questioning whether only the latter category would find explicit language 'frightening'.[70] This again reflected wider concerns in sex education—with the use of explicit language (penis, testicles, vagina) only emerging in 1960s handbooks directed at older children.[71]

In part, the interest in directing these texts towards parents reflected concerns about whether they may provoke negative childhood emotions, with an implied assumption that children who had faced abuse may develop different emotional ranges to those who had not. The primary purpose of these books was to help in 'opening up discussions … in a non-frightening and practical way'.[72] The idea was that children would then be able to question adults about the meaning of the products, and would not be distressed, with concern from contemporary commentators that child protection films may 'mystify' or 'possibly even harm' children unless used in a 'carefully prepared context'.[73] Notably, the primary descriptions of childhood emotions in these texts were in sections addressed to teachers and parents. While the child characters in the books did not discuss their emotions, manuals advised teachers and parents to help their children to discuss 'happy or sad', 'angry, hurt, fearful, sad, disgusted, mean, or furious' feelings, for example by making collages and through role-play and discussion.[74] The books emphasised that children may have a variety of reactions to abuse and violence, but that all were 'normal' and 'okay'.[75]

To an extent, these texts were designed to educate adults as well as children, teaching adults about child abuse and prevention, and calling for them to pay attention to children's inner emotional lives. *No More Secrets for Me* (1986), a book sold in America and Britain and written by a teacher and a clinician, contained both guidance to parents and a story for children. The text's preface argued that the 'most effective way' of eradicating child sexual abuse was 'to teach children to be aware of what could happen'. However, the text also emphasised that if parents were more aware, they too 'could be more effective in protecting their children from assault, whether from inside or outside the family'.[76] Notably, this book was introduced by a male psychologist, who argued that the 'role of men in today's world' was 'under pressure at home, at work, and in bed', and that a man may, as a consequence, become 'tyrannical to his family'.[77] Problematic power dynamics and assumptions continued to shape child protection debate, and arguments about child protection became proxies for broader arguments and anxieties about social change.

The direction of these books and films to parents as well as to children thus reflected a system of long-standing hierarchies that were not disrupted by the introduction of child protection programmes. The texts constructed a strict division between 'childhood' and 'adulthood', with adults acting from a position of greater power as producers and consumers, family leaders, teachers, and reviewers of these materials. The materials addressed parents as the caring protectors of children. Parents were advised to act on behalf of their children, and to maintain 'limits, structures and boundaries' in their children's lives, acting as 'parents first and friends second'.[78] The vision of parenthood was a positive one—with parents able to 'decide what is best for their own'—but also one entwined with ideas of protectionism, boundaries, and restriction.[79]

Parents as Teachers as Parents

Teachers, as well as parents, were gatekeepers in shaping how and when children accessed child protection education, particularly as the state imbued schools with new legal duties in this area.[80] The *Children Act* of 1989 placed duties on local education authorities (LEAs) to assist local authority social services departments acting on behalf of children in need or enquiring into allegations of child abuse.[81] In 1995, Circular 10/95 stated that every school should have a designated member of staff responsible for child protection and that the LEAs should have a list of these teachers.[82] A specific model of the compassion and abilities of teachers underpinned these additional burdens. Through the 1990s, educational researchers argued that teachers were well placed to detect child abuse and to enact child protection education because they were 'caring people', in close and regular contact with children, and because the majority of abuse occurred within the family home.[83]

Many teachers were reluctant to take such a key role in child protection education, feeling ill-equipped to work in this new area. In 1989, the *Guardian* quoted Peggy, a deputy head in an inner city comprehensive of 750 pupils. Peggy stated that teachers were reluctant to teach children about child protection because of the 'emotions' involved, but also that she still felt responsible, and that 'you can't walk away from the problem'.[84] Research by ChildLine testified that schools were enacting child protection measures in very different ways. Drawing on evidence from children's calls, the charity reported that some schools referred children to ChildLine and operated as safe spaces for children to report family violence. In other cases, however, callers reported that their teachers had: told them to come to terms with their parents' problems; immediately told their parents what they had reported, triggering physical retaliation; or disbelieved that 'such a nice father would behave like that'.[85]

In 1995, the Department for Education and Employment made funding available to support child protection training.[86] However, the courses offered were neither widespread nor effective. A study by Rosemary Webb and Graham Vulliamy published in 2001 noted that four out of five teachers had had no training from their local authority, and that even trained teachers credited their knowledge to personal experience, not training.[87] LEAs were struggling to provide sufficient training as Prime Minister Margaret Thatcher's reforms reduced their numbers and linked their funding to specific government targets.[88] Teachers trying to provide child protection education faced further challenges when trying to assess how school policies on abuse interacted with broader school environments, for example in terms of teachers' authority over pupils, policies on bullying, and biases around race and class.[89]

The shift towards teachers gaining authority in child protection education functioned in opposition to broader trends of education policy in the 1980s, in which parents were gaining more influence. The *Education Acts* of 1980 and 1986 mandated that school governing bodies would have the same number of parent governors as LEA governors, and also gave governors new responsibilities over the curriculum, discipline, and staffing.[90] The 1986 Act stated that governors must give parents clear information about the school's curriculum, produce an annual report, and hold an annual parents' meeting.[91] In terms of sex education more broadly, the parent was also gaining more power: the 1986 Act gave governors responsibility for sex education; included a requirement to consult with parents; and enabled parents to withdraw their children from sex education classes.[92] The confidence of teachers to engage in sex education also fell following guidance about responsibility to promote 'family life'.[93]

In this context, the voluntary sector became increasingly important as a provider of child protection education and as a support to teacher training. Kidscape was again significant, providing training for teachers and detailed lesson plans.[94] In terms of training, Kidscape offered short courses to train teachers in their methods focusing on: identifying the signs and symptoms of child abuse; learning about how offenders targeted children; developing basic questioning skills; thinking about the role of professional agencies; and, most significantly, techniques for teaching children how to protect themselves.[95] There was popular appetite for these courses: within months of the first workshops in 1986, Kidscape had a waiting list of over 800 schools and was dealing with over 120 inquiries a week.[96] By February 1987, the Kidscape programme was reaching more than 1000 schools who catered for almost 250,000 children.[97] Assessments of the effectiveness of the workshops were broadly positive, with teachers reporting substantial improvements in their knowledge of abuse and their ability to teach child protection after attendance.[98] The reach of Kidscape in this period demonstrated the successes of the charity, the concerns from teachers around this area, and the lack of broader state-provided training opportunities.

Kidscape also distributed many of their lesson plans and books. Kidscape's lesson plans produced three age-banded guides for under-fives, six- to eleven-year olds, and twelve-to-sixteen-year olds, encompassing lesson plans around bodily autonomy, self-determination, and assertiveness, and drawing on storytelling, role-play, and question and answer sessions.[99] These materials were relatively popular. For example, an under-fives colouring sheet was funded and sponsored by the Metropolitan Police, which distributed over 500,000 copies between 1990 and 1994.[100] The different lesson plans constructed differing, and 'age appropriate', ways in which schoolchildren would be able to become 'expert'. The under-fives programme instructed teachers to work closely with children to discuss and explain Kidscape's key messages, using puppets, colouring-in, and role-plays.[101] Spaces for interactivity remained, for example in terms of colouring-in sheets featuring Cosmo and Dibs and inviting children to draw their bodies and themselves saying no, and to practise running and thinking about who they could tell their problems to.

In the Teenscape programme, for twelve-to-sixteen-year olds, a more active model of childhood emerged. Students would discuss lessons in pairs, away from teacher involvement, and the programme advised them to write to newspapers and to approach local radio stations to 'present their views'.[102] In one key exercise, the children would pair up and label themselves 'teenager' and 'adult'. The teenager would make a statement to the 'adult', which the adult would repeatedly deny.[103] The students and teacher subsequently joined together to discuss collectively how difficult it may be for some children to challenge adults.[104] This represented an extent to which these models did seek to subvert adult-child relations, particularly for adolescents, as well as to manage them. Again, a clear model of child development emerged, with children capable of holding increasing levels of expertise in child protection as they aged. As with Kidscape's work with parents, however, there would also be flexibility in terms of the specific enactment of these programmes, with each teacher deciding when and whether it was 'appropriate' for children to complete the colouring-in activity, and how much 'drama' to inject into their role-plays.[105]

Nonetheless, the addressing of children significantly below the age of 11 in education relating to sex was relatively unusual in this period.[106] Facets of the government's broader sex education agenda were visible here—in terms of foisting 'responsibility' onto children and 'respect for themselves and others'.[107] At the same time, the broader Department for Education focus on using sex education to show the 'benefits of stable married life' or the 'responsibilities of parenthood' was absent from child protection education.[108] Also significant, the emphasis on the ages of different children, and their ability to attain and perform expertise, was not so present in the materials describing children's experiences and studied in Chap. 3. These materials were drawn from, and then written about, children, rather than directed to them, and represented a more homogenous and singular view of an ageless, genderless, classless child.

In addition to reflecting and reshaping relations between students and teachers, child protection education also represented a broader challenge to the relationships between teachers and parents. The Kidscape under-fives guide recognised the need to manage this relationship carefully, and opened with warning that it was 'recommended' that teachers sought the consent of all parents before teaching children these lessons, as well as providing guideline 'parental decision forms'.[109] At the same time, renewed concern around child sexual abuse in the 1980s also partially increased teachers' authority over parents, amid rising awareness of the prevalence of familial violence as well as limited evidence, from contemporary newspaper and televisual coverage, that many parents wanted teachers to take the primary responsibility for child protection education.[110]

Thus, the moral and legal frameworks guiding sex education and child protection education were notably different. In terms of the latter, while the teacher was not seen as a parent, he or she was increasingly represented as a pastoral caregiver. As such, the teacher became more responsible, and to an extent more accountable, for the child's welfare. In part, teachers acted in partnership with parents, providing child protection education to all children, but they also acted in conflict, with the teacher also deemed responsible for monitoring family life. Child protection education was firmly directed at children themselves, and such materials addressed children as active, intelligent, potentially expert subjects. However, such materials also magnified long-standing tensions between groups of adults; in this case, between parents and teachers, who had to negotiate how best to inculcate child expertise.

Child Experts and the 1980s

Chapters 3 and 4 of this book have in tandem assessed how debates around child protection developed new spaces for children's experiences, emotions, and expertise to be constructed by and expressed within public policy, family homes, and schools. These shifts built on longer-term developments. The emphasis on listening to minorities, and on thinking about family violence, owed much to second-wave feminism and the refuge movement. The work of Kidscape and children's fiction around child protection drew on thinking about 'authenticity' in 1960s children's literature, notably by Leila Berg. Kidscape's presentation of parents as capable of deciding 'what was best for their own', and acting on 'instinct', echoed the post-war parenting manuals of John Bowlby, Donald Winnicott, and Penelope Leach.[111]

While the developments in these chapters echoed longer-term changes, they were also reshaped in the distinct social, cultural, and political spaces of the 1980s. From the mid-1980s, media and political concerns about child sexual abuse reached new levels, drawing on long-standing knowledge from the voluntary sector and social services. Concerns about child protection were mobilised by feminist critics and by small charities to challenge and reshape broader ideas about children's position in society. By couching their discussions in terms of 'child protection', a framework which had become politically powerful, these groups were able to develop relatively radical programmes. For example, child protection education discussed consent with children from infancy, bypassing contemporary concern from conservative campaigners about child development and the maintenance of 'innocence' until 'adulthood'.[112]

This suggests, first, that discussions about child protection have not only acted as proxies for broader social and political concerns, but that they have also functioned as a shield for the promotion of specific agendas.

Second, this shows the gaps in the policy implementation of Thatcher's agendas on 'personal morality', 'family values', and 'Victorian values'.[113] Rhetoric around these ideas was reflected in the formation of policy about sex education, homosexuality, and censorship. However, the Thatcher governments were also pragmatic, and their social and moral agendas varied: the governments also rejected conservative shifts around abortion, contraception for the under-sixteens, and embryonic research.[114] While conservative shifts were made in sex education more broadly, child protection education to an extent developed outside of state control, and in a range of radical and progressive directions. In these contexts, a new, but historically grounded, vision of childhood expertise and child development emerged.

The voluntary sector fundamentally shaped this vision, acting influentially within the gaps of Thatcher's moral projects. Again, the idea of the voluntary sector as providing children's services, and as acting in a 'moving frontier' with the state, was not new to the 1980s. Notably, independent voluntary agencies had long played a significant role in providing information about sexually transmitted diseases and contraception.[115] However, this moment, following rising concerns about child sexual abuse, also saw the increasing significance of small voluntary organisations, such as Kidscape. In addition to the development of large and 'professional' 'non-governmental organisations' over this period, small charities began to emphasise their size as a strength, facilitating innovation, responsiveness, speed, and critique. Despite their small size, the work of these charities was used as a justification for state retrenchment.[116] Teachers, in particular, were not receiving significant state support for their child protection work.[117] The influence of Thatcher was cultural, as well as economic: the focus on individual consent, rather than community action, echoed Thatcherite emphasis on 'the individual' or 'popular individualism', in development from the 1960s and 1970s.[118] Following the second-wave feminist moment, and the increasing focus on small numbers of women as industry leaders, influential female figureheads led Kidscape and ChildLine. Media interest in strong women cannot be separated entirely from the cultural and media interests in Thatcher.

Overall, therefore, the construction of children as experiential and emotional experts drew on longer term trajectories, but was also a process magnified by, and influential within, the shifting cultural, political, and economic contexts of the 1980s, themselves shaped, but not wholly defined, by the agendas of Thatcher and Thatcherism.[119] The politics of experience as expertise extended beyond focus on children alone in this period, and indeed the following two chapters trace how parents, to a greater extent than children, were able to mobilise media and political interest in their emotions and experiences from the 1980s. Adult leaders of children's charities, likewise, were affected by this politics. For instance, Elliott, the leader of Kidscape, described the bases of her expertise variously as deriving from her status as a mother, as a former teacher, and as an educational psychologist.[120]

While parents and later survivors became increasingly significant as experiential experts from the 1980s and 1990s, childhood expertise met with new challenges. Growing concerns about childhood violence were significant, particularly following the murder of James Bulger by two boys in 1993.[121] Expressing a resurgence in discussions of parents' rights, Harry Hendrick cites a High Court ruling in March 1994 in support of a childminder's right to 'smack' children in her care with parental permission, and a level of 'interpretational backlash' against the Gillick ruling, which in 1985 enabled children to access contraceptives without parental permission.[122] The development of parents' advocacy movements further complicated the interpretation of children's experiences from the late 1980s and particularly in the 1990s. As the next chapter shows, parents who had been falsely accused of abuse began to challenge social work around children, and to call for the further instatement of privacy in family life, creating a more complex terrain for seeking out children's testimonies. Nonetheless, social policy interest in children's experiences, emotions, and expertise also continued through the 1990s and 2000s, for example in medical journals looking to access the accounts of child patients and in political rhetoric around how children were not only 'possessions' but 'individuals', not just 'future adults', but 'part of our society now'.[123]

Conclusion

This chapter has explored how successive governments, public health campaigners, and small charities sought to make children expert in the everyday work of child protection. In Britain, this was a new interest which emerged from the mid-1980s, though it followed and drew on research and personnel from American counterparts who began work in the 1960s and 1970s. This analysis is significant in two key ways. First, it demonstrates that public, political, and professional interest in childhood expertise developed significantly in the late twentieth century, in part motivated by concerns about child protection. Children's charities and psychologists became increasingly convinced that children *could* become expert, and newly invested in developing programmes to inculcate expertise. This analysis shows that growing public interest in understanding children's experiences was inflected by analysis of emotion; the expression of which was seen as a marker that adults had accessed an 'authentic' child testimony.

The second key facet of this analysis is in further exploring the extent to which adults mediated, represented, and shaped the ways in which children were made expert in the late twentieth century. Voluntary sector organisations run by adults were particularly significant in providing child protection education, often operating aside from state leadership or the priorities of larger voluntary organisations. On an everyday level, parents and teachers would determine whether, when, and how children were able to read storybooks or watch films about child protection. Culturally, adults also governed the production and creation of child protection products. While adults working in this area sought to represent the 'true' stories of children, and to produce their works collaboratively, at times the child subject which emerged was a very abstract one, not demarcated by class, race, age, or gender. While this chapter therefore traces the development of experiential and emotional expertise—the key theme of this book—it also shows that the processes through which this expertise was realised, manifested, and limited would vary significantly for children, parents, and survivors.

Notes

1. Hester Barron and Claire Langhamer, 'Feeling through Practice: Subjectivity and Emotion in Children's Writing', *Journal of Social History*, 51, no. 1 (2015): 108.
2. Kidscape's size can be examined through exploration of their historical Annual Reports, potentially available on request to researchers at the Kidscape Offices, and also through examination of accounts at Companies House. The organisation was significantly smaller than, say, Action for Children, which employed between 2200 and 6500 members of staff between 1991 and 2009 (see Matthew Hilton, Nick Crowson, Jean-Francois Mouhot and James McKay, *A Historical Guide to NGOs in Britain: Charities, Civil Society and the Voluntary Sector since 1945* (Basingstoke: Palgrave Macmillan, 2012), 84.

   In terms of markers of the organisation's significant influence, Kidscape's representatives participated in the Child Sex Offender Review Stakeholder Group, the Home Office Sex Tourism Policy Group, and the Children's Social Policy Group on the prevention of child abuse, and over 20,000 adults attended Kidscape's courses between 1984 and 1989 alone (see, Michele Elliott, *Teenscape: A Personal Safety Programme for*

Teenagers (London: Health Education Authority, 1990), 5; Michele Elliott, *Dealing with Child Abuse: The Kidscape Training Guide* (London: Kidscape, 1989)).

3. Jay Mechling, 'Advice to Historians on Advice to Mothers', *Journal of Social History*, 9 (1975): 56; Laura Tisdall, 'Education, parenting and concepts of childhood in England, c. 1945 to c. 1979', *Contemporary British History*, 31 (1): 24; Pascal Eitler, Stephanie Olsen, and Uffa Jensen, 'Introduction', in Ute Frevert et al., *Learning How to Feel. Children's Literature and Emotional Socialization, 1870–1970* (Oxford: Oxford University Press, 2014).
4. Jay Mechling, 'Advice to Historians on Advice to Mothers', *Journal of Social History*, 9 (1975), 56.
5. See, for example, Irma Joyce, *Never Talk to Strangers* (New York: Golden Books, 1967); Robin Lennett and Bob Crane, *It's OK to Say No!* (New York: Tom Doherty Associates, 1985); Oralee Wachter, *No More Secrets for Me: Helping to Safeguard Your Child Against Sexual Abuse* (London: Penguin Books, 1986).
6. Jenny Rees, 'Every child's right to a private life', *Daily Mail*, 14 September 1978, 13.
7. Idea of 'imported problem' raised by Michele Elliott in a retrospective interview: Nancy Stewart Books, 'Interview with Michele Elliot, Founder of British Charity, Kidscape', 16 February 2011 <http://nancystewartbooks.blogspot.co.uk/2011/02/interview-with-michele-elliott-founder.html> (2 January 2015).
8. See Nigel Parton, *The Politics of Child Protection: Contemporary Developments and Future Directions* (Basingstoke: Palgrave Macmillan, 2014), 24, 66–67; Phillip Jenkins, *Intimate Enemies: Moral Panics in Contemporary Great Britain* (New York: Aldine de Gruyter, 1992), xiii, 12–17, 101–107; Harry Hendrick, *Children, Childhood and English Society, 1880–1990* (Cambridge: Cambridge University Press, 1997), 60. Quote is from Hendrick, *Children, Childhood and English Society*, 101.
9. Michele Elliott, *501 Ways to Be A Good Parent: From the Frantic Fours to the Terrible Twelves* (London, 1996), p. 50; Victoria McKee, 'Let's not frighten them', says child abuse campaigner', *Daily Mail*, 10 February 1987, 13.
10. Elliott, *Teenscape*, 6.
11. Jane Pilcher, 'School sex education: policy and practice in England 1870 to 2000', *Sex Education*, 5, no. 2 (2005): 154–156.
12. James Hampshire and Jane Lewis, "The Ravages of Permissiveness': Sex Education and the Permissive Society', *Twentieth Century British History*, 15, no. 3 (2004): 291; Pilcher, 'School sex education': 159–160.

13. See, for example, the Central Advisory Council for Education's Plowden Report (1967), which includes a whole chapter on sex education but which does not mention child protection education within this. The only vague hints towards consideration of this topic is the idea that 'not all homes are happy' although this statement is provided alongside the idea that, 'some parents still find it embarrassing to discuss the physical details of sex with their children', rather than in the context of violence. (Central Advisory Council for Education England), *The Plowden Report: Children and their Primary Schools* (London: Her Majesty's Stationery Office, 1967), c. 716.
14. Jane Cousins Mills, '"Putting Ideas into Their Heads": Advising the Young', *Feminist Review*, 28 (1988): 163.
15. Ibid., 163.
16. See, for example, Hampshire and Lewis, "The Ravages of Permissiveness": 299–301. See also: Lawrence Black, 'There Was Something About Mary: The National Viewers' and Listeners' Association and Social Movement History', Nick Crowson, Matthew Hilton, and James McKay (eds), *NGOs in Contemporary Britain: Non-state Actors in Society and Politics since 1945* (London: Palgrave Macmillan, 2009): 182–200.
17. David Limond, 'Martin Cole, the Growing Up Controversy and the Limits of School Sex Education in 1970s England', *History of Education*, 37, no. 3 (2008): 409–429.
18. See: Hampshire and Lewis, "The Ravages of Permissiveness": 292–293; Rachel Thomson, 'Prevention, promotion and adolescent sexuality: The politics of school sex education in England and Wales, *Sexual and Marital Therapy*, 9, no. 2 (1994): 116. On how individual teachers renegoitated sex education in the classroom, see also: Hannah Elizabeth, 'Getting around the rules of sex education', *Wellcome Collection*, 7 June 2018.
19. See: Martin Durham, *Sex and Politics: The Family and Morality in the Thatcher Years* (London: Palgrave Macmillan, 1991); Eliza Filby, *God and Mrs Thatcher: the Battle for Britain's Soul* (London: Biteback Publishing, 2015), chapter 6.
20. Pilcher, 'School sex education': 163.
21. Ibid., 158.
22. Michele Elliott, *The Willow Street Kids: Play Safe Stay Safe* (1st edition, London, 1986), 71.
23. Ibid., 91.
24. Ibid., 57.
25. Ibid., 57.
26. Ibid., 17, 52, 99.
27. Ibid., 36. See also: Michele Elliott, *A Safety Guide for Young Children: Feeling Happy Feeling Safe* (London: Hodder Children's Books, 1991), 23.
28. Elliott, *The Willow Street Kids* (1st edition), 85.

29. Ibid., 88.
30. See, for example, Hampshire and Lewis, "The Ravages of Permissiveness": 299–301.
31. Gaby Weiner, 'New Era or Old Times: Class, Gender and Education, *International Journal of Inclusive Education*, 2 (1998): 189–207; Vicki Coppock, Deena Haydon and Ingrid Richter, 'Patronising Rita: The Myth of Equal Opportunities in Education' in Vicki Coppock et al. (eds) *The Illusions of 'Post-Feminism': New Women, Old Myths* (London: Routledge, 1995), 47–74. Given that education was a 'crucial component of the father's provider role', Laura King also demonstrates that insurance advertising 'capitalised on the idea of men as providers to target them in their campaigns, whilst certain adverts highlighted this role in their promotion of education projects such as encyclopaedias'. (Laura King, *Family Men: Fatherhood and Masculinity in Britain, c. 1914–1960* (Oxford: Oxford University Press, 2015), 30–39).
32. Jeffrey Weeks, *Sex, Politics and Society: The Regulation of Sexuality since 1800* (London: Longman, 1989), 251–252.
33. See, for example: Michele Elliott, *The Willow Street Kids: Be smart, stay safe* (3rd edition, London: Macmillan Children's Books, 1997), 1.
34. Mary MacLeod, *Talking with children about child abuse: ChildLine's first ten years* (London: ChildLine 1996).
35. While overall a critical voice, Herbert praised Kidscape's books, and particularly their illustrations, for representing children from different demographic groups (Carrie Herbert, 'A Safety Guide for Young Children: Feeling Happy, Feeling Safe', *Children & Society*, 5 (1991): 283.) Discussion of the norms of parenting manuals in: Tisdall, 'Education, parenting and concepts of childhood': 30. Discussion of child protection texts in these terms in: Cousins Mills, "Putting Ideas into Their Heads": 171.
36. Paul Vallely, 'How streetwise can a nine-year-old be?', *Independent*, 6 January 1997, 6.
37. Maureen Thom and Celia Macliver, *Bruce's Story* (London: The Children's Society, 1986).
38. John Rowe Townsend, *Gumble's Yard* (1961), as described in Gillian Avery, 'The family story', in Peter Hunt (ed.) *International Companion Encyclopaedia of Children's Literature* (London: Routledge, 2004), 338. Discussion of Leila Berg work in: 'Classmates for Janet and John', *The Times*, 13 January 1969, 5; 'Nippers on the Dump', *Guardian*, 3 February 1969, 9.
39. Herbert, 'A Safety Guide for Young Children': 282.
40. Ibid., 283.
41. See, for example: Wendy W. Williams, 'The Equality Crisis: Some Reflections no Culture, Courts, and Feminism', in Linda Nicholson (ed.), *The Second Wave: A Reader in Feminist Theory* (New York and

London: Routledge, 1997), 76, 83; Catharine A. Mackinnon, 'Sexuality', in Nicholson (ed.)., *The Second Wave*, 167–168, 171; Gayatri Spivak with Ellen Rooney, '"In a Word": Interview', in Nicholson (ed.), *The Second Wave*, 357.

42. Pilcher, 'School sex education': 157.
43. For example, Walt Disney produced *Now I Can Tell You My Secret* (1985) and the Californian company Educational Media International made *No More Secrets* (1985) (as cited in Michele Elliot, 'Caution', *Times Educational Supplement*, 18 April 1986, as reproduced in Elliott, *Dealing with Child Abuse*, 117.) In terms of how children related to television, see Joe Moran, *Armchair Nation: An intimate history of Britain in front of the tv* (London: Profile Books, 2013), 2.
44. 'Charley—Strangers', Central Office of Information for Home Office, 1973, <http://www.nationalarchives.gov.uk/films/1964to1979/filmpage_strangers.htm>).
45. Ibid.
46. See Thomson, *Lost Freedom*, 165–168.
47. 'Charley—Strangers', 1973.
48. 'And the winner is…', *BBC News*, 28 March 2006 <http://news.bbc.co.uk/1/hi/magazine/4853042.stm> (1 June 2017).
49. National Archives (hereafter TNA), Children Say No: Prevention of child abuse and molestation, on behalf of the Home Office, FM/COI/3181, May 1987–1989, First Revision to Children Say No: Correspondence, April 1987.
50. Sandy Sulaiman, 'Would your child go with a stranger?', *Independent*, 26 January 1992, 74.
51. Ibid., 74; Elliott, *Teenscape*, 71.
52. Sulaiman, 'Would your child go with a stranger?', 74.
53. Elliott, 'Caution'.
54. Thomson, *Lost Freedom*, 148.
55. Ibid., 148.
56. Peter Fiddick, 'TV puppets to fight child abuse', *Guardian*, 13 January 1987, 4.
57. BBC and Kidscape, Keeping Safe with Cosmo and Dibs—Harry's Cousin, 1987.
58. Ibid.
59. Victoria Neumark, 'It's not rude to say no', *Times Educational Supplement*, 6 February 1987.
60. TNA, Child Abuse: Aspects of Health Visitors Work, MH 152/166, 1975–1989, Extract from the agenda of a meeting of Berkshire Central Review Committee Held on 30 October 1987, 11.
61. TNA, Children Say No: Prevention of Child Abuse and Molestation, on behalf of the Home Office, FM/COI/3181, May 1987–1989, 'Say No: Fair': 60 Second TV filler, 5 November 1987, 1–5.

62. TNA, Children Say No: Prevention of Child Abuse and Molestation, on behalf of the Home Office, FM/COI/3181, May 1987–1989, 'Say No: Song', 5 November 1987, 1–4.
63. Julian Petley, '"Are We Insane?" The "Video Nasty"', *Recherches sociologiques et anthropologiques*, 43, no. 1 (2012): 35–57.
64. Cited in Jeni Harden, 'There's No Place Like Home: The Public/Private Distinction in Children's Theorizing of Risk and Safety', *Childhood*, 7, no. 1 (2000): 55.
65. Elliott, *Willow Street Kids* (1st edition), vi.
66. Caroline Moorehead, 'Child abuse: facing the unthinkable', *The Times*, 2 December 1995, 11.
67. Elliott, *Willow Street Kids* (1st edition), ii.
68. Discussed by Kidscape at: Michele Elliott, *Why My Child? Child-Centred Advice for Parents or Carers whose Children Have been Sexually Abused* (Dublin: Irish Society for the Prevention of Cruelty to Children, 1994), 7, 17; McKee, 'Let's not frighten them', 13; Elliott, *501 Ways to Be A Good Parent*, 152. See also criticism by Parents Against Injustice in similar terms in: Bodleian Library, M89.B00525, Susan Amphlett, 'Statement to the Cleveland Inquiry', 14 December 1987, 26.
69. Moorehead, 'Child abuse: facing the unthinkable', 11.
70. Hilary Macaskill, 'How to avoid close encounters of the worst kind', *Guardian*, 22 September 1987, 10.
71. Pilcher, 'School sex education': 160–162.
72. Elliott, *Willow Street Kids* (1st edition), vi; Wachter, *No More Secrets for Me*, 20.
73. Moorehead, 'Child abuse: facing the unthinkable': 11.
74. Elliott, *Teenscape*, 93; Elliott, *Why My Child?*, 16.
75. Elliott, *Teenscape*, 93; Elliott, *Why My Child?*, 3, 6.
76. Wachter, *No More Secrets for Me*, x.
77. Andrew Stanway, 'Introduction', Wachter, *No More Secrets for Me*, 15.
78. Elliott, *Why My Child*, 7; Elliott, *501 Ways to Be A Good Parent*, x.
79. Elliott, *Feeling Happy Feeling Safe*, 3.
80. *Children Act 1989* (London: Her Majesty's Stationery Office, 1989); Department for Education and Employment (hereafter DfEE), *Protecting Children from Abuse: the role of the Education Service*, Circular 10/95 (London, 1995).
81. *Children Act 1989.*
82. DfEE, *Protecting Children from Abuse.*
83. Dorit Braun and Anne Schonveld, 'Training teachers in child protection', in Tricia David (ed.) *Protecting Children from Abuse: multi-professionalism and the Children Act 1989* (Stoke-on-Trent: Trentham Books, 1994); Ben Whitney, *The Children Act and Schools: A Guide to Good Practice*

(London: Routledge Falmer, 1993); Rosemary Webb and Graham Vulliamy, 'The Primary Teacher's Role in Child Protection', *British Educational Research Journal*, 27 (2001): 59–77.

84. Julia Hagedorn, 'It doesn't happen in our school', *Guardian*, 25 April 1989, 25.
85. Carole Epstein and Gill Keep, 'What Children Tell ChildLine about Domestic Violence', in Alex Saunders, *"It hurts me too": Children's experiences of domestic violence and refuge life* (1995), 55.
86. DfEE, *Protecting Children from Abuse.*
87. Webb and Vulliamy, 'The Primary Teacher's Role in Child Protection': 61–65.
88. Derek Gillard, *Education in England: a brief history*, 2011 <http://www.educationengland.org.uk/history/chapter08.html> (21 July 2015).
89. Maureen O'Hara, 'Developing a Feminist School Policy on Child Sexual Abuse', *Feminist Review*, 28 (Spring, 1988): 159.
90. *Education Act 1980* (London: Her Majesty's Stationery Office, 1980), *Education Act 1986* (London: Her Majesty's Stationery Office, 1986).
91. *Education Act 1986*, Section 20, Sections 30–31. See also: Pilcher, 'School sex education': 165–166.
92. Thomson, 'Prevention, promotion and adolescent sexuality': 119. See page 121 for how this requirement was subsequently modified by the introduction of the National Curriculum in 1988.
93. Pilcher, 'School sex education': 165–166.
94. Theoni Mavrogianna, 'Child Abuse Prevention: Evaluation of the "Kidscape" Teacher Training Programme, Unpublished Thesis, Institute of Education, University of London, August 1993, 19.
95. Ibid., 19.
96. Christine Aziz, 'Teaching children to say no', *Guardian*, 6 January 1987, 10.
97. Ibid.; McKee, 'Let's not frighten them', 13.
98. Mavrogianna, 'Child Abuse Prevention', 38.
99. Kidscape, *Under Five's Programme*; Kidscape, *Kidscape Primary Kit: Children's Lesson for planning and teaching good sense defence to children* (London: Kidscape, 1986); Elliott, *Teenscape.*
100. Kidscape Offices, *Kidscape Annual Report 1993–4*, 'Colour-in Code Posters', 4.
101. Kidscape, *Under Five's Programme*, p. 21.
102. Elliott, *Teenscape*, 107.
103. Ibid., 40.
104. Ibid., 40.
105. Kidscape, *Under Five's Programme*, 8. 21.

106. Pilcher, 'Gillick and After': 83.
107. Department of Education and Science, *Circular 11/87: Sex Education at Schools* (London: Department of Education and Science, 1987), as cited in Thomson, 'Prevention, promotion and adolescent sexuality': 120.
108. Ibid.
109. Kidscape, *Under Five's Programme*, 4.
110. British Film Institute (hereafter BFI), *Kidscape*, Thames Help, Dir. Simon Buxton, 26 August 1986; Geraldine Bedell, 'Taking the X-factor out of sex', *Independent*, 27 June 1993, 42; Macaskill, 'How to avoid close encounters of the worst kind', 10.
111. Tisdall, 'Education, parenting and concepts of childhood': 37; Angela Davis, *Modern Motherhood: Women and the family in England, 1945–2000* (Manchester: Manchester University Press, 2012), see Chapter Five: 'Experts and childcare 'bibles': mothers and advice literature.
112. Pilcher, 'Gillick and After': 77.
113. For more on Thatcher's use of 'Victorian values', please see: Raphael Samuel, 'Mrs Thatcher's Return to Victorian Values', *Proceedings of the British Academy*, 78 (1992): 9–29.
114. Durham, *Sex and Politics*, as cited in Thomson, 'Prevention, promotion and adolescent sexuality': 119.
115. Thomson, 'Prevention, promotion and adolescent sexuality': 117.
116. Hansard, House of Commons, sixth series, vol. 160, col. 266, 15 November 1989.
117. See, for example: Paul Pierson, *Dismantling the Welfare State? Reagan, Thatcher, and the Politics of Retrenchment* (Cambridge: Cambridge University Press, 1994).
118. Arguing that visions of individual consent replaced those of public morality around sexuality from the 1960s: Weeks, *Sex, Politics and Society*, 251–252. Discussing the roots of popular individualism in the 1970s: Emily Robinson, Camilla Schofield, Florence Sutcliffe-Braithwaite, Natalie Thomlinson, 'Telling Stories about Post-war Britain: Popular Individualism and the 'Crisis' of the 1970s', *Twentieth Century British History*, 28, no. 2 (2017): 268–304.
119. Matthew Hilton, Chris Moores, and Florence Sutcliffe-Braithwaite, 'New Times revisited: Britain in the 1980s', *Contemporary British History*, 31, no. 2 (2017): 145–165.
120. Michele Elliott, *Keep Them Safe* (Swindon, 1990), 1; Sally Weale, 'Watch out with Mother', *Guardian*, 26 July 1993, 9.
121. Hendrick, *Children, Childhood and English Society*, 98.

122. Ibid., 99.
123. Hansard, House of Lords, fifth series, vol. 578, col. 725, 19 February 1997; National Commission of Inquiry into the Prevention of Child Abuse, *Childhood Matters: Report of the National Commission of Inquiry into the Prevention of Child Abuse. Volume Two* (London: Her Majesty's Stationery Office, 1996), 5; Cleone Hart and Rosemary Chesson, 'Children as consumers', *British Medical Journal,* 23 May 1998, 1600–1603.

Open Access This chapter is licensed under the terms of the Creative Commons Attribution 4.0 International License (http://creativecommons.org/licenses/by/4.0/), which permits use, sharing, adaptation, distribution and reproduction in any medium or format, as long as you give appropriate credit to the original author(s) and the source, provide a link to the Creative Commons license and indicate if changes were made.

The images or other third party material in this chapter are included in the chapter's Creative Commons license, unless indicated otherwise in a credit line to the material. If material is not included in the chapter's Creative Commons license and your intended use is not permitted by statutory regulation or exceeds the permitted use, you will need to obtain permission directly from the copyright holder.

CHAPTER 5

Collective Action by Parents and Complicating Family Life

This chapter explores how parents began to mobilise collectively from the 1960s, 1970s, and 1980s, and to contest child protection policy and practice. Initially, and in part in response to the studies of parental psychology analysed in Chap. 2, parents mobilised in partnership with long-standing professional agencies, notably the NSPCC. However, parents also began to mobilise independently, for example in the formation of new self-help groups and to establish new helplines. This activism was often inspired by the work of American support groups, but nonetheless was also shaped by a distinctly British context.

In particular, the development of British groups relied on growing interest in contesting family privacy and the 'stiff upper lip' by making the challenges of family life public.[1] Indeed, these new collective groups were significant in presenting a complex view of family life that was created by parents themselves. The groups also explicitly challenged the ability of professionals to understand family life, and sought to combat interventionist and paternalist interactions with social work and medical agencies. In the mid-1980s, support groups for parents who had been falsely accused of child abuse extended such challenges and argued that professionals in medicine and social work should themselves draw on experiential and emotional forms of expertise.

The ability of parents to conduct such critical work occurred in a context of reform for social services. The *Local Authority Social Services Act* of

© The Author(s) 2018

J. Crane, *Child Protection in England, 1960–2000*, Palgrave Studies in the History of Childhood,
https://doi.org/10.1007/978-3-319-94718-1_5

1970 consolidated previously disparate departments such as Children's Welfare, Physically Handicapped, and Mental Welfare into a broad and generic 'Social Services'. At a similar time, the *Children and Young Person Act* of 1969 introduced care orders, a new mechanism through which social services would manage all children when referred by local authorities, police, or the NSPCC.[2] Contemporary news coverage suggested that introducing both of these pieces of legislation at once was a 'fundamental political and administrative miscalculation', and gave examples of a system struggling to adapt.[3]

In these contexts, from the 1960s families were increasingly responding to crises of health, social life, and identity by writing to newspapers, reaching out to those with similar experiences and, indeed, by founding voluntary groups. Parental activism was likewise visible, for example, in the establishment of the Society for the Prevention of Cruelty to Pregnant Women in 1960 and in the foundation of the Stillbirth and Perinatal Death Association in 1978.[4] It was in these shifting contexts of professional, voluntary, and media life that parents themselves were able to enter debates around child protection for the first time in the late 1960s, 1970s, and 1980s. While these groups made significant criticism of professional expertise, their own activism remained reliant on the professional skills and emotional labours of their figurehead leaders. Because these leaders had significant skillsets, and were able to mobilise media and political interest in experience and emotion, parent activists yielded significant influence in the late twentieth century.

Parents as Partners

Chapter 2 of this book traced the ways in which clinicians and the NSPCC developed interests in parents who 'battered' their children, and positioned these parents within broader rhetoric about social problem groups. In part, this interest continued over the 1970s. The NSPCC maintained its research into the 'well-marked personality characteristics' of violent parents, pinpointing factors such as 'social inhibitions', shyness, immaturity, and vulnerability to emotional upset.[5] At the same time, from the 1960s and 1970s parents themselves were also able to work with the NSPCC's social workers to manage their own family situations, as well as, in a more limited sense, to reshape child protection policy. Parents, while being observed and categorised by professional agencies, also critiqued and challenged social work and medical practice.

Parents were partners in an everyday sense with NSPCC staff, working closely together. This was particularly the case in an NSPCC experiment which began operating in 1968—the Battered Child Research Project, which was organised by four social workers led by psychiatric social worker Joan Court.[6] Court was interested in the emotional, not the mechanical, side of her work and wanted to build up a 'trusting relationship' with parents, believing that parenthood did not necessarily come naturally to everyone.[7] The experiment provided twenty-four-hour advice and assistance to up to 50 families, recruited from the hospitals of London.[8] Parents played a role in shaping their relationships with this social service, governing when, how, and why the NSPCC entered their family homes.

Significantly, parents were also the NSPCC's partners in seeking political reform. Testifying to the Select Committee on Violence in the Family in November 1976, representatives from the NSPCC's National Advisory Centre for the Battered Child (the later name for the Battered Child Research Project) were joined by five parents who had used the organisation's programmes, identified as Mr and Mrs A., Mr and Mrs B., and Mrs C.[9] Discussions centred on the experiences of these parents, who the Committee's chairman, Labour Member of Parliament Joyce Butler, called 'parents who find that a child is too much to cope with'.[10] Mr and Mrs B., for example, came to the NSPCC 'in the middle of the night' when their child was eight months old, because they were struggling with his hyperactivity. The parents had since relied on the service to take the child into their care on a number of occasions and had seen a 'tremendous improvement' in his behaviour.[11] Mrs C. likewise referred herself, when her child was three. She was living in 'appalling conditions' in a small single room and had given her child 'superficial injuries'. She was aged 18, had no family support, and had separated from her husband, whom she had married at 16. She could not cope with her child and ultimately decided that he should be adopted.[12] These parents—Mr and Mrs B. and Mrs C.—then had very different experiences of child-rearing. The former were at risk of harming their child, while the latter had already been violent. The former family kept their child, while the latter decided to have hers adopted. The NSPCC hence worked with a variety of family situations daily, and, significantly, this interaction shaped its broad definitions of abuse and maltreatment.

One key narrative which emerged from the parents' testimony to the select committee was that professional services were failing. Mr A. reported that for two and a half years he and his wife had been 'everywhere', 'to hospitals and health visitors—quite a number of people', but that they had not received adequate help until their health visitor put them in contact with the NSPCC.[13] Mr and Mrs B. likewise had had a similar experience of struggling to access help from doctors and hospitals before reaching the NSPCC. Subsequently, they felt that doctors and 'normal welfare workers'—outside of the NSPCC—did not know enough about the 'social problems in connection with babies'.[14] These parents criticised doctors for forgetting to perform the social work of asking parents what was wrong, and for merely 'writing out a prescription as soon as you walk in the door', rather than listening to parents' complaints.[15]

Parents thus accompanied NSPCC representatives at the Select Committee on Violence in the Family hearings, and acted in partnership with social workers in the day-to-day interactions of the Battered Child Research Project. The dynamics of this partnership were not entirely equal: the NSPCC was the only organisation other than police and local authorities with the legal powers to apply for care orders on behalf of vulnerable children, and thus could theoretically prosecute parents, as well as offering rehabilitative support. At the same time, the parents testifying to the Select Committee at least were broadly supportive of these powers, arguing in fact that health visitors should also wield them, given that 'the child's life is far more important than anything else'.[16]

The NSPCC's work around battered children thus demonstrates the ways in which the social spaces of child protection were highly contested in the late 1960s and 1970s, involving parents, social workers, charities, and government. The idea of social life which emerged was the atomised, individualised family unit, rather than a broad vision of 'society' or 'community'. Medical expertise remained significant: the Battered Child Research Unit had a Scientific Advisory Committee chaired by a paediatrician and including representatives from psychiatry and radiology.[17] Nonetheless, the work of this organisation was revealing of a moment in which experiential expertise was also becoming significant on the public stage. Testifying to the Select Committee on Violence in the Family, Mrs A. emphasised that it was the 'personal contact' with the professional, 'not just a telephone number', that was important, and further that parents should interact with social workers and clinicians as equals, on a 'human' level.[18] Mrs A. also criticised how alienating it was to experience professionals at the clinic who 'never swear or lose their temper', giving the example, 'if a baby piddles over their hand they say "Oh, dear me, I must go and have a wash."'[19]

The calls made by Mrs A. and other parents in this context were not only for a shift in the management of child protection from medical to social professionals. Rather, this critique suggested that all professionals involved in child protection should draw on personal experience when working with parents, breaking down a hierarchical model of professional–parent relations through reference to common life experiences. While these calls were not necessarily heeded, they became influential within the limited space of this select committee, where individual politician members responded by sharing their own experiences of family life. One Member of Parliament, for example, reported that his youngest child would for 'a very long time' wake up 'almost every night', which 'created considerable problems'.[20] Likely—and as Selina Todd has argued with reference to Family Service Units and the Family Welfare Association—the work between parents, NSPCC staff, and indeed Parliamentarians modified the thinking of social workers and politicians.[21]

In working with parents in this way, promoting a 'more understanding approach', the NSPCC also forged a new role for itself, defying voluntary sector concerns that charities would cease to be important after the post-war extension of state provisions for children.[22] The long-established hierarchies between professions and the recipients of state and charitable 'aid' would not be flattened, but they would be reshaped. In the context of the 1970s, reductions in statutory medical and social work services provided new opportunities for voluntary action to become further impactful.

Early Self-Help Groups

Parents themselves began to have influence in the practice and policy of child protection not only through the mediatory agency of the NSPCC, but also through the establishment of self-help groups. In Britain, these groups were founded in the 1970s and 1980s for parents 'in crisis' and at risk of, or already, harming their children. Internationally, the first of such groups was Parents Anonymous, initially known as Mothers Anonymous, and established in America in 1967 by a parent, Jolly K., in collaboration with her psychiatric social worker Leonard Lieber. The group became a model for 500 chapters which developed across America by 1977, gaining federal and charitable funding.[23] Parents could self-refer or be referred by social agencies, courts, and police. Once members, parents were offered weekly meetings and a peer support network.[24] Parents Anonymous was subject to clinical and social interest, and its representatives spoke at the first International Congress on Child Abuse and Neglect, held at World Health Organisation in September 1976.[25] There, representatives described the case of a 21-year-old married mother of an infant diagnosed with 'failure to thrive' but returned to the family home under supervision by a public service agency. When referred to Parents Anonymous, fellow parents realised that the mother had no knowledge of infant care or nutrition and was scared of her social worker. Members provided 'basic education for parenthood' and role-playing techniques 'to ease her fear of authority', leading to 'marked improvement' in three weeks.[26]

Parents, social workers, nurses, and midwives established multiple similar groups across Britain: Dial-for-Help, a helpline in Ashton-under-Lyne; a walk-in centre in Cambridgeshire; Help-a-Mum in Glasgow; Target and Scope in Southampton; Tell-a-friend in Sittingbourne; Parent Child Concern; and Parents Anonymous.[27] The very names of these organisations positioned them in a tradition of mutual aid and self-help, providing a forum for collective action even as state social work pushed an individualist model of family and parental responsibility. Helplines were a key service provided by these organisations, but they often also offered regular meetings and personal contact.[28] The groups focused on overcoming social isolation and rehabilitating damaged relationships between parents and children by building parental confidence and skills.[29] Parents who had themselves been through the programme often led classes.

While overtly all parents were welcome, mothers were often the focus of these groups' work. Parent–Child Concern, for example, primarily cared for mothers and lobbied for further research into post-natal depression and pre-menstrual tension.[30] When presenting their work to the Select Committee on Violence in the Family, the group were asked whether husbands were 'rebellious' or resistant to the organisation's aims. One group representative answered that they would 'like to include them, but there is the question of baby-sitting'.[31] Nonetheless, the notion of the mother as the primary carer and also perhaps as the parent most likely to be engaged with, and rehabilitated through, talking therapies was prominent. Facets of this work held parallels with feminist consciousness-raising and community-based mental health provision, though this link was not made in published or Parliamentary documents.[32] Instead, Parliamentary reports and media coverage framed these projects as equally beneficial for all members of the nuclear family.

With parents themselves acting as partners, leaders, and evaluators of self-help groups, several things happened. First, the ideas of abuse offered by the groups—as defined with and by parents—were very broad. Both Parents Anonymous in England and America recognised, and were willing to help, parents who had committed physical abuse, physical neglect, emotional abuse, emotional deprivation, verbal assault, and sexual abuse.[33] Parent-Child Concern stated that their members 'define abuse and neglect in their own terms', which varied from verbal abuse to severe physical violence.[34] In a review of the American group, assessing 613 questionnaires provided by a sample of Parent Anonymous chapters, 77 per cent reported verbal abuse, 53 per cent physical abuse, 43 per cent emotional abuse, 28 per cent emotional neglect, 7 per cent physical neglect, and 4 per cent sexual abuse.[35] By recognising a range of forms of abuse, and particularly the interplay and overlapping nature of physical, verbal, and emotional forms, the groups broadened focus from the battered child syndrome alone, pointing to the ways in which abuse needed to be managed and prevented on a variety of levels.

A second result of parents becoming voluntary leaders was that they promoted a highly sympathetic approach. Parent group organisers argued that many parents had considered hitting their child at some point; that the boundaries between punishment and physical abuse were blurred; and that the majority of physical abuse cases emerged from people who desperately wanted to stop hurting their children.[36] These groups encountered sexual abuse only rarely, and saw this as a fundamentally different—and far more serious—issue. Parents Anonymous London, reporting in 1991 that one in ten calls they received surrounded sexual abuse, argued that this was never acceptable. The organisation stated that their more typical contacts were from women who wanted to change, whereas men who were 'ambivalent' about reforming were the typical perpetrators of sexual abuse.[37]

The reconstruction of physical, emotional, and verbal abuse as something which 'most parents' had perpetrated on one occasion, or as conducted by 'everyday mothers and fathers' as well as by 'seriously troubled people', marked a rejection of the psychological and charitable focus on parental pathology in the 1960s.[38] At the same time, this interpretation also represented a troubling normalisation of family violence, and a construction of boundaries between parental discipline and violence as blurred. Beyond the complex ethics of this position, such accounts suggested that listening to the lived experiences of parents, rather than studying parents, provided the best means through which to fulfil the social policy aims of family maintenance and child protection. These campaign groups recognised, to an extent, the controversial nature of their reinterpretation of 'abuse', emphasising that they were 'militantly anti-child abuse' and '[a]bove everything else ... a service for children'.[39] Nonetheless, they insisted that parental testimony was important, and expressed a level of confidence in conveying parental experiences in this area which both continued and also extended broader clinical and social work sympathies.

These groups sought to shift public and political focus towards the lived experiences of parents, which were conveyed through lengthy descriptions in published materials, newspaper interviews, and consultations with select committees. In 1977, the American Parents Anonymous contributed to the new international journal of *Child Abuse & Neglect,* including an appendix of testimonies from involved parents, making statements such as, 'We are human and want and need help', and 'It's a sickness that can be treated and even prevented if we can reach people in time'.[40] Attention was turned to the emotions as well as the experiences of parents involved—anger, frustration, fear, shame—which were said to be 'honest, human and universal feelings'.[41] In a *Guardian* interview of 1981, likewise, the parent-founder of Parents Anonymous in Britain stated that her desperation came as no one ever asked just how 'angry and tired' she was, and because of 'overwhelming guilt coupled with hostility' towards 'the authorities'.[42] She argued that the group's aim was to 'encourage people to just be more honest about their feelings'.[43] By sharing their emotions publicly to professional fora but also in media interviews, these parents sought to become human subjects of professional and public analysis, rather than research objects analysed in demographic studies and decoupled from their human experiences. The descriptions of emotion, again, as in the discussions in Chaps. 3 and 4, were seen as markers that an 'authentic' or 'real' form of experience had been accessed and portrayed.

This framing of parental emotions as intrinsically valuable—and universal—served to bring further attention to the inner lives of parents, but also to promote a radical model of peer support, with testimony from mothers of Parent-Child Concern stating that the group was 'so friendly', and provided a 'feeling that somebody cares' and 'emotional help'.[44] The emotions visible in professional accounts of the period remained—anger, hostility—but for parents, such emotions were directed against professional intervention. Intervention from peers meanwhile was coded in terms of empathy, care, help, and friendliness; descriptions not detached from the female-dominated membership of the groups. Ingrained in this model was professional critique, within which parents could support one another better than professionals could. The groups testified that many parents involved shared a 'mistrust of authority and fear of service providers' which would prevent them from seeking help, while voluntary organisations were perceived as 'more acceptable and less threatening'.[45]

At the same time, many groups were founded and run in partnership between parent volunteers and social work or therapeutic professionals and, the American Parents Anonymous testified, emerged 'out of an informal interchange of ideas between parents and professionals'.[46] For this group, including a professional as a consultant could beneficially create a 'positive image of an authority figure—a service provider' for parents.[47] Parent-Child Concern in England also invited professional speakers to its weekly meetings, including—and showing multiple frameworks of authority in late twentieth century Britain—a psychotherapist, a marriage guidance counsellor, a headmistress of an infants' school, and a teacher and counsellor from a local comprehensive.[48] These parent-support groups thus did not entirely dismiss professional expertise but rather mediated, tested, and evaluated it according to parental preferences. Furthermore, a blurring between professional and personal forms of expertise was also evident: one representative from Parent-Child Concern told the Select Committee on Violence in the Family that when attending weekly meetings, 'I do not go as a health visitor, I go as a parent'.[49]

Significantly, the success and reach of these self-help groups in part reflected broader aims in clinical and social work settings towards taking a sympathetic approach to parents, and to taking their emotional inner lives seriously—as was also visible in Chap. 2. Parents ran these self-help groups, but they also drew on advice, speakers, and support from social workers and clinicians involved in the everyday practices of child protection. At the same time, the collective action within these groups, by and between parents, marked a development from the NSPCC partnership work of the 1960s. Indeed, such groups signalled growing parental interest in forming collective solutions to individual problems, whether without, in conflict, or in partnership with professional interventions. This work became publicly visible, and was examined and interrogated by media, in following decades.

Falsely Accused Parents[50]

From the inception of concerns about the 'battered child syndrome' in the 1960s, clinicians in Britain and North America discussed the potential for false accusations to emerge against parents.[51] Writing to the *British Medical Journal* from Vancouver, Canada, in 1964, Reginald A. Wilson emphasised the 'danger' that the 'punitive pendulum may swing too far', giving an example of a case in which clinical scepticism about a parent's account was unwarranted.[52] This concern about false accusations remained on a low level throughout the 1960s and 1970s but did not fully emerge and become publicly contested until the 1980s, as multiple new voluntary groups were formed to defend parents falsely accused of abuse. These new groups contributed further to processes of making family life increasingly visible in press and policy, and portrayed the modern family as powerful—but also under siege.

The largest group working in this area, Parents Against Injustice (PAIN), was formed by two parents, Susan and Steve Amphlett. PAIN had clear and well-established aims, to lobby for: the creation of a complaints procedure for parents involved in child protection cases; greater rights for parents to challenge child protection proceedings; the right for parents to be assessed in their own homes; and the right to a secondary medical opinion in all cases.[53] To fulfil these aims, the group engaged in lobbying and in detailed support work with families—PAIN worked with 13,000 parents during its life course between 1985 and 1999.[54] Importantly, the Amphletts took parents' protestations of innocence at face value, believing that an 'anxious climate' had emerged where false accusations were common, and that guilty parents would not seek out further attention.[55]

Despite conducting significant work, PAIN was relatively small. The group's income was just £4428 in the financial year ending in April 1987, £19,169 in 1988, and £52,528 in 1989.[56] Nonetheless, the group found spaces for media and political influence and, importantly, also had some contact with its large-scale American equivalent—Victims of Child Abuse Laws, which was founded in 1984 and had over 10,000 members by 1992.[57] This transatlantic contact was limited, however, most likely due to lack of resources on both sides. Nonetheless, PAIN commonly used false accusation cases in America as a warning in its policy work, for example telling one public inquiry, 'Let us not take the same road as America, we can learn from their mistakes'.[58]

PAIN's work made family life visible. Notably, the organisation's leaders made their own experiences and life histories public in describing their work. The group's publicity materials described how the Amphletts' daughter had sustained bone fractures in 1983 and, when the child was taken to an accident and emergency ward, the parents were referred to social services and placed on the Child Abuse Register; a list of children considered at risk of abuse.[59] Nine months later, when the child sustained another fracture, the parents sought further medical advice and found that she had brittle bone disease. This explained why she had sustained fractures after relatively minor falls.[60] While the parents were removed from the Child Abuse Register, they wrote in publicity materials that they remained 'appalled' by their experiences.[61] They felt strongly that involved professionals had barely listened to their experiences and perspectives during the processes of this case. For example, during the key case conference to discuss the child's future, sixteen professionals attended, only one of whom (a general practitioner) knew the family. The parents were not allowed to attend but rather were nominally represented by a social worker who they had only briefly met.[62]

In addition to describing the challenges that their family had faced, and describing confrontations with social services which may have previously been kept secret, the Amphletts also made public the inner mechanics of how their organisation worked, and its relationship to their family life. Internal newsletters described how the group was run from the Amphletts' home with the assistance of secretaries, one of whom described this as an 'unusual' place to work, with piles of papers acting as 'an obstacle course across the floor'.[63] Suggestive of the significance of the familial relationship across this organisation, another secretary wrote for the group's newsletter that she did not just work for a charity but rather 'a Family … a very loving and caring family'.[64] This level of openness about the processes of running a voluntary organisation again marked a new level of visibility. The Parents Anonymous organisations of the 1960s and 1970s, by contrast, had not transparently discussed such logistical or material challenges.

In addition to sharing their own experiences, the Amphletts also shared testimonies from other parents, often focused on their emotions. PAIN's publicity materials and media comments emphasised 'anguish, anxiety, shame, helplessness', 'fear', 'anger', 'disbelief', 'despair', 'horror', 'terror', 'helplessness', and 'sheer desperation'.[65] PAIN further encouraged parents and affiliates to be self-representative, and to make their own struggles public. Notably, the group advised its supporters to write to elected officials and made submissions on their behalf to public inquiries.[66] PAIN gained most exposure through its media work and, through PAIN, many parents shared their experiences with journalists.[67]

PAIN sought to provide fora for children, as well as parents, involved in child protection cases to share their views. In 1989, PAIN established a 'children's sub-group', Children Against Injustice (CHAIN).[68] The group invited 'children old enough to voice their opinions' to use this as a vehicle to tell PAIN about their problems, how these could be alleviated, and what help they may wish to receive.[69] PAIN promised to facilitate the children's meetings and to 'help them to make representations to whomever they wish'.[70] While PAIN suggested a level of popular interest, stating that some children had asked them to put them in touch with their peers, there are few archival traces of CHAIN.[71] Nonetheless, its existence demonstrated the significance, for PAIN, of making the lived emotional and practical effects of child protection cases public.

Raising further media and political awareness of false accusations, local action groups also developed in response to alleged abuse cases in Cleveland, Rochdale, and Orkney. These groups varied significantly in terms of their shape and services provided. The Cleveland group was particularly large—formed of 45 parents meeting weekly under the supervision of Reverend Michael Wright, a clergyman who also managed a unit caring for the elderly and mentally infirm.[72] While Wright's role echoed the historic significance of religious figures as mediators and experts in local communities, the Amphletts represented a model of self-help led by parents themselves. Yet it was significant nonetheless that the establishment of a voluntary group for parents became a key response to false accusations in the 1980s.

Particularly significant were the ways in which these groups sought to make the dynamics of family life visible, but also that they were rarely successful in this endeavour until they found clear leadership. The groups in Rochdale and Orkney, established following the removal of children from their homes after allegations of satanic ritual abuse, relied on Susan Amphlett to inform their foundation and to hold initial press conferences.[73] Testifying further to this point, the public inquiry into the Cleveland case emphasised that the 'voices' of accused parents were not 'heard publicly' until they had met with Wright and, through this group, their local Member of Parliament, Stuart Bell, and a local police surgeon, Dr Irvine.[74] These men, in existing positions of power, were able to generate 'enormous media coverage' and to disseminate 'some of their [the parents'] stories'.[75]

Leaders and established political and professional figures were key to gathering media coverage, and to driving the work of these new voluntary organisations. Such leaders would shape the parental 'voice' that emerged, and would thus both amplify but also reshape the narration of parental experience. Media coverage, drawing on overarching cultural tropes, further reframed the experiences of involved parents. In the Cleveland case, for example, newspaper coverage was coded in clichéd and dramatic terms: interviews emphasised that parents were 'as white as a sheet', and lighting cigarettes with 'shaking fingers'.[76] Nonetheless, these parental groups were significant new sites of activism, which enabled parents to share their experiences and emotions and, to some extent, to guide media narration of false accusation cases.

Professional Tensions

In the 1960s and 1970s, parent groups worked both with professions and also critically against professional intervention. By the 1980s, groups of falsely accused parents raised new levels of critique against clinicians and social workers. Such critique became particularly significant and visible following the satanic ritual abuse cases, false memory 'wars', and Cleveland case of the 1980s. In this moment, and to a new extent, collective action by parents led the way in defining new spaces of professional reflection, and in pushing media commentators to rethink who they consulted as 'expert'.

In part, the critique offered by groups of falsely accused parents, such as PAIN, was agitating for a radical rethink of relations between parents and professionals, whereby the testimony of each would be placed as equally significant. Fundamentally, this was a challenge to the nature of professional 'evidence'. At the Cleveland public inquiry, for example, PAIN argued that medical opinions were neither 'objective' nor 'sacrosanct' but 'only an opinion', and that social workers could be unreliable and inexperienced.[77] As through the 1960s and 1970s, however, parental advocacy groups also continued to form strong relationships with specific professionals. PAIN, for example, had a trustee who was a social worker, and who testified in the group's newsletter that PAIN promoted 'the highest professional standards', making sure that social workers would have to reflect on the potential 'hardship and trauma' that parents may experience, and give them the benefit of the doubt.[78]

Hence, PAIN drew support from a social worker who placed value on hearing about the 'hardship', 'trauma', and experiences of the PAIN families, and who reflected on the ways in which parental experience could inform social work practice. Notably, this was a vision which extended beyond social workers acting in partnership with PAIN alone. When reviewing the work of case conferences in 1986, for instance, the social workers Jonathan Phillips and Mike Evans argued that 'great care' must be taken to respect parents, who may be innocent, in need of help, and would likely be going through 'the most stressful time' of their lives.[79] Suggesting that the willingness of accused parents to put forward their personal experiences may have shifted professional thinking, Phillips and Evans acknowledged that parental advocacy groups had played a key role in illustrating cases where 'professionals made poor recommendations based on insufficient information'.[80]

PAIN also formed a significant relationship with a controversial professional figure: Dr Colin Paterson, who invented the diagnostic category of 'Temporary Brittle Bone Disease' (TBBD).[81] Based on a study of 39 children who had fractures before they reached the age of one, Paterson argued that the disease caused temporary fragility of the bones, and that physicians may then subsequently mistake children's injuries for abuse.[82] PAIN put several families in touch with Paterson, and by 2003, he had given evidence in over 100 legal cases in Britain and America.[83] While PAIN consulted Paterson as expert, his theory was highly contested. In 1995 Mr Justice Wall stated during a High Court case that Paterson's evidence should be treated with 'the greatest caution and reserve'.[84] In 2000, the Royal College of Radiologists called the idea of TBBD 'an unproven theory promulgated by a one-man band'.[85] In 2004, Paterson was struck off by the General Medical Council for having provided misleading evidence in court.[86]

Paterson's relationship with PAIN spoke to a context in which, in the last two decades of the twentieth century, voluntary organisations were forging themselves a role in deciding *who* held expertise. In 1987, for example, PAIN spokespeople expressed significant gratitude and deference to Paterson, telling *New Society* that he had provided 'expert medical advice' to families who had been the 'victims of inadequate medical knowledge'.[87] Even as Paterson's work was increasingly challenged in the 2000s, Susan Amphlett nonetheless told the *Daily Mail*, 'Parents would be devastated that think that Dr Paterson's career is in trouble.'[88] In the *Daily Mail* article discussing this case, Amphlett's testimony about parental feelings was placed alongside quotes from a senior law lecturer at Sheffield University and a chairman of the health union Unison.[89] Voluntary leaders, as well as academics, lawyers, trade unionists, and clinicians, had a role to play in criticising or promoting 'experts', in part because of their ability to represent the experiences of marginalised communities.

This voluntary sector role—in constructing expertise—was further visible in media coverage of Roy Meadow, a paediatrician who, in the late 1990s and early 2000s, argued that having multiple cot deaths in one family was highly improbable. Meadow's evidence was used as part of several criminal trials in which mothers were convicted of child murder, but later exonerated. Parents and voluntary organisations played a key role in protests that challenged the legitimacy of this evidence. In 2003, the *Daily Mail* reported that a 'handful of mothers and fathers' who had had their children taken away were demonstrating outside the High Court in London.[90] The article quoted one involved mother, who stated that the protest aimed to 'expose the secrecy of the family courts in which Professor Meadow and other experts have given evidence'.[91] Acting as informed readers and critics of media representations, also, in 1999 the Foundation for the Study of Infant Death wrote to the *Independent* to criticise how the paper had reported on Meadow's research.[92] Criticising the headline, 'Some "cot deaths" may be murders', the group argued it paid too much attention to the low number of cases in which cot deaths were unnatural, and would cause parents 'renewed grief, pain and anguish'.[93] From the 1980s, therefore, voluntary leaders and individual parents used representations of experience and emotion to challenge the expertise of clinical and legal witnesses—even entering into debates around controversial cases.

Further indeed, small parental campaign groups demanded that professionals were sensitive to, and indeed themselves displayed, experiential and emotional expertise. PAIN newsletters featured one social worker arguing that the experiences of falsely accused parents were 'the other side of the coin' to the 'fear and anguish' which social workers faced when working on child protection cases.[94] In broader media coverage, Susan Amphlett told the *Independent on Sunday* in July 1995 that 'social workers need to be more aware of the realities of normal family life'.[95] Social workers took up PAIN's expectation—and indeed argued that they already had 'normal lives as children … [and] children of our own'.[96] Echoing the paediatric radiologists discussed in Chap. 2, Paterson and Meadow likewise stated that they were 'upset' and made 'physically sick' by child abuse cases.[97] The 1980s thus marked a period in which professionals explained and explored their emotions and experiences in order to justify and defend claims to expertise. While these types of clinical explanation echoed accounts offered in the 1940s, 1950s, and 1960s, from the 1980s, the boundaries between 'professional' and 'experiential' expertise were increasingly blurred. Parental activism and media interest in child protection also increased, calling for and providing spaces in which professionals could offer personal accounts.

The process of breaking down hierarchies between professional and personal expertise went two ways. While social workers and clinicians increasingly discussed their family life with media, parent campaigners also, particularly in discussion with public inquiries and conferences, emphasised their professional credentials. In evidence to the Cleveland inquiry, Susan Amphlett opened by stating that she was a nurse before working for PAIN—as, indeed, were two of the group's regional co-ordinators.[98] By making their family dynamics public, and by challenging professional decisions, parent campaigners thus opened up a range of questions about what types of evidence and expertise were of value. The work of parent campaigners was contested. For example, in the aftermath of the Cleveland case, a husband and wife team, a pathologist and a medical secretary, formed the 'Campaign for Justice for Abused Children'. The group organised a letter to the *Guardian* from 11 paediatric consultants, which was published in 1989 and criticised the media for having, 'blown up the criticism of the paediatricians out of all proportion'.[99] This letter therefore challenged the representativeness of small voluntary groups, and the ways in which they directed and shaped media attention. This kind of challenge showed that experiential and emotional expertise were becoming important, but also foreshadowed a broader professional backlash which developed in the 1990s and 2000s.

Emotional Labour

Through the mid-1980s and the 1990s, as parent campaigners made their family lives more visible, they were also increasingly open about the emotional labours of campaigning work, and about the struggles of maintaining multiple roles as parents, professionals, campaigners, supporters, and lobbyists. In 1991, parent volunteers running crisis phone lines told the *Independent* that they felt that they could 'catch people's problems, especially if they touch your own unresolved feelings'.[100] Collective action groups examining this problem recognised that it was gendered. In draft responses to government, PAIN staff wrote that mothers felt particular pressure to leave their jobs after they were accused of abuse, motivated by 'fear' that they would be perceived as 'uncaring' should they remain at work.[101] One regional co-ordinator wrote in PAIN's newsletter that she felt she did not spend enough time volunteering for PAIN while her children, she interpreted, 'feel that I spent too much'.[102] In both examples, the maternal role was constructed in terms of emotions of fear and expectations of care, notably in the latter example around the co-ordinator's wistful testimony that, 'many a bedtime story is missed'.[103]

Psychologists and media, as well as parents themselves, began to discuss the emotional burdens of activism in the 1980s and 1990s. In 1989, a psychotherapist from the Tavistock Institute of Marital Studies examined the emotional labour that volunteer helpline leaders performed. Running workshops for helpline volunteers at Parents Anonymous London, the psychotherapist found that the 50–60 primarily female helpline volunteers were placing unrealistic demands on themselves, and were left with 'feelings of helplessness, inadequacy', and 'sick with anxiety'.[104] Volunteers also reported difficulties in understanding the situations which were reported and in distinguishing between real and hoax calls; a concern that echoed criticisms of the volunteer workforce at ChildLine, seen in Chap. 3.[105]

In part, media, voluntary, and psychological concern about the emotive effects of child protection work were not new. Such concerns had been raised around the work of social workers at the NSPCC since the mid-1970s, for example.[106] However, interest in the mental states of parents emerged hand-in-hand with closer examination of family life, and with the mobilisation of collective parental activism through the 1970s and particularly in the 1980s. This developing concern thus in part reflected the lived difficulties for individual figurehead leaders looking to run voluntary organisations, to provide services and support, and to critique and reshape social policy, all the while adeptly manifesting and utilising experiential and professional forms of expertise. The next chapter further explores the emotional pressures placed on mothers to narrate their experiences and emotions in the late twentieth century; an analysis which is key to understanding the gendered politics of experiential expertise.

Conclusion

This chapter has explored the emergence of collective action by parents around child protection. Such action first emerged in the 1960s. At the same time as parents were becoming objects of psychological and clinical research, the NSPCC also made innovative efforts to engage parents as partners through their Battered Child Research Project. Through this project, NSPCC social workers collaborated with parents in the daily practices of child protection, and NSPCC leaders gave parents platforms from which to represent their own experiences to Parliament. While parental activism initially started in partnership with statutory agencies, it later developed as an alternative to professional interaction. This shift—from partnership to opposition—was fuelled by the challenges which social work and statutory agencies faced from the 1960s and 1970s. As these professions were reorganised and lost resources, parental support groups newly conceptualised their role as 'relieving some of the pressures' on the state.[107] As well as acting to support state work, parental activism also policed and criticised it, particularly from the late 1980s. Activism from falsely accused parents looked to reshape professional practice, and to encourage social workers and clinicians to discuss and to use their own personal, experiential, and emotional resources.

Disparate forms of parental activism developed between the 1960s and the 1990s, as this chapter has demonstrated. However, common themes have emerged. All of the strands of activism studied here created collective responses to child protection issues: peer support, pastoral services, legal advice, and media representation. At the same time, individual figurehead leaders directed this collective action. Notably nonetheless, the groups in this chapter all represented the challenges of family life. The groups displayed and discussed complex experiences and emotions through media collaboration, working particularly with print journalists to represent the emotional labours of activism, the family politics of violence, and the lived effects of false accusations. Making these experiences visible reflected the will of parent leaders and parent members of these groups, as well as growing media interest.

From the late 1990s, many of the parent groups traced in this chapter had faded away. Phone lines and support groups run by and for parents at risk of committing violence had dissipated, and professional intervention instead managed this complex terrain. PAIN lost its grant money and employees after 1999. Susan Amphlett believed that the organisation had lost momentum, and that prospective funders no longer regarded it as 'new and innovative'.[108] In part, the spaces in which parent groups emerged and gained media and political attention were reactionary ones, dependent on these groups being subversive and 'new'. A change in government was also significant, and the following two chapters examine how the New Labour governments worked with parent and survivor communities through partnership with individual figurehead leaders.

Nonetheless, while the influence of the specific groups studied in this chapter faded, a social policy interest in consulting with parents had formed between the early 1960s and the late 1980s. By the end of this period, the *Children Act* of 1989 stated that professionals and parents must work in partnership to protect children. This meant that those involved in child protection proceedings must 'seek the views' of parents, and that the state should avoid intervention unless there was evidence that a child was at risk of 'significant harm'.[109] This policy was driven by social policy research, public inquiries, daily social work, and, relatedly, by the entwined and prominent campaigning of parents.[110] Parental activism in child protection took a specific collective form in the 1960s, 1970s, and 1980s, and in that moment such activism was able to influence media and social policy debate, representing complex—and at times controversial—visions of family, voluntary, and professional experience, emotion, and expertise.

Notes

1. Deborah Cohen, *Family Secrets: The Things We Tried To Hide* (London: Penguin, 2014), 233.
2. Ray Jones, 'Children Acts 1948–2008: the drivers for legislative change in England over 60 years', *Journal of Children's Services*, 4, no. 4 (2009): 43–44.
3. Marcel Berlins and Geoffrey Wansell, 'Overloading the Care Circuit', *The Times*, 10 November 1972, 16.
4. On the letter that founded the Society for the Prevention of Cruelty to Pregnant Women see: Sonia Willington, 'Letters to the editor', *Observer*, 1 April 1960, 7. On description of the media coverage which led to the establishment of Sands see, 'Our History', Sands: Stillbirth & neonatal death charity <https://www.sands.org.uk/about-sands/who-we-are/our-history>.
5. Clare A. Hyman, 'A report on the psychological test results of battering parents', *British Journal of Clinical Psychology*, 16 (1977): 221–224.
6. Jerman, 'You seen a clean pinny. The bruises are underneath', 10.
7. Ibid., 10.
8. Ibid., 10.
9. *First report from the Select Committee on Violence in the Family*, session 1976–1977. Volume II. Evidence, 346–358.
10. Ibid., 355.

11. Ibid., 346–347.
12. Ibid., 347.
13. Ibid., 347.
14. Ibid., 350.
15. Ibid., 356.
16. Ibid., 356.
17. Jerman, 'You seen a clean pinny. The bruises are underneath', 10.
18. *First report from the Select Committee on Violence in the Family*, 355, 357.
19. Ibid., 357.
20. Ibid., 348, 351.
21. Selina Todd, 'Family Welfare and Social Work in Post-War England, c. 1948–1970', *English Historical Review*, CXXIX (537) (2014): 363.
22. The Children's Society and Barnardos also recognised the popularity of the idea that there would be less need for voluntary childcare organisations in the post-war period: Liverpool University Special Collections and Archives, Barnardos Archives, D239 A3/1/98, *Annual Report for 1962*, 2; Children's Society Archives, Annual Reports, AR85.0063.46, *Annual Report for 1968*, 1.
23. Leonard L. Lieber and Jean M. Baker, 'Parents Anonymous—Self-Help Treatment for Child Abusing Parents. A Review and An Evaluation', *Child Abuse & Neglect*, 1 (1977): 133–148.
24. Ibid., 133–148.
25. Ferrier, 'Foreword', iii–iv.
26. Lieber and Baker, 'Parents Anonymous': 137.
27. 'Sidelines: parent self-help', *Guardian*, 18 December 1978, 13.
28. *First report from the Select Committee on Violence in the Family: Violence to children*, session 1976–77. Vol III: Appendices, 554.
29. Ibid., 554.
30. *First report from the Select Committee on Violence in the Family*, session 1976–1977. Volume II. Evidence, p. 361, 370.
31. Ibid., 374.
32. See the work of Kate Mahoney, including unpublished PhD thesis, 'Finding Our Own Solutions: The Womens Movement and Mental Health Activism in Late Twentieth-Century England', Centre for the History of Medicine, University of Warwick, 2017.
33. Lieber and Baker, 'Parents Anonymous': 133–148; *First report from the Select Committee on Violence in the Family. Violence to children*. Session 1976–1977, Vol III: Appendices, 553.
34. *First report from the Select Committee on Violence in the Family*, session 1976–1977. Volume II. Evidence, 361.
35. Lieber and Baker, 'Parents Anonymous': 140.

36. Lee Rodwell, 'I was really afraid I'd kill her', *Independent*, 6 February 1991, 16.
37. Ibid., 16.
38. First report from the Select Committee on Violence in the Family. Violence to children. Vol III: Appendices, 553; *First report from the Select Committee on Violence in the Family*, session 1976–1977. Volume II. Evidence, 361.
39. Lieber and Baker, 'Parents Anonymous': 133–148; Barbara Brandenburger, 'Kid gloves', *Guardian*, 6 January 1975, 9.
40. Lieber and Baker, 'Parents Anonymous': 147.
41. *First report from the Select Committee on Violence in the Family*, session 1976–1977. Volume II. Evidence, 362.
42. 'Safety in numbers', *Guardian*, 4 August 1981, 10.
43. Ibid., 10.
44. *First report from the Select Committee on Violence in the Family*, session 1976–1977. Volume II. Evidence, 360.
45. Lieber and Baker, 'Parents Anonymous': 133–148; *First report from the Select Committee on Violence in the Family*. Violence to children. Vol III: Appendices, 552.
46. Lieber and Baker, 'Parents Anonymous': 133–148.
47. Ibid., 133–148.
48. *First report from the Select Committee on Violence in the Family*, session 1976–1977. Volume II. Evidence, 359.
49. *First report from the Select Committee on Violence in the Family*, session 1976–1977. Volume II. Evidence, 363.
50. Parts of the following section were first tested out, in slightly different form, in my article, Jennifer Crane, 'Painful Times: The Emergence and Campaigning of Parents Against Injustice in 1980s Britain', *Twentieth Century British History*, 26, no. 3 (2015): 450–476. Select archival quotations and my own ideas are reused here in line with the article's open access status, as it was published under a Creative Commons CC-BY license.
51. John Caffey, 'Significance of the history in the diagnosis of traumatic injury to children', The *Journal of Pediatrics*, 67, no. 5 (1965), 1013; Reginald A. Wilson, '"Battered baby" syndrome', *British Medical Journal*, 4 July 1964, 57.
52. Wilson, '"Battered baby" syndrome', 57.
53. Bod, 'Susan Amphlett's statement to the Cleveland Inquiry', 3, 6, 14–17.
54. David Brindle, 'Painful departure', *Guardian*, 14 April 1999, 6.
55. James Erlichman, 'Ordeal of the innocent: Of course the young must be protected, but…', *Guardian*, 10 June 1997, 17.

56. BL, Parents Against Injustice Newsletters, Newsletter 1: January 1987, 'General Account', 8; BL, Parents Against Injustice Newsletters, Newsletter 2: July 1987, 'General Account', 22–23; BL, Parents Against Injustice Newsletters, Newsletter 6: August 1989, 'Income and Expenditure Account', Insert to booklet.
57. For a discussant of VOCAL, see: Gary Alan Fine, 'Public Narration and Group Culture: Discerning Discourse in Social Movements', Hank Johnston and Bert Klandermans (eds) *Social Movements and Culture* (Minnesota: University of Minnesota Press, 1995), 138; Lela Costin, Howard Jacob Karger, and David Stoez, *The Politics of Child Abuse in America* (New York: Oxford University Press, 1996), 35.
58. Bodleian Library (Hereafter Bod), Oxford, M89.B00525, Susan Amphlett, 'Susan Amphlett's statement to the Cleveland Inquiry', 14 December 1987, 28.
59. Modern Records Centre (Hereafter MRC), Coventry, MSS.378/ BASW/7/28, Susan and Steve Amphlett, 'PAIN—Parents Against Injustice Publicity Material', Untitled and Undated Statement, 1.
60. Ibid., 1.
61. Ibid., 2.
62. Bod, 'Susan Amphlett's statement to the Cleveland Inquiry', 6.
63. British Library (hereafter BL), Parents Against Injustice Newsletters, ZK.9.b.1682, Newsletter 3: August 1988, 'Have you ever wondered….?', 19.
64. BL, Parents Against Injustice Newsletters, Newsletter 3: August 1988, '…And now, for my next trick', 21.
65. MRC, Parents Against Injustice Publicity Material, Untitled Pamphlet, Undated; British Film Institute (hereafter BFI), LCPW008X, *Open Space: Innocents At Risk*, Dir. Stephanie Cartwright, 17 March 1986.; Anthea Gerrie, 'How can they call this 'care'?', *Daily Mail*, 4 July 1987, 6; Nicola Tyrer and Chris Tighe, 'The Cleveland Dilemma', *Irish Independent*, 26 June 1987, 8; BL, Parents Against Injustice, A response to Child Abuse—Working Together, 35; BL, Parents Against Injustice Newsletters, Newsletter 1: January 1989, 'Dear Members', Susan Amphlett, 1–2.
66. Bod, Amphlett, 'Statement to the Cleveland Inquiry', 1–26; BL, Parents Against Injustice, A response to Child Abuse—Working Together, 1–31; BL, Parents Against Injustice Newsletters, Newsletter 1: January 1987, 'How PAIN has grown', 5–6.
67. For contemporary journalistic descriptions of the work of PAIN, see for example: Anthea Gerrie, 'Victims of the abuse 'experts'', *Daily Mail*, 24 June 1987, 12; Gerrie, 'How can they call this 'care'?', 6; Rosie Waterhouse, 'Innocent suffer during inquiries into child abuse', *Independent*, 1 December 1992, 8; Rosie Waterhouse, 'At Breaking

Point', *Independent*, 25 October 1992, 6; David Brindle, 'Parents 'still lose rights' in abuse cases', *Guardian*, 1 December 1992, 4; Brindle, 'Painful departure', p. 6; Erlichman, 'Ordeal of the innocent', 17.

68. British Library, Parents Against Injustice Newsletters, Newsletter 6: August 1989, 'Children's Subgroup', 17.
69. Ibid., 17.
70. Ibid., 17.
71. Ibid., 17.
72. National Archives (hereafter NA), BN 68/15, Inquiry into Child Abuse in Cleveland 1987: Report and Papers, Evidence and Papers Submitted to the Inquiry, Parents and Cleveland Parents' Support Group: Statements from Reverend Michael Wright (Group Co-ordinator), 13 August 1987, 1, 4.
73. Jack O'Sullivan, 'Rochdale abuse case transferred', *Independent*, 20 September 1990, 5; J. J. Clyde, *The Report of the Inquiry into the removal of Children from Orkney in February 1991* (Edinburgh: Her Majesty's Stationery Office, 1992), 126.
74. Elizabeth Butler-Sloss, *Report of the Inquiry into Child Abuse in Cleveland 1987* (London: Her Majesty's Stationery Office, 1988), 36, 160, 161.
75. Ibid., 36, 161.
76. Anthea Gerrie, 'The hospital ward full of boisterous children', *Daily Mail*, 24 June 1987, 2.
77. Bod, Amphlett, 'Statement to the Cleveland Inquiry', 3–4, 11.
78. BL, Parents Against Injustice Newsletters, Newsletter 3: August 1988, 'Statements from the New Trustees', 3.
79. MRC, FSU 748/7/15, Jonathan Phillips and Mike Evans, *Participating Parents—An Examination of the issues for and against parental participation in child abuse case conferences* (Bradford, 1986), 30–32.
80. Ibid., 16.
81. For Paterson's initial article on this topic, see: C. R. Paterson, J. Burns, S. J. McAllion, 'Osteogenesis imperfect: the distinction from child abuse and the recognition of a variant form', *American Journal of Medical Genetics*, 15, no. 45 (1993): 187–192.
82. Useful description of Paterson's work and of the subsequent response from medical communities is available in: Alan Sprigg, 'Temporary brittle bone disease versus suspected non-accidental skeletal injury', *Archives of Disease in Childhood*, 96 (2011): 411–413.
83. Grace McLean, 'Doctor who put 'abuse' down to brittle bones may be banned', *Daily Mail*, 15 November 2003, 17.
84. Ibid., 17.
85. Ibid., 17.
86. 'Child injury 'expert' struck off', *BBC News*, 4 March 2004, <http://news.bbc.co.uk/1/hi/scotland/3533487.stm> (8 March 2015).

87. Howard Sharron, 'Parent Abuse', *New Society*, 13 March 1987, 22–23.
88. McLean, 'Doctor who put 'abuse' down to brittle bones may be banned', 17.
89. Ibid., 17.
90. Rebecca Allison, 'Wrongly accused parents demand public inquiry', *Guardian*, July 2003, 7.
91. Ibid., 7.
92. Reverend Ron Robinson, 'Cot death mysteries', *Independent*, 12 January 1999, 2.
93. Ibid., 2.
94. BL, Parents Against Injustice Newsletters, Newsletter 1: January 1987, 'Foreword', 3.
95. Gary Clapton and Maggie Mellor, 'Scapegoats over child abuse', *Independent on Sunday*, 30 July 1995, 22.
96. Ibid., 22.
97. Anne Johnstone, 'When doctors disagree', *The Herald*, 26 January 2001; John Sweeney, 'Cot deaths and justice: Crown prosecutors use Sir Roy Meadow as their experts witness in infant fatalities. They shouldn't.', *The Observer*, 15 June 2003, 27.
98. Bod, Amphlett, 'Statement to the Cleveland Inquiry', 1.
99. William Condary, 'Cleveland childcare mythology must be exploded', *Guardian*, 18 February 1989, 20.
100. Rodwell, 'I was really afraid I'd kill her', 16.
101. BL, YC.1999.b.9251, Parents Against Injustice, A response to Child Abuse—Working Together: A Draft Guide to Arrangement for Inter-agency Co-operation For the Protection of Children, October 1986, 36.
102. BL, Parents Against Injustice Newsletters, Newsletter 6: August 1989, 'Regional Administrator Reports: East of England', 5.
103. Ibid., 5.
104. Beverly Loughlin, 'Review of W. Colman, On Call: The Work of a Telephone Helpline for Child Abusers', *Journal of Social Work Practice*, 4, no. 2 (1990): 118.
105. Ibid., 118.
106. Edwina Baher, Clare Hyman, Carolyn Jones, Ronald Jones, Anna Kerr, Ruth Mitchell, *At Risk: An Account of the Work of the Battered Child Research Department, NSPCC* (London and Boston: Routledge & Kegan Paul, 1976), 2.
107. *First report from the Select Committee on Violence in the Family*, session 1976–1977. Volume II. Evidence, 365, 371; *First report from the Select Committee on Violence in the Family. Violence to children.* Vol III: Appendices, 552.
108. Brindle, 'Painful departure', 6.

109. *The Children Act 1989* (London: Her Majesty's Stationery Office, 1989), see: Section 26: Review of cases and enquiries into representations.
110. Ann Macaskill and Peter Ashworth, 'Parental Participation in Child Protection Case Conferences: The Social Worker's View', *British Journal of Social Work*, 25 (1995): 582; Panel of Inquiry into the Circumstances Surrounding the Death of Jasmine Beckford, *A Child in Trust: The Report of the Panel of Inquiry into the Circumstances Surrounding the Death of Jasmine Beckford* (London: London Borough of Brent, 1985), 249; Butler-Sloss, Report of the inquiry into child abuse in Cleveland, as discussed in Jenkins, *Intimate Enemies*, 138–139; Sharratt, 'Inquiry urged into ritual abuse allegations', 20; MRC, *Participating Parents*, 7; BFI, *Innocents At Risk*.

Open Access This chapter is licensed under the terms of the Creative Commons Attribution 4.0 International License (http://creativecommons.org/licenses/by/4.0/), which permits use, sharing, adaptation, distribution and reproduction in any medium or format, as long as you give appropriate credit to the original author(s) and the source, provide a link to the Creative Commons license and indicate if changes were made.

The images or other third party material in this chapter are included in the chapter's Creative Commons license, unless indicated otherwise in a credit line to the material. If material is not included in the chapter's Creative Commons license and your intended use is not permitted by statutory regulation or exceeds the permitted use, you will need to obtain permission directly from the copyright holder.

CHAPTER 6

Mothers, Media, and Individualism in Public Policy

This chapter examines the role of mothers in reshaping concerns about child protection over the late twentieth century, particularly through becoming subjects of—and at times active partners in guiding—gendered media coverage. The chapter explores a series of case studies: anti-paedophile protests by mothers in the 1970s, the partnership between Parents Against Injustice and the BBC *Open Space* series in the 1980s, and the work of Sara Payne as an individual spokesperson in the early 2000s. While thus crosscutting the work of Chap. 5, this chapter also makes new contributions to this book. Most significantly, 'Mothers, Media, and Individualism' explores the gendered media representations of parents involved in child protection, and the ways in which journalistic interest in women's experiences and emotions also reconstructed mothers as irrational and hysterical.[1]

At the same time, the chapter also demonstrates that mothers were at times empowered in their work with media. Collectively and individually through the late twentieth century, mothers utilised and subverted media interest in their emotional states to direct and govern popular coverage, shaping a self-representation that could drive forward specific personal and political agendas.[2] As such, mothers were both empowered and marginalised by media coverage of child protection and by public interest in their inner lives and social roles; a position which was negotiated during the rise and realisation of second-wave feminism and amidst increasing female participation

© The Author(s) 2018
J. Crane, *Child Protection in England, 1960–2000*, Palgrave Studies in the History of Childhood,
https://doi.org/10.1007/978-3-319-94718-1_6

in the workforce. The chapter therefore focuses on the gendering of the politics of experience, emotion, and expertise, again emphasising that the growing social and political focus on individual experience challenged, but did not overthrow nor entirely counterbalance, long-standing structural hierarchies.

'[T]he Sickness of the Twentieth Century'

In the 1970s, much journalistic attention was paid to anti-paedophile protests launched by mothers. Public discussion of paedophilia developed in the late nineteenth century, when the term 'paedophile' was first invented.[3] Yet public awareness of sexual relations between adults and children—and the construction of this new term—did not immediately precipitate activism. Indeed, Steven Angelides has argued that within Victorian society paedophilia was 'seldom discussed', except by sexologists such as Havelock Ellis, Sigmund Freud, and Richard von Krafft-Ebing, who considered it a highly 'rare occurrence'.[4] Looking at the early-to-mid twentieth century, Mathew Thomson argues that 'post-Freudian' ideas about child sexuality did not only ignore but actively averted social concerns about paedophilia, by suggesting that children were not damaged, nor innocent, in adult–child sexual relations.[5] Thomson emphasises also that perpetrators were represented first as mentally deficient and later as psychologically flawed; characterisations which saw this group subjected to medical, rather than legal or public, interventions.[6] While parents may have informally warned others about certain individuals in their communities, they rarely took collective political action against them.

From the 1970s, concerns about paedophiles became a 'major public issue', and the paedophile was newly considered 'the most terrifying folk devil imaginable'.[7] The rapid development of concerns about paedophilia were linked to broader media anxieties about child sexual abuse, child pornography, satanic rituals, and serial murder emergent in this decade.[8] Paedophile liberation groups also developed in the 1970s, further bringing this group to public attention. Two such groups were founded in 1974: Paedophile Action for Liberation and the Paedophile Information Exchange (PIE). These groups had some structural differences, but both sought to create an analytical distinction between 'the paedophile' and 'the child molester'. They argued that the former group only engaged in consensual relations with children, while the latter did not. The groups couched this argument in terms of the topical discourses of rights, choice, and freedom of association and speech.[9]

These groups formed some—albeit often tense and tenuous—links with larger liberationist organisations, which brought them further to political and public attention. Many gay rights groups at this time were arguing that the 'sexual revolution' of the 1960s had not gone far enough in terms of, for example, creating an equal age of consent for heterosexual and homosexual sexual activities.[10] Lucy Robinson has demonstrated that, in this context, the Gay Left Collective perceived paedophilia as 'a new battlefield from which to extend sexual liberation', opening up debates about the fluidity of sexuality.[11] Other gay rights groups—notably the Campaign for Homosexual Equality (CHE)—defended the rights of paedophiles to associate and to speak publicly but sought to emphasise that this was the only connection between their organisations. CHE's annual conference of 1983 passed a resolution condemning attempts to use public concern over assault cases to conduct 'witch hunts' against minority groups such as PIE, but framed this decision as 'entirely a question of freedom of speech'.[12]

Utilising contemporary anxieties about freedom, in 1975 the PIE also affiliated to the National Council for Civil Liberties (NCCL); a loose association granted to nearly 1000 organisations upon the payment of a small fee.[13] Chris Moores has shown that the relationship between the PIE and the NCCL was formed mainly through the NCCL's Gay Rights Sub-Committee, primarily in order to discuss freedoms of speech, movement, and association, and the uses of 'public morality' legislation.[14] Thomson and Moores have additionally argued that paedophile movements also found some support from certain radical academics in medicine, sociology, and law at this time, who were 'uncomfortable about using the law to police sexual boundaries', as well as among child welfare workers, psychologists, and educational theorists.[15]

Paedophile rights groups were marginal and relatively small in the 1970s and early 1980s, but nonetheless also held loose relationships with factions of counter-cultural and radical thought. The development of these groups was an international phenomenon, and British paedophile groups formed fiscal and emotional connections with concurrent movements developing in Western Europe and North America; exchanging letters, newsletters, and occasionally donations.[16] The development of paedophilia movements on a global scale was ardently criticised. Mary Whitehouse stated that the PIE, 'encapsulates the sickness of the twentieth century'.[17] In the Commons, Conservative Members branded the organisation as 'an abominable child sex group', whose membership were 'publicity-seeking freaks' and 'crackpots'.[18]

Second-wave feminists also mounted a powerful challenge to paedophile rights groups. For example, in *Spare Rib* in 1981, workers from London's Rape Crisis Centre strongly rejected these groups' attempts to function within broader movements of sexual politics.[19] Rather, the authors wrote, paedophile advocacy groups should be analysed and critiqued as part of a society in which men held power over women and children.[20] This argument foreshadowed continuing links between female activism and sexual danger, whereby women—notably mothers—became the key figures in anti-paedophile protest. These critiques—from the moral right and second-wave feminists alike—also demonstrated that paedophile organisations had failed to disassociate 'the paedophile' and 'the child molester': both figures were seen as equivalent. Any analytical distinction between these terms, indeed, dissolved further when many leaders and members of paedophile rights groups were arrested for sexual offences against children in the late 1970s.[21]

'Mothers on the Warpath'

As men associated with paedophile rights groups were convicted of sexual offences, public awareness of—and disgust about—these groups grew. In this context, newspapers focused on isolated incidences of anti-paedophile protest by individual women. The *Guardian* reported in 1977 that a woman from Swansea had 'drenched' the leader of the PIE in beer when she saw him in a local pub.[22] In the same year, another woman became a self-styled 'Campaigner against Sex Offences on Children', launching a national questionnaire and a petition to demand increased legal restrictions against sexual offences.[23] The *Guardian's* coverage of these stories noted that both women had the title, 'Mrs', and indeed that the former was a 'mother of two' and a 'woman teacher', motivated in her actions by the 'upset' caused to her family.[24]

Newspapers continued to emphasise the gendered nature of anti-paedophile protest. One notable thread of this discussion centred on the coverage of the first—and only—public meeting of the PIE in September 1977. PIE held this meeting at Conway Hall in London and priced tickets at £1.50.[25] On the day, newspapers estimated that approximately 100 people gathered outside the venue to protest. This protest did not receive mass media attention; however two substantial articles in the *Daily Mail* and *Guardian* provided coverage. In these articles, journalists suggested that the protesters were primarily working-class women, joined by a smaller group of male members of the National Front.[26] Despite the evidence of popular right-wing political agitation, it was the mothers who were the key focus of analysis. The articles were titled: 'Mothers on the Warpath' and 'Mothers in child sex protest'.[27]

Using the language of contemporary industrial relations, the *Mail* article claimed that men from the National Front had made 'burly pickets', and 'kicked, punched and spat on' conference delegates.[28] Protesting women, meanwhile, were represented as 'near-hysterical mothers' and 'young mothers', who stood outside the building 'closely-huddled and with arms linked'.[29] In contrast to this communitarian and gentle view of femininity, newspapers also reported that those at the conference received 'deep scratches on their faces from [the] women's nails'.[30] The *Mail* reported that the women threw domestic items, including 'rotten eggs, tomatoes, apples and peaches'.[31] The *Guardian* added that in addition to throwing 'eggs', 'fruit', and 'vegetables', the women also launched 'stink bombs' and 'insults'.[32] Newspaper coverage in part represented female activism as a manifestation of a mothering 'instinct'. Indeed, a subsequent letter to the *Daily Mail* from a member of the public went as far as to state that the women's 'missiles', the fruit and vegetables, expressed 'the natural and God-given instincts of mothers in protecting their children'.[33] At the same time, media descriptions of the women's physical violence were also to an extent at odds with representations of their youth, docility, and nurturing femininity, manifested, for example, in descriptions about 'huddling'.

Media coverage did not only focus on the women's 'instincts' but also discussed their stated aims, which were, first, to register 'revulsion and disgust at the sickness of these people' and, second, to lobby for paedophile organisations to be banned.[34] The latter aim was not fulfilled, although a Conservative Member of Parliament, Geoffrey Dickens, did suggest a bill to this effect in 1984.[35] Female protest had not necessarily inspired Dickens' bill however, since it had only received minimal newspaper coverage years beforehand. Furthermore, Dickens' bill was unpopular. Other Members of Parliament argued that this was a radical move, since only two groups had previously been proscribed: the Irish National Liberation Army and the Provisional Irish Republican Army, both on the grounds of advocating violence.[36] Further demonstrative that political representatives did not take up the messages of female anti-paedophile protesters, Parliamentarians also argued that they should ban acts, not organisations.[37]

This case illuminates a complex chain of relationships between small campaign groups, media attention, and legislative change. The 'mothers on the warpath' did not receive substantial media attention; however, their protest was documented in two significant articles which contributed to a broader media narrative in this period, focused on stoking up public disgust about paedophile advocacy groups. This media narrative had an effect on one such group: Paedophile Action for Liberation, which closed in 1977 in part in response to the *Sunday People*'s front page calling them the 'vilest men in Britain'.[38] Yet media coverage did not affect the ongoing work of the PIE. Indeed, the organisation's Chairperson (1977–1984), Tom O'Carroll, to an extent courted such attention and had, the *Guardian* reported, 'an obvious flair for publicity'.[39]

What ultimately led to the closure of the PIE in 1984 was legal and logistical pressure, raised after police arrested several of the group's members and leaders for conspiracy, obscenity, and postal offences. These offences related to the organisation's newsletter, which provided a contact sheet of its membership that, courts ruled, may have enabled paedophiles to arrange to meet up in order to abuse children.[40] These prosecutions related to broader media debates of the period about the meaning of 'obscenity', and the PIE was again used by the moral right to demand that firm legislative limits were placed around acts, texts, and organisations.[41]

The aims of the 'mothers on the warpath' were thus ultimately fulfilled. However, this was not a clear-cut case of experience or emotion becoming expertise. Indeed, the parents who were protesting were not purposefully harnessing their experiences as mothers in order to claim authority in deciding how to cope with the rise of paedophile rights movements. Rather, media coverage used their overlapping identities as women, mothers, working-class people, and protesters as an analytical framework imposed from above to bolster broader reporting narratives. The women's activism was presented dismissively as hysterical, passive, violent, and mothering, and contrasted to the male identities of the paedophiles involved. Despite this, however, the media coverage did not simultaneously reflect on the relationships between patriarchy, violence, and sexual abuse.

In part, the lens of motherhood represented the stated factors driving the women's activism. The woman from Cardiff, for example, argued that it was for her family that she threw her drink. Another protester at the

Conway Hall protest told the *Daily Mail* that these women had all acted because, '[w]e're frightened for the sake of our children'.[42] At the same time, the media emphasis on gender was also a disempowering framework, preventing the women's arguments from being taken seriously. The leaders of the PIE certainly attempted to entwine and discount the women's experiences, emotions, and identities in this way. The group's newsletter argued that the women were 'hysterical' (a term also used in the *Daily Mail* coverage) and had acted because the PIE 'poses a threat to the traditional mother role'.[43]

While problematic, the representation of women's 'hysteria' in mainstream media also marked a significant historical moment in which women's emotions and experiences were being brought to public attention by the press. The representation of these women joining together, 'closely-huddled and with arms linked', echoed concurrent coverage of the Women's Liberation Movement.[44] Although media coverage did not make this connection explicitly, these mothers were in a similar period drawing on their personal experiences to take political action; in this case demanding that their individual concerns for children should be translated into a ban on paedophile groups. The women were insisting that their individual beliefs were authoritative and worthy of attention, or expert. Newspapers documented these beliefs in terms of the gendered tropes of emotion and instinct, but nonetheless the women's activism had also commanded a media response, and shaped a broader critique of paedophile advocacy groups. In years to come, media interest in women's experiences and emotions radically extended. In response, women collectivised into formal groups, and capitalised on this interest to disseminate their arguments powerfully.

Gender and False Accusations[45]

In the 1980s, women harnessed media interest in motherhood to add complexity to visions of child protection and to drive televisual analysis. Significantly, Parents Against Injustice (PAIN)—the campaign group for parents who had been falsely accused of abuse—worked closely with the BBC's Community Programme Unit in 1986. The Unit's *Open Space* series allowed members of the public to work with BBC staff to design and produce half-hour documentaries about their lives. Between 1983 and 1997, several of these programmes were aired per year in popular mid-evening timeslots on BBC Two.[46] PAIN had the opportunity to create one of these programmes, which was entitled *Innocents at Risk* and which aired on 17 March 1986. The programme featured extended interviews with the Amphletts and with three other families represented by PAIN. These testimonies, discussing the case histories and emotions of the parents ('guilt', 'despair', and 'helplessness'), were at the forefront of the documentary.[47] Periodically, parental accounts were interspersed with narratives provided by a doctor and a social worker, but parents' self-narratives and experiences were central.

Significantly, PAIN's role in co-curating and designing this documentary meant that the organisation was able to present a complex view of family, gender, and child protection, in contrast to the simplistic vision of female hysteria offered by 1970s newspapers. Notably, *Innocents at Risk* referred to 'family' and to 'parents', rather than to mothers alone, and also offered visual representation of mothers and fathers.[48] Indeed, when fathers were interviewed, they discussed their emotions, stating that it had been 'hard' to live without their child, and that they were finding their experiences within the child protection system 'frightening', 'harrowing', and isolating.[49] Masculine discussion of working patterns and repressed emotion in part framed fathers' accounts: one father discussed how his work schedule made it particularly difficult to see his child while they were in care. Another father contended that it was hard to describe the emotions that he felt about this intrusion into his family life. As a result, he was feeling both 'intense anger'—paralleling the masculine constructions of emotion offered by 1960s paediatric radiologists in Chap. 2—but also, he admitted, 'helplessness'.[50]

Interviews with mothers likewise featured discussion of the maternal role. One mother stated that when her child was taken away, and she could no longer breastfeed, she felt that, 'I was just another person, I wasn't her [the child's] mother'.[51] When her child was returned, she felt, 'Brilliant… I'm a Mum again'.[52] Susan Amphlett further stated that being involved in child protection investigations made her 'begin to doubt my capabilities as a mother'.[53] The emphasis on mothers as the key caregivers, and as those particularly affected by issues of child protection, was thus to an extent continued from the 'mothers on the warpath' coverage of the 1970s. At the same time, and offering a more complex vision than previous media representations, another mother—who was presented without a partner in the documentary—reversed hackneyed gender tropes. Describing the first admission of her child into hospital, she emphasised that she had tried to 'reason' with a male doctor, and to 'explain to him how things had happened', but that he had behaved irrationally.[54] This account confronted a long-standing Western vision of hysteria as female and rationality as male, and further challenged the ability of clinicians, as experts, to respond to evidence.[55]

The documentary indeed represented mothers and fathers in complex ways as both 'rational' and 'emotional', facing stress but also mobilising to regain custody of their children and to protect other parents. Gendered tropes of motherhood, visible in the newspaper coverage of the 1970s, were not absent here, but they were modified, mediated, and re-interpreted by parents themselves, drawing on their lived experiences. While a more complex vision of gender emerged from this work, therefore, explicit and implicit representations of class continued to bolster and fortify the parents' claims. The documentary opened by portraying two parents in a smartly furnished home, carefully putting on earrings and a tie. Looking to frame the testimonies of PAIN's members, Susan Amphlett stated in the piece that none of the families had been involved with the police before. Steve Amphlett, furthermore, attested that if the Amphletts could be accused of abuse, 'knowing what kind of parents we are', then anyone could be.[56] This representation of universal—perhaps 'ordinary'—respectability was significant in PAIN's broader work.[57] The group's submission to a public consultation in 1986, for example, likewise stated that their parents were the 'type of people' who made use of state health and social work services, enabling these authorities to ensure that their children were 'weighed and examined ... up to date with the vaccinations'.[58] PAIN's representations therefore drew on a vision of compliance, respectability, articulacy, and relative affluence; characteristics which framed the narration of experience and emotion in authoritative terms.

While visions of class and gender framed the work of many prominent parent campaigners, parent activists did also find new opportunities to represent their own experiences and emotions in their own terms in the 1980s. In doing so, parents did not challenge all forms of structural inequality; however, they did challenge professional competency, and they did challenge media representations of family life and motherhood. These representations became relatively influential. A small but significant proportion of the UK population—around 1.4 million viewers—saw *Innocents at Risk*.[59] This was among the highest viewing figures which the programme had ever had, and PAIN received over 400 responses after the documentary had aired.[60] PAIN claimed that all responses had been 'favourable', and that falsely accused parents had written 75 per cent, and interested professionals the remainder.[61]

This evidence speaks to the kind of audiences that PAIN's media work was reaching. Even when aired at primetime in the 'age of one-nation television', the organisation's programme was not watched universally, but rather primarily by parents facing similar experiences.[62] Nonetheless, the programme did also attract the attention of a small but significant cohort of policy-makers and professionals interested in child protection. *Innocents at Risk* may have challenged visions of gender, family life, and child protection for its viewers but, as the following sections will demonstrate, media emphasis on mothers—and indeed on individual mothers—was extended and continued through the 1990s and 2000s.

Sara Payne and Mothers in the Media

In the 2000s, Sara Payne led a highly prominent parental campaign, which illustrated ongoing media focus on the experiences of women, but also new pathways through which individual parents could influence New Labour thinking. Sara and her husband Michael Payne came to public attention after their daughter, the eight-year-old Sarah Payne, was abducted and murdered by the paedophile Roy Whiting in 2000. Whiting had previously been convicted of abducting and indecently assaulting another young girl in 1995. All mainstream newspapers provided substantial coverage of the Paynes' personal tragedy—the hunt for Sarah when missing, the grief of her parents, and the search for, and conviction of, her killer.

As with the PAIN families in the 1980s, Sara's emotional inner life was central to this coverage, particularly in the popular tabloid press. News stories discussed Sara's 'tears' and praised her 'dignified and courteous' statements to the courts.[63] One *Daily Mail* article suggested that, as the case continued, Sara's 'dignity' and her 'passionate' demeanour had shifted to a 'calmer' and 'quieter' way of being, 'as if somehow a flame has gone out'.[64] News stories entwined descriptions of Sara's emotional and domestic lives, for example writing that her home was 'a tip, both dirty and untidy… It is perhaps symbolic of her depressed state of mind.'[65] Sara herself expressed emotions clearly to newspapers, telling the *Mail* in 2002 that her pain remained 'raw', but that she had 'got used to it' and 'built a brick wall around my heart'.[66] Interlinked descriptions of Sara's devastation and her resilience were thus key to framing this case, and to constructing Sara as a significant individual spokesperson.

While Sara was the primary focus of much newspaper reporting, at times newspapers also emphasised the partnership between the Paynes and the protective role of Michael. For instance, newspaper coverage described Michael putting his arm around his wife and Sara 'clasping the hand of her husband' and 'collapsing into the arms of her husband'.[67] Nonetheless, on the whole newspapers provided less representation of Michael's grief and, when paying attention to him, often focused on his quietness, for example stating that he 'trembled uncontrollably at her [Sara's] side' or was 'so distraught that he was unable to speak'.[68] In 2003, discussing the Paynes' separation, the *Daily Mail* argued that Michael felt guilt for not having been able to protect his daughter; a description tied to a masculine vision of fatherhood protectiveness.[69] While the primary media focus was on the Payne parents, the experiences of their other children were also represented in gendered terms, for example with the oldest boy, a teenager, described as 'trying to be strong and unemotional', while the youngest daughter was 'walking around bewildered'.[70]

While the ongoing news coverage of the Payne case was far more substantial than that around the PAIN families, like the parent campaigners of the 1980s, Payne asserted that her personal experiences entitled her to speak authoritatively about child protection. Payne later recorded that she had initially questioned whether it was her 'place to get involved in something like this' since she was part of an 'ordinary family', with no particular knowledge about politics.[71] However Payne subsequently asserted her own claims to expertise, stating that she was in fact one of 'the most qualified people' to campaign on issues of family safety, because she had had personal experience in this regard.[72] The Paynes' self-framing as 'ordinary' continued in 2003, as Sara told the *Daily Mail*, explaining the emotional burden of this case, that she was part of 'a very ordinary couple catapulted into the spotlight'.[73] Newspapers subsequently linked this vision of ordinariness to working-class aspiration, describing the Payne parents as 'cheerfully struggling along, making ends meet, in and out of jobs' and as 'all squashed into a council house', for example.[74] While inflected by visions of class, *The Times* also used this construction to invite 'all parents' to reflect on their own lives and to consider, 'how we would bear up had it been one of us standing there yesterday?'[75] In this statement, the identity of 'parent' was seen to supersede class identity, and to provide an element of collective feeling across all families.

A key difference between the parental campaigning in the 1960s, 1970s, and 1980s and that in the 2000s was that the criticism of professional authority had in part diminished by this latter period. Payne's promotion of experiential expertise, and her testimonies about her own emotions, were not tied up with criticism of clinicians, social workers, or other professional bodies. Indeed, Payne testified that she was 'extremely lucky' as she experienced 'support' and 'respect' during her dealings with the criminal justice system.[76] The Paynes made public statements of thanks to the police involved in their case.[77] Appearing on *BBC News* in 2001, Sara also offered a moderate analysis of the judge who had previously sentenced Whiting to four years in jail following a previous sexual assault of 1995. While the director of the Victims Crime Trust told newspapers that there was 'never too high a [jail] sentence for a paedophile', Payne stated that she did not 'blame' the judge, but rather recognised that he had acted with the information he was given at the time.[78]

Payne's lack of critique for professional services thus reflected her own experiences but also, importantly, a broader context in the 1990s and 2000s in which media critiques of professional authority had, to an extent, been replaced by a focus on multi-disciplinary action and partnership working with families. In this context, newspaper reporting emphasised that Sara Payne referred to 'we' and 'us' as the family, police, and media. Newspaper coverage presented Sara as empowered within this network of actors—for example, reporting that she had made suggestions about how best to publicise the missing person case.[79] Newspapers presented Sara's empowerment as at odds with her working-class background and her feminine emotions, however, and charted a narrative transition from 'working-class Sussex family' and 'terrified mother' to 'articulate, persuasive campaigner'.[80]

While Sara thus became 'expert' in interactions with media and police, newspapers were also increasingly interested in describing the personal experiences and emotions of involved professionals, continuing developments charted in Chap. 5. Newspapers reported, for example, that detectives had 'wiped tears' from their eyes at Whiting's trial, while Sara stated that the judge who sentenced Whiting in 1995 would have 'to live with the "if onlys…"'.[81] Media coverage therefore constructed police and legal professionals as emotional and reflexive subjects. This construction was relatively new, and was not as present in the descriptions offered of, nor by, the clinicians working on the battered child syndrome in the 1940s, 1950s, and 1960s, discussed in Chap. 2.

Media Partnership

The Paynes' work, like earlier parental activism, relied on collaboration with newspapers, though the Paynes became more deeply embedded with media contacts than previous campaigners. Sara Payne was potentially more empowered in interactions with media than previous parents, and harnessed the public interest in her experiences to lobby for change. Once police found her daughter's body, Sara began sustained research about paedophilia and child protection law. When Payne was contacted by a journalist from the *News of the World*, looking for an interview, she asked the paper to investigate Megan's Law: American legislation designed in 1994 to create a publicly accessible database of the names, addresses, and convictions of all sexual offenders.[82] Days later, the *News of the World* contacted Payne again to propose the 'For Sarah' campaign, which would lobby for a range of child protection measures, including enabling concerned parents controlled access to the Sex Offenders Register (already established by the *Sex Offenders Act* of 1997).[83] Sara was not a naïve actor in interaction with newspapers but, rather, reshaped media interest to drive change. Acknowledging and indeed analysing this complex relationship, one contemporary reporter argued that interaction with the media was a way for the Paynes to contribute to the search and to cope with their personal distress.[84]

The first effort by the *News of the World* to promote the 'For Sarah' project was a 'Name and Shame' campaign, which published the names and photographs of people on the Sex Offenders Register. The Home Office, the NSPCC, the Children's Society, ChildLine, and the police condemned this as dangerous, potentially driving paedophiles underground, further endangering children, or leading to mistaken attacks.[85] In terms of the latter, some people were mistaken for those on the list, and their homes surrounded by protestors.[86] Despite its controversial start, this campaign was ultimately influential. The *News of the World* began to collaborate with the NSPCC, police, and probation services, and constructed proposals that were partially enacted in the *Criminal Justice and Court Services Act* of 2000. This act established new laws to prevent paedophiles from working with children, ensured that police would inform victims of sexual abuse if their abuser left jail, and strengthened the resources in place to monitor sexual offenders.[87] Following this, four police areas piloted controlled access to the Sex Offenders Register.[88] This act also introduced Multi-Agency Public Protection Arrangements: new panels to manage offenders in the community and composed of representatives from police, probation, prison, health, housing, education, and social services—again demonstrative of a shift towards co-operation between professional services in the 1990s and 2000s.[89]

The Paynes' campaigning hence in a sense followed a similar pattern to the work of parent campaigners in the 1980s: parents, particularly mothers, provided emotional and experiential testimony, which the media disseminated and interpreted. However, newspaper discussions of the lives and feelings of the Paynes were far more extensive than ever before, led by tabloid press but also echoed in broadsheet newspapers.[90] The tabloid media also worked more directly and closely with Sara than it had with campaigners of the 1980s. *News of the World* journalists became, for Sara, 'good and trusted friends'.[91] Indeed, for journalists Sara was both a grieving mother and a powerful activist. These dual roles were expressed by the *Daily Mail* in 2002, which described how Sara had 'channelled her relentless grief into a one-woman campaign to change the law to protect the nation's children'.[92] This campaign created a debate about who should be able to access information about crime, and about whether parents were equipped to understand and utilise this information, or whether it should be left within the criminal justice system.

While the Paynes, and particularly Sara, were in part empowered in interactions with newspaper outlets, by making their experiences public they also became subject to press intrusion and sensationalism. In 2001, the *Independent* reported that when the police were telling Michael and Sara that they had found Sarah's body, the other Payne children were already hearing this news from a television in another room.[93] Newspapers thus critically reported on the level of press interest into the Paynes' family lives, while also contributing to it. In a related line of analysis, in 2001 the *Daily Mail* questioned whether the parents were 'more confident in front of cameras than the police'; again reporting on this case while also raising a set of issues about whether such coverage inhibited the Paynes' relationships with statutory authorities.[94] In 2011, such debates—about the relationships between Paynes and press—came to the fore with allegations that the *News of the World* may have hacked Sara's phone.[95] Hence, parents had new access to journalists in the 2000s, and were in part empowered in guiding the object of media coverage. However, the ethical and legal boundaries of this new terrain had not yet been established.

Individualism in Public Policy

Through Sara Payne, parental campaigning may have directly influenced legislative change. In addition to forming significant connections at the *News of the World*, Payne also developed important links in the political world; a new space for parent campaigners. In September 2000, the Paynes met with Jack Straw, the first Home Secretary appointed under the New Labour government of 1997. Demonstrative of multiple sources of influence in this encounter, the Paynes were accompanied by Sarah's grandparents and by Rebekah Wade, *News of the World*'s editor. The parents also promised to present Straw with a petition containing one million signatures from members of the public.[96] The network between policy and public thinking—connected through petitions, political representatives, and media—was not new, but the entry of parents and grandparents into political discussions, directly through meeting with politicians, was significant.

Meeting with a home secretary did not guarantee parental influence, nor the fundamental disruption of public–political relations. Following a 90-minute meeting, the press reported that Straw had 'told the parents' that the *Sex Offenders Act* would be changed. While this was what the Paynes had called for, Home Office spokespeople looked to frame the level of parental influence carefully. One department spokesman told *The Times* that the home secretary had 'an opportunity to give Mr and Mrs Payne an indication of the direction the Government will be taking'; a statement which presented discussions with the Paynes as intended to disseminate, rather than to reshape, policy.[97]

While parental influence was not instant or guaranteed, Sara Payne did form important and new informal relationships with successive home secretaries under New Labour. In 2002, the *Mail* reported that Sara and Michael met regularly with David Blunkett, the home secretary between 2001 and 2004. In interview, Sara called Blunkett 'lovely'. Further—and again demonstrating interest in discussing the experiential expertise of public figures in this period—Payne also iterated that Blunkett 'always asks about the children before we get down to any business'.[98] Emphasising the informal nature of her relationships with politicians in her own book of 2009, Payne reported being phoned on a Sunday morning 'while lounging about in her bed' by John Reid, home secretary between 2006 and 2007. Payne reported that Reid had called to warn her that a judge had mistakenly released a sexual offender, and that the media would soon be in touch.[99]

While New Labour spokespeople may have initially distanced themselves from the influence of the Paynes, the parents did find informal pathways to influence from the early 2000s and were consulted as expert. From the late 2000s, furthermore, Sara Payne also gained formal influence: in January 2009, she was named as the first 'Victims' Champion' at the Ministry of Justice, part of a broader 'explosion' in the number of outside experts appointed by New Labour.[100] The idea of utilising external experts had roots dating back to Harold Wilson's governments, but over 100 'tsars', 'advisors', 'independent reviewers', 'commissioners', and 'champions' were appointed between 1997 and 2010.[101] Many of these appointments were high-profile individuals, for example Lord Alan Sugar (Enterprise Champion), Tim Berners-Lee (Information Advisor), and Sir Steve Redgrave (Sports Legacy Champion).[102] These experts had no one clearly defined mandate, but generally their roles were as 'innovators', appointed to co-ordinate and inspire 'a range of actors' and to 'deal with particularly intractable problems'.[103]

The appointment of tsars such as Payne marked new opportunities for parents to influence policy—providing a further source of expertise for media discussion, as well as access to politicians and political events. The appointment of tsars also marked a shifting relationship between New Labour and the voluntary sector, moving focus from working with organisations towards appointing individuals. This strategy increased the policy capacity of central government but also changed interactions between parents and politicians. Previously, in the 1960s, 1970s, and 1980s, voluntary groups represented parents and took their concerns, collectively, to public inquiries, select committees, and media. From the late 1990s and 2000s, individuals such as Payne embodied parental concerns. As an individual, Payne was able to speak informally with politicians, and to be appointed for a formal political role.

To an extent, the creation of tsars and the passing of the *Criminal Justice and Court Services Act* of 2000 represented an individualist policy moment. In this act, individual parents were encouraged to be increasingly 'responsible' for overseeing and monitoring their children's development. The idea that parents had rights, as long as they exercised their responsibilities, while key in the *Children Act* of 1989, was extended by New Labour governments, for example in the creation of parental control orders, curfew orders, and legislation around anti-social behaviour.[104] One of the key tenets of the Sarah's Law campaign was 'empowering parents to protect children': parents would have the 'right' to controlled information about offenders in their neighbourhood but, with this, the conferred responsibility of ensuring that they monitored their neighbours to keep their children safe. The parent, rather than the family or indeed the mother, was to be the key object of social policy, and the agent responsible for promoting change. This escalated the interest seen throughout the 1960s, 1970s, and 1980s in engaging families, children, and parents in child protection practice. Newly however, the state and statutory agencies—as well as the voluntary sector—would support and facilitate familial responsibility.

Professional Retaliation

While the Paynes became influential, contemporary journalists, psychologists, and children's charities challenged the significance of experiential expertise. Lynda Lee-Potter from the *Daily Mail* argued that the government should not 'concede to the emotional pressure' of passing the *Criminal Justice and Court Services* bill. She further suggested that the bill's passing would evoke emotional public responses, such as 'mobs' or even murder.[105] Writing for the *Guardian*, the clinical psychologist Oliver James made a different critique: he argued that Sara Payne was not being treated as an expert by professional agencies, but rather that parent campaigners were 'wheeled out to express their concern' and exploited to sell newspapers.[106] These accounts portrayed emotions as powerful motivators for policy reform, and as underpinning popular appetite for newspapers. At the same time, these accounts also expressed concern about who controlled the portrayal and expression of parental emotion and experience.

Furthermore, and demonstrative of the pervasiveness of this hierarchy, newspapers also continued to contrast the experiential knowledge of the Paynes to 'professional' expertise.[107] This critique continued even when Sara Payne was appointed the Victims' Champion tsar. On the publication of her first report, *Redefining Justice*, the *Independent* suggested that 'some lobbying groups' had 'hinted heavily that it said nothing new'. The newspaper interpreted this to reveal an underlying attitude that 'Payne was an amateur stumbling through territory better left to professionals like them'.[108] This contrast between the 'amateur' and the 'professional' signified continuing challenges for parent campaigners. Even as they began to speak in the most influential circles, their testimony was often still interpreted as 'emotional', unoriginal, or 'amateur'. The holding of personal experience could confer *access* to media and policy spokespeople but could not guarantee influence. As with the 'mothers on the warpath', parents were encouraged to share their emotions publicly, particularly through press, and yet the visibility of their emotions was also used to undermine their arguments.

Payne therefore gained a prominent position in British politics, yet was also reliant on a level of patronage and support from politicians at the Ministry of Justice and the Home Office. Significantly nonetheless, by the 2000s parents were not only influencing policy from the 'outside', through street protests, but also through collaboration with the most influential figures in politics and media. The Home Secretary John Reid presented this as a broader process whereby the 'sincere views of the public, represented by parents such as Sara Payne', were politically powerful.[109] Other politicians though, such as Home Affairs spokesman Nick Clegg, questioned whether the government was using these reforms as 'populist headline-grabbing announcements', rather than to fundamentally shift public–political relationships.[110] Certainly, while Payne's campaign had substantial traction, other contemporary groups representing parents struggled to be heard. The shift in parents' campaigning from a collective to an individual phenomenon, and the increasing media fixation on campaign figureheads, did not wholly confront nor subvert long-standing debates about how communities, families, and policy should work together to protect children.

Conclusion

Chapters 5 and 6 of this book have analysed a series of moments in which parents sought out influence over policy and public debate in the late twentieth century. The 'mothers on the warpath' had some opportunities to disseminate their aims in the popular press. The subsequent articles published however were somewhat dismissive. Through the 1980s and the 1990s, numerous newspaper articles reproduced the narratives of falsely accused parents at length and near verbatim. The television show *Open Space: Innocents at Risk* also disseminated the experiences of these parents. Very small parental advocacy groups such as PAIN acted as mediators in this process, recording the stories of falsely accused parents and presenting them to press and policy. By the 2000s, the experiences and emotions of Sara and Michael Payne were documented daily by newspapers, and Sara was appointed as a special advisor to government, as part of New Labour's focus on appointing 'tsars'.

Looking across these case studies, one may be tempted to draw a smooth narrative, whereby parental campaigners assumed increasing influence over policy and media in the late twentieth and early twenty-first centuries. This may seem like a linear progression of the increasing influence of experiential and emotional expertise, amidst the rise of an investigatory media. To an extent, this narrative holds significance; however, this is by no means such a linear history. Chapters 5 and 6 also demonstrate that the extent to which parents successfully gained influence was shaped by their successes in negotiating relationships with journalists, policy-makers, social workers, and medical professionals. In the 1980s, parents had to both assert that their experiential expertise was more significant than the knowledge held by clinicians and social workers, and yet also to demonstrate that they had support from such professional groups. Media and parental focus on criticising professional practice also contributed to a moment in which social workers and clinicians defended their work in experiential terms. People's experiences and emotions became significant as sources of evidence, placed alongside medical and research reports, though such evidence was sometimes seen as irrational, as well as powerful.

Women's testimonies in particular were the focus of much media coverage in the late twentieth century. A media and policy focus on mothers—their bodies, emotions, and daily lives—has a long history throughout the nineteenth and twentieth centuries.[111] What was new, however, was the reshaping of these broader trajectories in terms of unprecedented media interest in women's narration of their own experiences, shaped by right-wing anxieties around increasing female participation in the workplace and the development of second-wave feminism. Descriptions of women's experiences and emotions were both empowering and disempowering in this moment. The protest of the 'mothers on the warpath' was explained by newspapers as a communitarian act, in the context of Women's Liberation, and yet also somewhat dismissed, and presented as a hysterical, 'womanly' reaction. Mothers were questioned from the 1980s about how their campaigning would affect their parental duties, and many felt expected to give up their jobs when contesting accusations of abuse. Mothers such as Amphlett and Payne understood the processes of media work and were able, to an extent, to channel media interest towards their own campaigning. Nonetheless, to gain influence, the women also faced significant press intrusion and the multiple burdens of parenting, activism, media work, and workplace life. Media coverage rarely analysed the position and role of fathers in child protection debates. Indeed, this absence itself motivated the activism of Fathers 4 Justice, which was founded in 2001 and undertook a variety of high-profile stunts to critique the treatment of fathers in family courts. In contrast to press coverage of protesting mothers in the 1970s and 1980s, newspaper articles about Fathers 4 Justice emphasised and explored the men's 'masculine' identities: their vigour, anger, and use of physically demanding feats.[112] Ideas of cultural masculinity were further represented in the organisation's own publicity materials, which invited men to join the group 'for less than the price of a pint a month', and made heavy use of the iconography of superheroes, particularly Superman.[113]

In these ways, the processes through which parents came to assume influence in the late twentieth century were complex and disordered, heavily shaped by perceptions of gender, and deeply reliant on collaboration and conflict with media, medicine, and social work. Nonetheless, the case studies of this chapter were also revealing of a space in which experiential and emotional expertise was somewhat further valued—or at least further visible—by the 2000s. The next chapter of this book analyses how survivor experiences and emotions also became visible in public policy and media from the 1980s and particularly from the 1990s. In doing so, it traces many parallels with parental activism—in terms of collaboration with media, the role of voluntary groups, and the focus on individual spokespeople under New Labour. At the same time, Chap. 7 also demonstrates that survivor campaigners faced further challenges to speaking out, as literary, social policy, and media actors were often reluctant to confront and analyse the long-term effects of childhood abuse, and to consider its lived effects on adult life.

Notes

1. On the Western philosophical tradition of constructing female emotion as 'irrational', and male 'objectivity' as 'rational', please see: Leena Rossi and Tuija Aarnio, 'Feelings Matter: Historians' Emotions', *Historyka. Stuidia Metodologiczne*, 88 (2012): 172–173; Alison M. Jaggar, 'Love and Knowledge: Emotion in Feminist Methodology', *Inquiry*, 32 (1989): 163–164.
2. Analysis in this area draws on the work of Peter Bailey in terms of assessing how working-class Victorians 'move[d] through several different roles' and performed respectability as a 'choice of role', rather than a 'universal normative mode'. Peter Bailey, '"Will the real Bill Banks please stand up?": Towards a Role Analysis of mid-Victorian Working-Class Respectability', *Journal of Social History*, 12 (1979): 341–343.
3. Mathew Thomson, *Lost Freedom: The Landscape of the Child and the British Post-War Settlement* (Oxford: Oxford University Press, 2013), 157.
4. Steven Angelides, 'The Emergence of the Paedophile in the Late Twentieth Century', *Australian Historical Studies*, 36 (2005): 272–295;

Sigmund Freud, *On Sexuality—Three Essays on the Theory of Sexuality and Other Works* (New York, 1962), as cited in ibid., 272.

5. Thomson, *Lost Freedom*, 157–158.
6. Ibid., 153–183.
7. Thomson, *Lost Freedom*, 168; Phillip Jenkins, *Intimate Enemies: Moral Panics in Contemporary Great Britain* (New York: Aldine de Gruyter, 1992), 9, 24, 99.
8. Jenkins, *Intimate Enemies*, 9, 24.
9. British Library (hereafter BL), PIE, *Childhood Rights*, Vol. 1 No. 3, 1977, 'Principles', 3.
10. Lucy Robinson, *Gay Men and the Left in Post-War Britain* (Manchester: Manchester University Press, 2011), 129–139.
11. Ibid., 127–129.
12. Described in: Conor Cruise O'Brien, 'Moles, Witches and the rest of us', *The Observer*, 4 September 1983, 7; Conor Cruise O'Brien, 'Cruelty, and other tests of tolerance', *Guardian*, 18 September 1983, 7.
13. Chris Moores, 'The Paedophile Information Exchange was a product of a different time and culture', The Conversation, 27 February 2014 <https://theconversation.com/the-paedophile-information-exchange-was-a-product-of-a-different-time-and-culture-23735> (23 March 2015).
14. Chris Moores, *Civil Liberties and Human Rights in Twentieth-Century Britain* (Cambridge: Cambridge University Press, 2017), 190–198.
15. Ibid., 201; Thomson, *Lost Freedom*, 183.
16. Mary De Young, 'The Indignant Page: Techniques of Neutralisation in the Publications of Pedophile Organisations', *Child Abuse and Neglect*, 12 (1988): 593; Julian Bourg, 'Boy Trouble: French Pedophiliac Discourse of the 1970s' in Axel Schildt and Detlef Siegfried (eds), *Between Marx and Coca-Cola: Youth Cultures in Changing European Societies, 1960–1980* (New York: Berghahn Books, 2006), 285–313; Phillip Jenkins, *Decade of Nightmares: The End of the Sixties and the Making of Eighties America* (Oxford: Oxford University Press, 2006), pp. 259–268; Phillip Jenkins, *Moral Panic: Changing Concepts of the Child Molester in Modern America* (New Haven, Connecticut: Yale University Press, 1998). Archival materials—primarily newsletters—of the North American Man-Boy Love Association are available at the Beinecke Rare Book and Manuscript Library at the University of Yale.
17. Tom Crabtree, 'Adults only', *Guardian*, 19 May 1977, 11.
18. Hansard, House of Commons, fifth series, vol. 941 col. 901, 15 December 1977; Hansard, House of Commons, fifth series, vol. 943 col. 1833–1879, 10 February 1978.
19. Romi Bowen and Angela Hamblin, 'Sexual Abuse of Children', *Spare Rib*, May 1981, Issue 106.
20. Ibid.

21. Robinson, *Gay Men and the Left*, 133–134; 'Judge attacks paedophile group', *Guardian*, 1 April 1978, 3.
22. 'Paedophile chairman 'soaked with beer'', *Guardian*, 8 December 1977, 4.
23. Crabtree, 'Adults only', 11.
24. 'Paedophile chairman 'soaked with beer'', 4; 'Why child-sex man got a pub drenching', *Daily Mail*, 8 December 1977, 16–17.
25. 'Paedophile conference plans 'age of consent' meeting', *Guardian*, 1 September 1977, 4.
26. Philip Jordan, 'Mothers in child sex protest to continue anti-PIE campaign', *Guardian*, 21 September 1977, 5; Hencke, 'Street battle after paedophilia meeting, *Guardian*, 20 September 1977, 1; William Langley and Stuart Collier, 'Mothers on the Warpath', *Daily Mail*, 20 September 1977, 1; 'Paedophile conference plans 'age of consent' meeting', 4.
27. Langley and Collier, 'Mothers on the Warpath', 1; Philip Jordan, 'Mothers in child sex protest to continue anti-PIE campaign', *Guardian*, 21 September 1977, 5.
28. Langley and Collier, 'Mothers on the Warpath', 1.
29. Ibid., 1.
30. Ibid., 1.
31. Ibid., 1.
32. Jordan, 'Mothers in child sex protest', 5.
33. Robin Ball, 'Top marks to the stink bombers!', *Daily Mail*, 26 September 1977, 30.
34. Langley and Collier, 'Mothers on the Warpath', 1.
35. Hansard, House of Commons, sixth series, vol. 62 col. 975, 27 June 1984.
36. Malcolm Dean, 'Scotland Yard sends two new reports on PIE to ministers', *Guardian*, 25 August 1983, 2.
37. 'Note of a meeting held at 3.00PM on 23 November 1983: Paedophile Information Exchange', as cited in Shelley Phelps, 'Leon Brittan and Geoffrey Dickens notes from 1980s released', *BBC News*, 4 June 2015 <http://www.bbc.co.uk/news/uk-politics-32992155> (23 June 2015).
38. A. Mayer and H. Warschauer, 'The Vilest Men in Britain', *Sunday People*, 25 May 1975 as cited in Robinson, *Gay Men and the Left*, 129.
39. 'Why the DPP resurrected an ancient law to deal with paedophiles', *Guardian*, 14 March 1981, 17.
40. 'Man jailed for conspiracy to corrupt morals', *The Times*, 14 March 1981, 2.
41. For accounts of the debates around obscenity laws, please see: David J. Cox, Kim Stevenson, Candida Harris, Judith Rowbotham, *Public indecency in England, 1857–1960: 'a serious and growing evil'* (London: Routledge, 2014); Christopher Hilliard, 'Is It a Book That You Would Even Wish Your Wife or Your Servants to Read? Obscenity Law and the Politics of Reading in Modern England', *American Historical Review*,

118, no. 3 (2013): 653–678; David Bradshaw, Rachel Potter (eds), *Prudes on the prowl: fiction and obscenity in England, 1850 to the present day* (Oxford: Oxford University Press, 2013).

42. Langley and Collier, 'Mothers on the Warpath', 1.
43. Hall Carpenter Archives (hereafter HCA), Paedophile Information Exchange, *Magpie*, Issue 9, 1977, Keith Hose, 'Proud to be a pig', 8–9.
44. Langley and Collier, 'Mothers on the Warpath', 1.
45. Parts of the following section were first tested out, in slightly different form, in my article, Jennifer Crane, 'Painful Times: The Emergence and Campaigning of Parents Against Injustice in 1980s Britain', *Twentieth Century British History*, 26, no. 3 (2015): 450–476. Select archival quotations and my own ideas are reused here in line with the article's open access status, as it was published under a Creative Commons CC-BY license.
46. Giles Oakley with Peter Lee-Wright, 'Opening Doors: the BBC's Community Programme Unit 193-2002', *History Workshop Journal*, 82, no. 1 (2016): 213–234; Richard Kilborn and John Izod, *An Introduction to Television Documentary: Confronting Reality* (Manchester: Manchester University Press, 1997), 82–83.
47. British Film Institute (hereafter BFI), LCPW008X, *Open Space: Innocents At Risk*, Dir. Stephanie Cartwright, 17 March 1986.
48. Ibid.
49. Ibid.
50. Ibid.
51. Ibid.
52. Ibid.
53. Ibid.
54. Ibid.
55. See: Rossi and Aarnio, 'Feelings Matter': 172–173; Alison M. Jaggar, 'Love and Knowledge': 163–164.
56. BFI, *Open Space.*
57. For an interesting analysis of 'ordinariness' as constructed in the 1980s, please see: Chris Moores, 'Thatcher's troops? Neighbourhood Watch schemes and the search for "ordinary" Thatcherism in 1980s Britain', *Contemporary British History*, 31, no. 2 (2017): 230–255.
58. BL, Parents Against Injustice, *A response to Child Abuse—Working Together: A Draft Guide to Arrangement for Inter-agency Co-operation For the Protection of Children*, October 1986, 8.
59. British Broadcasting Corporation Written Archives (hereafter BBC), BARB Viewing Figures 17 March 1986, 1; BL, 'How PAIN has grown', 5; Karen Dunnell, *The Changing Demographic Picture of the UK: National Statistician's Annual Article on the Population* (Newport: Office for National Statistics, 2007), 10.
60. BL, 'How PAIN has grown', 5.

61. Ibid., 5.
62. Joe Moran, *Armchair Nation: An intimate history of Britain in front of the TV* (London: Profile Books, 2013), 2.
63. Lynda Lee-Potter, 'Sarah's Law is not the best way', *Daily Mail*, 19 December 2001, 11.
64. Angela Levin, 'I've built a brick wall around my heart', *Daily Mail*, 29 June 2002, 30.
65. Ibid., 30.
66. Ibid., 30.
67. Julia Stewart, 'Tears and fears of a distraught family fighting to cope with the loss of their 'little princess'', *Independent*, 13 December 2001, 3; Paul Peachey, 'Sarah Payne jury is told of gruesome discovery', *Independent*, 21 November 2001, 11; Terri Judd, 'Paynes face murder suspect in court', *Independent*, 20 February 2001, 2. Describing hand-holding: Paul Harris, 'At least their daughter could now rest in peace', *Daily Mail*, 13 December 2001, 8–9.
68. Stewart, 'Tears and fears of a distraught family', 3.
69. Stephen Wright, 'Our marriage has ended, say Sarah Payne's parents', *Daily Mail*, 8 September 2003, 17.
70. Stewart, 'Tears and fears of a distraught family', 3.
71. Sara Payne, *A Mother's Story* (London: Hodder & Stoughton, 2005), 94–95.
72. Ibid., 94–95.
73. Wright, 'Our marriage has ended', 17.
74. Val Hennessy, 'A family ravaged by grief', *Daily Mail*, 18 June 2004, 55; David Mattin, 'The Face: A Mother with a Mission', *The Times*, 20 June 2006, 2.
75. Miranda Ingram, 'The Courage of Sarah's mother', *The Times*, 20 July 2000, 8.
76. 'Justice 'must focus on victims'', *BBC News*, 5 November 2009 <http://news.bbc.co.uk/1/hi/uk/8343313.stm> (31 August 2017).
77. Harris, 'At least their daughter could now rest in peace', 8–9.
78. Christian Gysin, 'No regrets', *Daily Mail*, 18 December 2001, 5.
79. Ingram, 'The Courage of Sarah's mother', 8.
80. Mattin, 'The Face: A Mother with a Mission', 2.
81. Christian Gysin, 'No regrets', *Daily Mail*, 18 December 2001, 5; Harris, 'At least their daughter could now rest in peace', 8–9. See also the analysis in *The Times* that the confirmation of Sarah's death, when the body was found, 'hit all those working on the inquiry' and led to an 'emotional press conference', Michael Harvey, 'Sarah's parents visit site where body lay', *The Times*, 19 July 2000.
82. Shy Keenan and Sara Payne, *Where Angels Fear: two courageous women bringing hope out of horror* (London: Hodder & Stoughton, 2009), 38–39.

83. Ibid., 39.
84. Ingram, 'The Courage of Sarah's mother', 8.
85. Cahal Milmo, 'Police say "naming and shaming" paedophiles puts children at risk', *Independent*, 24 July 2000, 1; Mark Gould, 'Paynes call for open sex-offenders register', *Independent*, 30 July 2000, 4.
86. Ian Burrell, 'Innocent man is attacked after tabloid "naming"', *Independent*, 25 July 2000, 9.
87. Payne and Keenan, *Where Angels Fear*, 42–46.
88. Hazel Kemshall and Jason Wood, *Child Sex Offender Review (CSOR) Public Disclosure Pilots: a process evaluation—2nd edition* (London: Home Office, 2010), 2.
89. Payne and Keenan, *Where Angels Fear*, 44–45.
90. For example, the speech given by Sara Payne at Sarah's funeral was recreated at length—as in the tabloids—in: Steve Bird, 'Mother's farewell to murdered daughter', *The Times*, 1 September 2000. A valedictory account of Sara's strength and resilience, again echoing tabloid coverage, was provided in: Ingram, 'The Courage of Sarah's mother', 8.
91. James Robinson, 'Sara Payne: the people at News of the World became my trusted friends', *Guardian*, 28 July 2011 <https://www.theguardian.com/media/2011/jul/28/sara-payne-news-of-the-world> (31 August 2017).
92. Levin, 'I've built a brick wall around my heart', 30.
93. Stewart, 'Tears and fears of a distraught family', 3.
94. Harris, 'At least their daughter could now rest in peace', 8–9.
95. 'Sara Payne 'on phone-hack' list', *BBC News*, 29 July 2011 <http://www.bbc.co.uk/news/world-14332689> (26 April 2018).
96. Conal Urquhart, 'Straw to change sex offenders law', *The Times*, 12 September 2000.
97. Ibid.
98. Levin, 'I've built a brick wall around my heart', 30.
99. Payne and Keenan, *Where Angels Fear*, 169–170.
100. Martin Smith, *Goats and Tsars: Ministerial and other appointments from outside Parliament*, Public Administration Select Committee, Eight Report of Session 2009–2010, (London: Her Majesty's Stationery Office, 2010), 42.
101. Prime Minister Harold Wilson also notably attempted to use politically sympathetic outside experts for advice in his administration. Please see: Andrew Blick, 'Harold Wilson, Labour and the Machinery of Government', *Contemporary British History*, 20, no. 3 (2006): 343–362. In terms of appointments under New Labour please see: Ruth Levitt and William Solesbury, 'Debate: Tsars—are they the 'experts' now?', *Public Money & Management*, 32, no. 1 (2012): 47.
102. Smith, *Goats and Tsars*, 41.

103. Ibid., 42.
104. Harry Hendrick, *Children, Childhood and English Society, 1880–1990* (Cambridge: Cambridge University Press, 1997), 60–65; Nigel Parton, *The Politics of Child Protection: Contemporary Developments and Future Directions* (Basingstoke: Palgrave Macmillan, 2014), 30, 35–36.
105. Lynda Lee-Potter, 'Sarah's Law is not the best way', *Daily Mail*, 19 December 2001, 11.
106. Oliver James, 'Sarah Payne: turning a tragedy into a sales opportunity', *Guardian*, 19 July 2000 <https://www.theguardian.com/lifeandstyle/2000/jul/19/healthandwellbeing> (5 June 2017).
107. Jo Dillon and Louise Jury, '"Sarah's Law" unworkable, say paedophilia experts', *Independent*, 6 August 2000, 1.
108. Joanna Moorhead, 'Parent power: Sara Payne on being an ordinary mother in Whitehall', *Independent*, 12 November 2009 <http://www.independent.co.uk/news/people/profiles/parent-power-sara-payne-on-being-an-ordinary-mother-in-whitehall-1818835.html> (7 July 2017). Notably however, the Chief Executive of Victim Support wrote to the *Independent* to criticise this initial article, and to challenge in particular the 'damaging implication' that Payne was viewed as an 'amateur' (Gillian Guy, 'Victim Support offers selfless aid', *Independent*, 16 November 2009, 30).
109. Hansard, House of Commons, 13 June 2007, col. 761, 'Child Sex Offender Review'.
110. Ibid.
111. See, for example: Vicky Long and Hilary Marland, 'From Danger and Motherhood to Health and Beauty: Health Advice for the Factory Girl in Early Twentieth Century Britain', *Twentieth Century British History*, 20 (2009): 454–481; Rima Apple, 'Constructing Mothers: Scientific Motherhood in the Nineteenth and Twentieth Centuries', *Social History of Medicine*, 8 (1995): 178.
112. See for example: 'Profile: Fathers 4 Justice', *BBC News*, 22 April 2008 <http://news.bbc.co.uk/1/hi/uk/3653112.stm> (3 August 2018); 'Good Morning Britain hosts stunned as Fathers for Justice founder undoes trousers and threatens to expose himself live on air', *Evening Standard*, 15 June 2018 <https://www.standard.co.uk/news/uk/good-morning-britain-hosts-stunned-as-fathers-for-justice-founder-undoes-trousers-and-threatens-to-a3863726.html> (3 August 2018).
113. See: 'Our Story', Fathers 4 Justice website < http://www.fathers-4-justice.org/about-f4j/our-story/ > (10 July 2017); Richard Collier, 'Fathers 4 Justice, law and the new politics of fatherhood', *Child and Family Law Quarterly*, 17, no. 4 (2005): 511–33; Ana Jordan, '"Dads aren't Demons. Mums aren't Madonnas." Constructions of fatherhood and masculinities in the (real) Fathers 4 Justice campaign', *Journal of Social Welfare and Family Law*, 31, no. 4 (2009): 419–33.

Open Access This chapter is licensed under the terms of the Creative Commons Attribution 4.0 International License (http://creativecommons.org/licenses/by/4.0/), which permits use, sharing, adaptation, distribution and reproduction in any medium or format, as long as you give appropriate credit to the original author(s) and the source, provide a link to the Creative Commons license and indicate if changes were made.

The images or other third party material in this chapter are included in the chapter's Creative Commons license, unless indicated otherwise in a credit line to the material. If material is not included in the chapter's Creative Commons license and your intended use is not permitted by statutory regulation or exceeds the permitted use, you will need to obtain permission directly from the copyright holder.

CHAPTER 7

The Visibility of Survivors and Experience as Expertise

This chapter examines the multi-layered processes through which adults who had been abused in childhood—survivors—began to discuss their experiences of abuse in public, often for the first time, through published letters, autobiography, newspaper interviews, and testimonies offered to academia and social policy. These spaces were shaped by and reshaped the narration of individual experiences and emotions, entwining personal processes of thinking and remembering with the changing interests of publishing houses, newspaper editors, and researchers. The chapter argues that public and political attention shifted to the long-term effects of child abuse for the first time only in the 1980s, and particularly from the 1990s, decades after attention had been paid to the experiences and emotions of children and parents. It took time for survivors to come forward, and for public and policy attention to consider the long-term effects of abuse on children. While the chapter uses the word 'survivor' as shorthand, echoing contemporary accounts and the activism of multiple voluntary groups, survivor testimonies—influential in social policy and media interviews from the 1990s and 2000s—have also demonstrated the complexity and range of lived experiences of abuse.

As attention was turned towards survivor experiences and emotions, several processes traced through this book solidified at the turn of the twenty-first century. Notably, experiential knowledge became a key

© The Author(s) 2018
J. Crane, *Child Protection in England, 1960–2000*, Palgrave Studies in the History of Childhood,
https://doi.org/10.1007/978-3-319-94718-1_7

resource for framing—and for criticising—political and media analysis. Continuing a process traced throughout this book, consultation with voluntary groups remained the key mechanism to access survivor views and, to a new extent, representative groups grew and consciously entwined experiential and professional expertise. As we saw in the previous chapter, under New Labour individual voluntary leaders found new opportunities to influence public inquiries—although survivor spokespeople remained critical of state legislation and services. These spokespeople operated at a juncture: at times reliant on state-funding, often lobbying for legislative change, but also seeking to work productively with social services, police, and law.

Relationships between survivor representatives and specific journalists cross-cut this policy work, and survivors used media interest to express their viewpoints and to criticise child protection practice. This chapter hence demonstrates that the expertise of experience and emotion had become significant by the year 2000 and that, in this context, survivors themselves were able to play a significant role in reshaping policy and media debate about child protection. This new role, primarily assumed through voluntary groups, intervened in long-standing relationships between policy, media, and publics, and raised questions, which would become key in the twenty-first century, about *whose* experiences and emotions were being represented on the public stage.

Confessional Cultures?

From the mid-1960s, amidst renewed interest in child protection, social policy and medical texts made only occasional mention of the potential long-term effects of childhood abuse. Adults who were abused in childhood may have been speaking privately with agony aunts, counsellors, psychologists, and to one another before this decade, but their accounts were not yet heard publicly. Survivor accounts indeed were notably absent from broader 'confessional cultures' and 'cultures of self-expression' which, Deborah Cohen and Martin Francis have argued, emerged from the 1930s to the 1970s, or from the late 1950s and early 1960s.[1] Without open discussions about child protection at this time, survivors could not yet discuss their personal experiences or emotions on the public stage.

From the 1980s, however, early accounts about the long-term effects of childhood violence began to surface. Developing psychological research about trauma was also important in this moment, and the category of post-traumatic stress disorder was first included in the 1980 edition of the *Diagnostic and Statistical Manual of Mental Disorders*.[2] In this context, psychologists discussed the 'long-term effects' of guilt, trauma, betrayal, and secrecy for children, and the 'psychological scars' that may 'remain for a lifetime' following childhood abuse.[3] Social surveys—conducted by academics, popular magazines, and the voluntary sector—likewise were looking to uncover the long-term effects of abuse. A survey in *Woman* magazine in 1983 found that of 15,000 respondents, one-twelfth had suffered sexual abuse within their family.[4]

Social policy documents likewise began from the 1980s to consider this issue. The report of the public inquiry into the Cleveland case, published in 1987, included one paragraph mentioning that the Member of Parliament Frank Cook had provided information from three brothers who had revealed after many years that their father had sexually abused them as children.[5] The report did not present further details, simply writing that this did not come within its remit. Nonetheless, it emphasised that this suggested broader and long-term problems, that: perpetrators may remain in communities; abused children may require counselling in their futures; and authorities may face 'insuperable difficulties' confronting retrospective accusations of abuse.[6] While not addressing these issues at length, the report stated that this was an area 'we feel should be recognised and consideration given to it'.[7]

To an extent then, psychological, sociological, and policy researchers working in child protection were increasingly confronting the long-term effects of childhood abuse through the 1980s. This analysis signalled an important shift in terms of thinking about abuse over the life course, and in terms of its long-term effects—points notably absent from earlier debates which focused solely on the child in their childhood, rather than the child as a long-term, reflexive, living, and ageing subject. Survivors themselves in part drove this increased focus on their experiences. A range of charities—the NSPCC, ChildLine, Kidscape, Samaritans, Phoenix Survivors, and Relate—all testified that adults who were abused in childhood started to contact them, seeking help, in the 1980s and 1990s.[8] Survivors later testifying to select committee inquiries in the early 2000s emphasised that they had been 'too scared' to come forward as children, and that they had needed time to 'feel strong enough to give evidence'.[9]

These personal journeys of reflection occurred at the same time as new spaces opened up for children to disclose their experiences in the 1970s and 1980s, and alongside broader psychological interest in trauma. While survivors played a significant role in this process by coming forward in the 1980s and 1990s, professions also mediated the ways in which their experiences would be heard, disseminated, and used. The complex interactions between survivors—calling for assistance—and media, the voluntary sector, and policy may be analysed through a series of case studies: the work of agony aunts, autobiographies, and the NSPCC's *Childhood Matters* project.

Agony Aunts

Agony aunts are an important case study, demonstrating how the public narration of private experiences by survivors was mediated by the norms, cultures, and agendas of national institutions—newspapers—and by 'new experts' in confessional culture. Agony aunts turned to focus on child sexual abuse as a topic from the early 1990s, initially thinking about children but, later, shifting their focus towards adults. In these years, agony aunts told newspapers that they received a 'distressingly large' number of letters on child abuse—with indeed Deidre Sanders, agony aunt for the *Sun*, stating that one in five of her letters discussed this topic.[10] Accordingly, Sanders began to respond to many such letters in her column, publishing almost 400 letters about abuse and violence between 1998 and August 2015. Suggesting a further increase in openness about this area over the early twenty-first century, over half of these letters were published between January 2013 and August 2015.[11]

Agony aunts played a significant role in publicly disseminating lengthy individual and qualitative accounts, adding to the quantitative data collected by social surveys and the private qualitative information recorded by psychologists and public inquiries. People's experiences were framed in emotional terms: letters to the *Sun*'s 'Dear Deidre' page described life histories and, following this, testified that people felt 'so full of anger and hate' or 'frightened' about discussing their childhood abuse.[12] Sanders emphasised that abuse may leave 'emotional scars' and could surface in later relationships.[13] While the bylines chosen for these letters emphasised negative emotions—for example, 'Haunted by years of childhood abuse' and 'So hurt by evil abuser'—the letters' content also often reported therapeutic progress. In 2002, one young person of 26 wrote to the *Sun* to announce that, after Sanders had provided information and recommended counselling, they had 'moved on enormously' in their thinking.[14] While agony aunts therefore provided important support, the selection, publication, and framing of public letters also demonstrated significant interest in this period in lived experiences and the power of emotion. Emotion was coded as a motivational force; encouraging people to write to newspapers, to bring their perpetrators to justice, or to reach out to others. However, emotion was also presented a barrier to action—described as stopping adults from having spoken out before, and as a hindrance to developing relationships or careers.

These letters were therefore not only a product of shifting openness in discussing child abuse, nor of increasing disclosures from survivors about their life experiences. The publication of these letters also reflected the shifting interests of newspaper editors—issues that they thought would sell papers—and the assumed interests of members of the public. In 1993, agony aunt Suzie Hayman of *Woman's Own* discussed public letters as a commercial entity, as well as a therapeutic forum, emphasising that newspapers 'put a lot of money' into providing 'an enormously expensive reader service', and that they 'can't justify that unless the column's entertaining'.[15] While the agony aunt column was a 'service' to the public, the content of letters chosen for publication also revealed shifting ideas about what would 'entertain' newspaper readerships. Indeed, and reflecting different norms around discussing abuse, *Independent* agony aunt Virginia Ironside argued in 1993 that the 'very, very nervous broadsheets and posher papers' were later to offer agony aunt columns than tabloids, fearing initially that such columns may be 'tacky and silly'.[16]

Nonetheless, in curating and responding to these letters, agony aunts from tabloids and broadsheets alike emerged as a new type of visible and highly accessible expert in child protection. Agony aunts testified that they were often the first people who survivors shared their accounts with, and that many had previously 'kept the feelings bottled up inside themselves'.[17] In becoming expert, agony aunts further blurred the boundaries between professional and personal forms of expertise. Continuing a shift towards professional reflexiveness, visible throughout this book, agony aunts discussed their own emotional responses to receiving these letters, discussing how they were 'really upsetting' and made them 'sad' and 'angry'.[18] In addition, and extending the professional openness traced in Chaps. 5 and 6 through the 1980s, agony aunts also disclosed their own life stories, and indeed argued that personal histories of counselling, mental health, and family challenges, for example, provided key 'qualifications' with which to answer public letters.[19]

Tied in with their focus on experiential expertise as a resource, and with their own provision of expert help, agony aunts both replaced and challenged statutory services in child protection. Interviewing agony aunts in 1993, the *Observer* argued that letters were sent by people who had been ignored by teachers, doctors, and 'others in authority'.[20] Ironside testified that people often wrote to agony aunts 'because the experts have failed them'.[21] Agony aunts acted politically and used this analysis of expertise to challenge broader social policies and social changes. While some agony aunts argued that 'resources are dwindling for social work', Philip Hodson, writing for *News of the World*, contended that child abuse had risen in response to parental employment and the divorce rate.[22]

Agony aunts therefore gleaned significant personal authority as individuals, and were able to challenge social and political change beyond child protection issues alone, but nonetheless with expertise based on their exposure to, and grasp of, public experiences and emotions. Recognising that public accounts were key to the construction of their expertise, agony aunts regularly deferred to self-help organisations, directing public inquiries to these groups, and also explicitly stating that many survivors wrote to their columns because others had.[23] Through the emergence of agony aunts, therefore, the experiences and emotions of survivors became visible. The sharing of these experiences and emotions bolstered the expertise of survivors, but also constructed the media as a provider of therapeutic care, a voice for marginalised populations, and a key critic of state services.

Autobiography

Autobiographies, like letters to agony aunts, became an important medium through which to express and share experiences of childhood abuse from the 1970s, 1980s, and 1990s. Again, this medium reflected both increasing willingness from members of the public to discuss their childhood experiences openly, but also a new commercial appetite—in this case from the publishing industry—for sharing experiences and emotions. The confessional memoir has a long history. Deborah Cohen has shown that interwar memoirs were highly candid, capitalising on a primarily female market which 'liked to read about family skeletons'.[24] In the late twentieth century, new forms of the confessional memoir emerged, linked in with developments in second-wave feminism, the interests of commercial publishers, and increasing social explicitness about the internal mechanisms of family life.

From the 1970s, second-wave feminists offered new accounts of childhood abuse which looked to mobilise descriptions of experiences and emotions to lobby for political change, and to draw together thinking about violence against women and children. Demonstrative of the growing production of such work by voluntary groups, writing from the London Rape Crisis Centre in 1981, one *Spare Rib* article emphasised that adult women who faced sexual abuse may experience vivid flashbacks, leaving them 'numb, depressed or acutely anxious', and experiencing feelings of blame, betrayal, humiliation, outrage, anger, and upset.[25] Feminist authors also produced memoirs and autobiographies describing their own experiences and those of others. Louise Armstrong's *Kiss Daddy Goodnight* (1978) was significant in this regard. Drawing on testimony from 183 women, recruited through adverts and peer networks, the book contained letters about incest written by women of 'every class, every family structure', charting experiences of fear and trauma, confusion and denial.[26] The book's back cover emphasised that Armstrong had written this text 'through the words of the victims themselves', breaking a 'conspiracy of silence'.[27] Reflecting in 2008, an obituary of Armstrong offered a similar perspective, arguing that her work had given many survivors 'the courage to speak out'.[28]

Within Armstrong's book, descriptions of emotion were central to women's accounts of their experiences, and contributors expressed hurt, guilt, fear, disbelief, denial, anguish, and rage.[29] One contributor questioned why she had never received help, given the transparency of her 'obvious emotional trauma', clear to 'anybody who had an IQ of more than one point above a ripe cucumber'.[30] The text therefore framed descriptions of experience and emotion as challenging existing professional services, and as challenging structural systems of patriarchy and power. In 2003, Armstrong argued that since 1978, and the publication of her book, 'experts' had sought to appropriate the experiences of survivors and of women and to 'dismiss feminist analysis as biased, political, unprofessional'.[31] Her book and subsequent works, therefore, positioned experiential expertise as authoritative, continuing women's efforts to present their own experiences, and those of others, publicly.

From the 1990s and 2000s, decades after the development of feminist memoirs about child abuse and incest, another distinctive form of child protection autobiography was popularised.[32] Informally titled 'misery lit', Victoria Bates has argued that such works were framed by a feminist-psychoanalytic model and centred around a single traumatised female, her traumatic memories, and a traumatic event.[33] These works, providing explicit accounts of childhood trauma, were written by men as well as women: the books *A Child Called It* (1995), *The Lost Boy* (1997), and *A Man Named Dave* (2000), all written by Dave Pelzer, were important in this genre.[34] Like earlier feminist accounts, these works brought narratives about the experiences and emotions involved in recalling historic abuse to wider audiences. Pelzer's first book, for example, described how his 'will to somehow survive' continued despite significant abuse by his mother, including physical violence, neglect, enforced labour, and 'using food as her weapon'.[35]

A Child Called It included graphic descriptions of Pelzer's childhood abuse, recalling his sensory environment and emotions. For example, in one passage Pelzer described how his mother burnt him on a hot stove, and he described the feeling of his skin—which 'seemed to explode from the heat'—and the smell of the 'scorched hairs from my burnt arm'.[36] Significantly, and demonstrative of public interest in such graphic accounts, 'misery lit' became an incredibly popular genre. In 2006, 11 of the top 100 bestselling paperbacks were memoirs about surviving abuse. Newspapers and publishers reported that supermarkets were a key space in which these books were sold, and that their purchasers were 80–90 per cent female.[37] The popularity of 'misery lit' declined from 2008, in part as journalists challenged the veracity of some accounts—including those offered by Pelzer—but also shaped by a changing economic climate.[38] The journalistic concern about the 'truth' of these accounts reflected a growing mode of investigative research, but also showed that long-standing sites of expertise would police, criticise, and analyse survivors' expressions of experience and emotion, once made public.

In part, there was tension between the genres of the 1970s and 1990s autobiographies. The trauma scholar Anne Rothe has argued that while Armstrong's book was 'part of her feminist activism', and a call for cultural and political change, 'misery lit' sought 'to sell the pain of others as entertainment'.[39] Contemporary journalists echoed this argument: an article in the *New York Times* about Pelzer was titled 'Dysfunction For Dollars', while the *Observer* wrote about 'Child abuse as entertainment', and the *Independent* described 'A million-dollar industry called Dave'.[40] Nonetheless, the publication, popularity, and dissemination of all of these texts marked a key shift in late twentieth-century British society. Survivors were able to share their own experiences in public, in their own terms, often for the first time, and these accounts were commercially, publicly, and politically significant. Survivor accounts provided in feminist and 'misery lit' texts alike were not solely framed around 'misery', 'cruelty', and 'despair', but also in terms of 'hope', 'resilience', 'survival', and 'triumph'.[41] Enabling survivors to provide their own accounts led to complex representations of emotion over the life course. These works presented the confrontation of experience and emotion as a liberating process, and were supported by concurrent accounts from survivors in newspapers about the entwined and long-term physical, emotional, and mental effects of childhood abuse.[42]

The ways in which survivor autobiographies were promoted and discussed in this late twentieth-century moment were distinct to the British context. While journalists in British newspapers criticised the idea that suffering had become entertainment, national publishers also sought to frame these books carefully, in comparison to how the same books were packaged and marketed in America. Making this point in 1988, an article in *Feminist Review* argued that the American marketing of *Kiss Daddy Goodnight* involved 'disgusting, almost titillating hype', presenting the book as 'A shocking, challenging expose of our ultimate sexual taboo!'[43] In 2001, the *Observer* reported that most British publishers had initially rejected Pelzer's book, even though it had been on the *New York Times* bestseller list for three years. The newspaper reported a 'consensus' among British publishers that this type of descriptive account 'wouldn't work here'.[44] When Pelzer's first book was published in Britain, the *Observer* stated, publishers replaced its 'garish' packaging with a 'classy-looking' cover.[45] British audiences, like American ones, were interested to read these graphic recollections of childhood experience and emotion, but they were marketed in Britain in more careful, discrete, and private terms.

Examination of autobiographies relating to child abuse thus demonstrates another new space in which survivor experiences and emotions were shared from the late twentieth century. This space was governed by survivors themselves—sharing positive as well as negative accounts—but also by the interests of commercial publishers and members of the public, and by overarching cultural frameworks of trauma and emotion. Discussing childhood abuse was constructed variously as therapeutic, politically powerful, and as public entertainment. Yet discussions were also modified by distinctly British assumptions about when and how private family experiences should be shared and made public, and policed by concerns about whether descriptions of personal experience were 'authentic' or 'true'.

Childhood Matters

In addition to growing focus from newspapers and publishing houses, academic and charitable interest in the long-term effects of childhood abuse was also developing from the mid-1990s. The National Commission of Inquiry into the Prevention of Child Abuse was notable in this context, established in 1994 by the NSPCC to consider the 'different ways in which children are harmed, how this can best be prevented, and to make recommendations for developing a national strategy for reducing the incidence of child abuse'.[46] The Commission members hailed from a range of professions and backgrounds. The Chair was former lawyer and Labour life peer Lord Williams of Mostyn, while other members were drawn from social work, academia, paediatrics, and Parliament. The NSPCC also appointed the chief executive of Channel Four, Michael Grade, and *Sun* agony aunt, Deidre Sanders, with the hope of gaining 'more coverage in the popular press and on television'—again indicative of growing public interest in this topic, and increased political recognition of the significance of media support.[47]

The Commission did not directly appoint individuals personally affected by abuse, though it did seek out their written contributions, as well as those from educationalists, clinicians, lawyers, researchers, and journalists. The Commission collected 10,000 testimonies in total.[48] Significantly, one chapter of the final report's 'Background Papers', co-written by the sociologists Corinne Wattam and Claire Woodward, focused on learning about prevention from those personally affected by abuse.[49] Following a parallel system to Armstrong, Wattam and Woodward placed adverts in agony aunt pages looking for the 'experiences' of 'victims of abuse', and received 1121 letters.[50] The majority of these (721) told the author's life story; 130 responded directly to the Commission's terms of reference; and the remainder were written by concerned relatives, friends, and professionals.[51] People who identified as female wrote 88 per cent of life-story letters. This gender disparity—in addition to reflecting the market for 'misery lit'—was also replicated in the responses to surveys conducted in the 2010s, suggesting an extent to which women felt more comfortable, or expected, to disclose, read about, and discuss historic abuse.[52]

In analysing these letters, Wattam and Woodward aimed to assess the common causes and types of child abuse, the ages at which abuse typically started, and the person believed responsible. Wattam and Woodward also analysed whether, when, and how the authors had reported abuse, and the strategies for recovery and prevention which they had found helpful.[53] This represented a focus, again present in earlier sociological and policy work, in using survivor experience to draw 'lessons' for future practice. The key lessons drawn echoed the points made by agony aunts. Many letters received pinpointed a culture of denial within which abused children and surviving adults were encouraged to remain silent. Thirteen per cent of the 721 life-story letters were written by authors who had never spoken about being abused before.[54] Authors suggested that the majority of Britons would rather pretend that child abuse did not exist than address its unpleasant realities.[55] Within the life-story category, only 32 per cent of authors had told someone about their abuse as a child, and 29 per cent of these people had received a 'negative' reaction and been ignored, dismissed, or even punished.[56]

A suspicion of child protection professions and systems emerged in Wattam and Woodward's study. Respondents described the 'child abuse system' as a 'faceless group' which had treated them abusively, and made particular criticism of health, psychiatric, and social and legal services.[57] Demonstrating an appetite for peer support, one respondent wrote that 'the last thing we need is someone who knows nothing apart from what they have read in books or through so-called training'.[58] Others argued that child protection professionals should have 'firsthand experience' or 'have been abused in childhood themselves'.[59] A study published in 2002 also directly addressed this belief in peer support, and was written by Christine Walby, a member of this NSPCC Commission, Matthew Colton, a child welfare academic, and Maurice Vanstone, a lecturer in criminology. On carrying out detailed interviews with 24 individuals who were abused in residential homes, Walby, Colton, and Vanstone found that 'several subjects' of their interviews emphasised the importance of self-help groups, and that 'some felt that such groups offer the most effective form of help for survivors'.[60]

As such, the National Commission of Inquiry into the Prevention of Child Abuse directly sought out and took seriously the experiences of adults who had been abused in childhood, foreshadowing later work in child welfare and criminology.[61] While this type of consultation was becoming increasingly important in policy and academic analysis, it was not the central focus of the Commission's final report, *Childhood Matters* (1996). Rather, the report focused primarily on providing recommendations to prevent future abuse, notably encouraging: better co-operation between health, children's services, probation services, teachers, and voluntary groups; and the creation of mechanisms for community reporting.[62] Discussing the project, Members of Parliament and journalists likewise focused on prevention, and often on the recommendations to instate a Minister for Children and to see children as individuals, not possessions.[63]

Discussion of the long-term experiences of survivors was nonetheless present in *Childhood Matters*, which argued that the contemporary legal system was sometimes 'as damaging as the original abuse itself'.[64] Furthermore, covering the report, the *Guardian* reprinted a comment from Lord Williams that 'the voices of survivors ... were constantly in our minds'.[65] Bolstered by broader shifts in confessional culture, and by the recognition of the long-term effects of trauma, social policy and the voluntary sector—along with commercial agencies—were turning their attention to the experiences and emotions of survivors, for the first time, from the 1980s and particularly from the 1990s. Social policy-makers and researchers were also beginning, for the first time, to couch the significance of their work in terms of accessing experiential expertise.

Childhood Matters was important also in extending debates from the 1980s, analysed in Chaps. 5 and 6, which encouraged practitioners and researchers to reflect on and share their own emotions and experiences, particularly when analysing child protection. Again, this belief was later addressed directly in the research of Walby, Colton, and Vanstone. Testifying to the range of emotions which survivors themselves expressed, the researchers found that their survey respondents felt 'anger' and 'pain' but that they also described the 'dignity of survival'.[66] Walby, Colton, and Vanstone argued that listening to these stories was 'humbling and traumatic', and that they were concerned about the impact which their own research and 'intrusion' was having on their interviewees.[67]

Turning their gaze to social work and police, Walby, Colton, and Vanstone also argued that 'emotional distancing' by professions could be received very negatively, and could leave survivors 'being defined as "other" and in a sense dehumanized'.[68] Criticism of the legal system in this regard was echoed in 2002 by survivors providing evidence to the Home Affairs select committee, one of whom argued that, 'my experiences were viewed as pieces of paper' when seeking redress.[69] While another respondent to this committee argued that the Criminal Prosecution Service had done a 'good job', the entry of adult survivors into child protection debate nonetheless invited further professional reflection.[70]

Collective Action

Echoing the focus on community support in *Childhood Matters*, new voluntary and self-help groups emerged in the late-1990s and 2000s to support survivors in Britain, developing alongside parallel groups in America, Europe, and Australia.[71] These groups sought to enable survivors themselves to provide narrative accounts of their experiences in collective terms, adding to representations collected and constructed by state, professional, and commercial organisations. In Britain, new voluntary organisations included national groups such as the National Association for People Abused in Childhood (NAPAC), One in Four UK, and Phoenix Survivors, and regional groups such as Survivors Swindon, Nottinghamshire's Survivors Helping Each other, and Norfolk's Surviving Together. By 2015, there were at least 135 of these national and regional groups united under the umbrella organisation The Survivors Trust.[72]

The shape, aims, and membership of each of these groups varied markedly. Some groups had specific foci, such as the Male Survivors Trust, Childhood Incest Survivors, and Minister and Clergy Sexual Abuse Survivors.[73] Regional groups were usually small and primarily constituted by weekly or fortnightly support meetings, although some created leaflets, newsletters, and helplines. Other groups also engaged in campaign work. For example, Phoenix Survivors organised several national campaigns and spoke to Members of Parliament and journalists to lobby for restrictions in where sexual offenders could live and work.[74] Notably, Phoenix Survivors took a broad approach to the problems of survivors—for instance helping people to pay their bills—as the group argued that challenges to material living situations reflected and contributed to people's 'bleak emotional state[s]'.[75]

One key parallel across these disparate groups was that many were founded by adults who had themselves faced historic abuse, and who had struggled to access professional help. Phoenix Survivors was established by Shy Keenan in 2001, who wanted to use her experiences of physical and sexual abuse and neglect to help others. Keenan was joined in 2006 by Sara Payne, whose activism was discussed in Chap. 6, and the group's mandate was extended to also provide support for families of murdered children—indicative of how leaders governed and reshaped the priorities of voluntary groups.[76] Peter Saunders founded NAPAC, one of the largest groups working in this area, in 1997. Saunders had come to reflect on his childhood experiences of abuse when he was in his late 30s, in the mid-1990s.[77] He had struggled to find support, telling newspapers that telling his family had 'torn' them apart and that he had tried to call ChildLine and the NSPCC to no avail.[78]

Following this, a second shared premise underlying many of these support groups was the idea that adults who had been affected by historic abuse may be able to help one another, more than professionals could; an idea echoed in the concurrent academic studies by Wattam, Woodward, Walby, Colton, and Vanstone. Discussing this explicitly with *The Times* in 1996, Saunders argued, 'The one thing that bastard gave me is an ability to empathise with victims of child abuse.'[79] Testifying to the Home Affairs select committee in 2002, another survivor argued that through institutional abuse, in particular, they had been 'linked' to other victims by the 'perversion' of one perpetrator.[80]

While the value of experiential expertise was thus promoted by survivors speaking to social policy, select committees, and newspapers, many leaders of survivor support groups themselves initially questioned its worth, or their own status as expert. When Keenan first began to receive requests for help, she reported that she had felt 'lost', not only because she did not have the time or the money to reply to all requests, but also because she doubted her 'authority' to do so, in comparison to those working in legal, police, social work, or medical fields.[81] In further interviews and in their own academic publications, nonetheless, the leaders of Phoenix Survivors and NAPAC came to assert that their personal experiences had given them the expertise to become spokespeople and had developed their emotional expertise and empathy.[82]

This premise shaped the specific types of support typically offered by these groups: phone lines staffed by other adults affected by abuse; websites with fora to talk to others; and online spaces in which adults could creatively express their feelings about the past, for example through paintings, poetry, and prose. As well as suggesting a growing culture of self-expression in late twentieth-century Britain, these spaces also reflected the argument of Joanna Bourke that the communication of pain has forged 'bonds of community' throughout time.[83] Memories of childhood abuse had forged informal interpersonal and community bonds previously, but these bonds became publicly visible, and to an extent publicly powerful, from the 1990s. A sense of community between and within survivor communities was fostered not only through the description of pain but also by sharing positive experiences of joy, strength, and happiness.[84] Again, voluntary organisations provided a means for survivors to rebuff and challenge professional categorisations of survivorship, and to present complexity. While challenging professional interests, this activism also represented a radical model whereby the long-term impacts of child abuse would be defined, analysed, and even managed through collective peer support, which could supplement, or if necessary bypass, statutory, community, or family provisions.

These groups continued a significant new mode of voluntary action emergent since the 1960s. Like other groups studied in this book, they bridged the 'new politics' of identity and New Social Movements and more long-standing forms of self-help and mutual aid. The groups represented experiential knowledge, but were also not lacking in professionalism nor formal organisation: NAPAC, for example, won grants from the Department of Health, Home Office, National Lottery, charitable trusts, and private companies, as well as through fundraising.[85] NAPAC also appointed formal boards of trustees and worked 'professionally' by establishing new helplines and websites and, as the chapter later outlines, working with policy and media. This book has analysed numerous such small voluntary groups who emerged around child protection and who, similarly, bridged 'professional' and 'expert', 'support' and 'advocacy' roles. The history of late twentieth-century Britain is incomplete without examination of such organisations.

Survivors as Experts

While policy-makers had consulted certain types of patient and service-user from the 1960s, it was only in the late 1990s that researchers began to acknowledge the long-term impact of childhood abuse and to consult survivors, with experience of abuse, as expert.[86] The potential mental health consequences of childhood abuse were first recognised by the state in the *Mental Health National Service Framework* (1999), the *Women's Mental Health Strategy: Into the Mainstream* (2002), and the Social Exclusion Unit Report on *Mental Health and Social Exclusion* (2004).[87] In a related shift, the *National Suicide Prevention Strategy* of 2001 included an explicit objective 'to promote the mental health of victims and survivors of abuse, including child sexual abuse'.[88]

By the early-to-mid-2000s, policy-makers began to consult survivors, often in terms of soliciting or reading select committee evidence about their experiences and emotions, as collated by voluntary organisations.[89] A range of models of consultation, all of which became important, were apparent in the Victims of Violence and Abuse Prevention Programme (VVAPP). The programme was established in 2005 by the Department of Health, the National Institute for Mental Health in England, and the Home Office. It aimed to consider the nature, extent, and effects of child sexual abuse, domestic violence, sexual assault, sexual exploitation, stalking, sexual harassment, forced marriage, female genital mutilation, and 'honour crimes'.[90] This broad approach to multiple issues demonstrated that, to an extent, social policy-makers were beginning to assess different types of violence in tandem in this period, following the late twentieth-century contexts of the 1960s, 1970s, and 1980s in which child abuse and domestic violence were often approached separately.

The first stage of the VVAPP was to gather evidence and six teams consisting of professionals, academics, and voluntary organisations were established.[91] One of these teams aimed to consider adult survivors of childhood sexual abuse.[92] Twenty-one 'expert advisors' composed this group, including academics, police, mental health specialists, clinicians, and representatives from the Home Office. Also included were seven members of voluntary organisations representing NAPAC, the Women's Therapy Centre, Rape Crisis, First Person Plural, and The Survivors Trust.[93] Suggestive that credence was paid to the experiential knowledge of survivors, Gillian Finch, the chair of The Survivors Trust, co-chaired this expert group alongside a Consultant Nurse on Sexual Abuse, Chris Holley.[94] The expert groups established the aims and scope of the VVAPP, which ultimately produced several outputs: mapping the common pathways from childhood victimisation to subsequent re-victimisation and the health and mental health of adults, producing a directory of the 180 voluntary organisations providing counselling for victims, and creating a Delphi method consultation.[95]

The Delphi consultation was significant because it not only demonstrated an appetite to consult with survivors as experts but also a social policy desire to find singular policy 'solutions' from a diverse and complex group. The consultation gave questionnaires to 285 'experts', including representatives from medicine, law, policy, children's charities, and survivor groups. The questionnaires sought out opinions about the existing provision of therapeutic services for child, adolescent, and adult victims, survivors, and perpetrators of abuse.[96] Responses were drawn through several rounds, whereby the survey was revised and redistributed after each round looking to uncover common responses. Of the 285 experts consulted, 123 responded to questions about adult survivors of childhood sexual abuse.[97] In the relevant section, the experts were asked about the 'most important principles and core beliefs' to inform work with 'victims/survivors', the most effective interventions, how to manage safety and risk, how to train people, prevention, and improving outcomes.[98] While it is not clear how many survivors were consulted, a fixed question on the survey did ask those with 'expertise from personal experience' to explain what strategies had helped them to recover from violence and abuse.[99]

The final reports produced by the VVAPP documented several conclusions relevant to the care of adults abused as children. Analysis of the Delphi consultation found strong agreement that no 'single therapeutic approach' would be effective for all survivors—indicating that there was no simple, singular policy response.[100] Participants agreed that any measures taken from the programme should be 'needs-led and victim/survivor centred', with all involved parties thinking carefully about survivor experiences, and giving survivors 'control' and 'choice'.[101] While experts agreed on these broad principles, they disagreed about the efficacy of specific forms of therapy for survivors (namely regression, hypnotherapy, and inner child techniques) and also over whether therapy should be offered on an 'open-ended basis' or not.[102] Experts also disagreed about whether those providing therapy needed qualifications and training, demonstrating that a level of professional suspicion remained about the value of peer support.[103]

The production, conclusions, and dissemination of the VVAPP demonstrated several key points about the ways in which survivors' experiences and emotions were becoming expertise in the 2000s. Notably, this project's survey consulted people with experiences of childhood abuse at the same time and in the same ways as those with professional experiences in law, social work, and medicine. This focus on experiential expertise was also highly visible in later analysis and framing of the programme and its results. In a subsequent book describing the VVAPP, the programme's director Catherine Itzin referred to the importance of consulting 'experts by both experience and profession'.[104] At the press release for this programme in November 2006, the Minister of State for Public Health, Caroline Flint, stated that the VVAPP was 'essentially informed by the strong voice of victims and survivors, of all ages and from all backgrounds'.[105]

Significantly, leaders of voluntary organisations would mediate, represent, and interpret the 'strong voice' of survivors. Indeed, one summary report produced by the VVAPP stated that the voluntary sector 'represents the interests—and the voice—of victims and survivors'.[106] Small voluntary groups had also played a significant role in representing the experiences and emotions of children and parents, as seen throughout this book. However, by the 1990s and 2000s, new spaces were also opening up for such small groups to yield significant influence over social policy and research. While the NSPCC's National Commission of Inquiry into the Prevention of Child Abuse, held in 1994, had invited survivors to write letters to its researchers, the VVAPP also appointed survivors, found through voluntary organisations, on to its advisory structures. One VVAPP publication released in 2006 even argued that 'survivor organisations' should become a key component in a broader system of multi-agency co-operation, working as service providers alongside statutory services—a position in tension with survivor critique of such agencies.[107]

To an extent therefore, survivors had further opportunities to contribute to policy construction in the 1990s and 2000s, and spokespeople couched the significance of policy work in terms of accessing survivor experience. This marked a significant transition from the 1970s and 1980s, when the long-term effects of child abuse were rarely the focus of political inquiry, and in part reflected the work of survivors to represent their own experiences and emotions in autobiography, newspapers, and through collective action. Nonetheless, significant limitations remained in the extent to which survivors were able to influence social policy.[108] Research by criminologists and by the parent representative Sara Payne emphasised that there was a significant 'implementation gap' between the rhetoric about victim and survivor support and the help provided.[109]

Further, voluntary survivor groups continued to struggle to gain financial support from successive governments, and statutory services were often the key beneficiaries of new financial commitments in victim support.[110] Survivor representatives and groups also had to continue to assert their rights to be heard, and to justify the significance of experiential expertise. Saunders, the founder of NAPAC, stated in 2013 that his organisation was only represented during Operation Yewtree, looking into the sexual offences of Jimmy Savile, after a journalist asked why survivors themselves were absent from debate.[111] Therefore, through voluntary groups, survivors found new pathways to share their experiences with policy-makers. Nonetheless, they were not always successful in disrupting existing processes of policy-construction, nor in making their experiences and emotions influential.

Role of the Media

Newspaper and televisual interest played a significant role in bringing public and political attention towards survivor experience and emotion, often through partnership between specific individuals in the media and leaders of voluntary organisations. Survivors guided these partnerships, but broader media tropes, interests, and agendas also shaped the narration of experience. One regular arena for survivor visibility and influence was in terms of, from the 2000s, leaders of voluntary groups offering expert comment on prevailing news stories, for example commenting on the appointments of new Ministers for Children, the issue of smacking as punishment, and the sentencing of sexual offences.[112] Published letters and quotations by voluntary leaders were printed and placed alongside those written by politicians and the leaders of large children's charities, demonstrating the authority of survivor groups.[113]

Survivor representatives often used this media space to make significant critiques of policy and practice. For example, Saunders wrote to the *London Evening Standard* that the appointment of Margaret Hodge as the first Minister for Children was a 'bad appointment' and that 'jaws dropped', because of the cases of sexual abuse in local care homes while she had been the leader of Islington council between 1982 and 1992.[114] Saunders emphasised that his critique represented the emotions and experiences of a broader community, arguing that this appointment had left survivors 'feeling disillusioned and saddened'.[115] Saunders' role in representing survivor experience continued in coverage from 2005, when the European Court of Human Rights awarded damage payments to a convicted paedophile, because of delays in setting his trial date. This case accrued much tabloid interest, and the *Daily Mirror*, *Daily Mail*, and *Daily Express* all quoted Saunders, who told the *Mail* that he felt 'bewilderment' while survivors would experience 'pain' and 'heartbreak'.[116]

In addition to responding to political, legislative, and social changes, survivor organisations also drove newspaper agendas, particularly through their appointment of celebrity patrons who, by sharing their own experiences, directed journalistic attention towards the lived experiences of child abuse and the fundraising efforts of voluntary groups. NAPAC, for example, appointed celebrity chef Antony Worrall Thompson and model Jerry Hall as patrons. Both spoke out about their childhood experiences for the charity. Hall discussed how her father 'had a lot of rages' and was 'quite violent', meaning that she knew 'the trauma of being a child and living in fear'.[117] Hall's statement, made while relaunching the NAPAC's helpline in 2006, received coverage in the *London Evening Standard*, the *Sun*, and the *Express*, leading *Third Sector* magazine to comment that 'the right celebrity with the right story can put a small charity on the front pages'.[118]

Survivor representatives also worked with television—for example Shy Keenan, of Phoenix Survivors, and Colm O'Gorman, of the charity One in Four, both made documentaries in partnership with the producer Sarah MacDonald, which aired on the BBC. These documentaries made the experiences and emotions of these voluntary leaders their primary subject, extending interest in the ability of such leaders to channel and represent broader communities of survivors. Keenan's programme was a sixty-minute Newsnight documentary, *A Family Affair*, which aired in November 2000. This documentary discussed Keenan's childhood and adulthood experiences, and featured undercover footage she had taken of her stepfather, Stanley Claridge, confessing to having sexually assaulted her and her sister, and to having allowed his friends to do so also, on multiple occasions.[119] While Keenan's childhood had been in the 1960s and 1970s, she sought to confront Claridge again in 2000, in her late-thirties, feeling that her own life was more established, and out of concern that her stepfather may again have access to children.[120] Keenan approached O'Gorman, who helped her to approach the BBC.[121] After *A Family Affair* was aired more of Claridge's victims came forward and the police launched 'Operation Phoenix'. On the basis of this, Claridge was sentenced to 15 years in prison at the age of 82.[122]

Keenan therefore exerted significant influence in contributing to the creation and shape of *A Family Affair*. Her persistence brought her case to the attention of the BBC, and she provided the crucial undercover footage. Keenan also shaped a critique of professional services which ran through this documentary and its subsequent news coverage. The programme itself discussed how perpetrators remained 'unchallenged by the authorities', and featured a reassessment of Keenan's childhood case files, which had barely mentioned Claridge.[123] In subsequent newspaper coverage, Keenan positioned her work as empowering, stating that she would fight for victims when they could not fight for themselves.[124] While Keenan was thus empowered in terms of using her experiences to shape this call for change, visions of vulnerability also framed media coverage. The documentary, for example, showed footage of Keenan being sick on the side of a motorway after her encounter with Claridge.[125] Subsequent media interviews described both Keenan's 'incredible bravery' and her 'vulnerability'.[126]

Continuing this close focus on the experiences and emotions of survivors, guided both by media interests and by survivors themselves, O'Gorman worked again with the director of *A Family Affair*, Sarah MacDonald, to make the documentary *Suing the Pope* (2002).[127] *Suing the Pope* followed O'Gorman as he returned to his birthplace, County Wexford in Ireland, to expose a Catholic Priest who had sexually abused him between the ages of 14 and 16, and to highlight the institutional failings that had enabled this abuse. The programme highlighted the institutional barriers for individuals coming forward about child abuse, with particular focus on the power and insularism of Catholicism in this small community.[128] O'Gorman was significant in directing the focus and content of this documentary. He reported that this work had given him a sense that religious and community power dynamics had shifted significantly, with the Catholic Church becoming the 'subject' of investigation, rather than the 'masters' of it.[129] In later years, other survivor organisations also framed media responses to clerical abuse, and NAPAC called for the Pope to review historic cases, make an apology, and talk directly to community representatives.[130]

While O'Gorman was highly important in shaping the content of *Suing the Pope*, and the representation of his experiences on the screen, community and public responses to this television programme could not be controlled. The response to *Suing the Pope* was, an updated version reported, primarily dominated by more victims coming forward and by an outpouring of public sympathy for those involved. A radio presenter in Wexford told the programme that they had 'people ringing in crying', and, notably, 'women in tears'. However, a minority response made threats of violence towards the programme's interviewees.[131] One interviewee later reported that they had initially struggled to cope with community attention after the documentary aired. They reported feeling like 'a goldfish in a goldfish bowl' and facing severe depression, although they later developed a sense of 'serenity'.[132]

Thus, by the 2000s survivors were in part able to drive media narratives around child protection, and were hailed by media as 'renowned expert[s]'.[133] The expertise of these individual survivor representatives derived from their personal experiences of abuse, but also from their ability to represent the emotions of broader communities of survivors.

Newspapers published critical letters from survivor leaders, but also complimented those who were 'measured and articulate', suggesting the ways in which tacit norms of 'appropriateness' governed which survivors became representatives and how.[134] Indeed, not all survivors were convinced by the value of media relationships. One anonymous survivor of institutional abuse, for example, in 2002 told the Home Affairs select committee that the media 'seems to paint survivors of child abuse as money grabbing liars'.[135] This testimony showed that, for some, suspicion of 'authority' and statutory services also extended towards the media. Further, the statement portrayed the challenges for voluntary leaders hoping to represent all survivor opinion publicly.

An early reconstruction of the Independent Inquiry into Child Sexual Abuse, founded in 2014 to explore historic cases, further probed this challenge. In 2014, the *Guardian* reported that panel members believed Home Secretary Theresa May was giving disproportionate influence to 'a vocal minority instead of the majority of abuse survivors', and that a 'small number of individuals and survivor groups' were exercising undue influence, particularly through their work with 'social media and the press'.[136] In the early twenty-first century, therefore, as survivor groups further developed and became empowered partners in forming media relationships, the role of specific groups and leaders also faced new critique. This critique raised questions of representativeness and inclusion, but was also in part a revived challenge to the power and authority of experiential and emotional expertise.

Childhood and Survivorship

A complex relationship emerged between the constructed rights and responsibilities of survivors and children. On the one hand, interest in the experiences and emotions of children—traced in Chaps. 3 and 4 of this book—had lain the groundwork for professions and policy to listen to, and care about, the experiences and emotions of survivors in later years. Certain channels that were established in the 1980s for children, such as ChildLine, were later used by adult survivors looking to seek help and to raise awareness of the long-term effects of abuse. At the same time, the accounts provided by survivors in the 1990s and 2000s also demonstrated the limitations to the shifts traced in Chaps. 3 and 4. While there was increasing rhetoric from charities and social policy about 'listening to children' over these years, later survivor testimonies demonstrated that many were unable to report abuse in these decades, nor to discuss their experiences publicly.

In the 1990s and 2000s, policy researchers looking for participants often suggested that survivors would be driven by a desire to protect future children, or that they even owed these children a duty of care, as part of a related community. Many survivors echoed this sentiment. Replying to Woodward and Wattam, one adult wrote that while 'we can't undo what happened to us', 'we can do a lot more to protect future generations'.[137] Providing evidence to the Home Affairs select committee in 2002, another survivor argued for the prosecution of all historic perpetrators, because they posed 'a threat to other innocent children'.[138] Politicians echoed the idea that survivors discussed their experiences and emotions in order to help future children, and that these testimonies could be mobilised to prevent future cases.[139]

While concern for present and future children was a significant driver for participation in social policy, survivors did not only speak out seeking to protect present and future children. Survivors also at times discussed their experiences and emotions as part of an individual therapeutic process, and to encourage other adults to seek help. Further, voluntary survivor organisations also sought to shift the focus of social policy and academic research from children alone towards analysis of the lifelong effects of abuse and neglect—areas which had been overlooked from the 1960s. Testimonies collated and published by voluntary organisations provided space for survivors to discuss their childhood experiences and the ways in which they had processed these as adults.[140] To an extent, survivor groups felt that they faced a more challenging task than children's charities in forcing publics to confront these issues, and that their cause was less 'fashionable' than that of the 'cosy, cuddly charities' which focused on children.[141] This tension between self-protection and protecting future children was also felt by individuals: one contributor to Armstrong's collection, for example, grappling with her decision to leave her children, asked, 'what about my needs as a child? What about my needs?'[142]

By presenting the long-term effects of violence, testimonies provided by adult survivors changed the public and political perceptions of children facing abuse, emphasising that surviving children may face long-term emotional, physical, and mental issues which would require significant support. Testimonies in this area called for a reconceptualisation of childhood—to be approached as a transient state and assessed as part of a broader process of lifelong development, rather than separated off from thinking about adulthood. In this way, survivor campaigning challenged the broader post-war fixation on segregating childhood by 'stage' or 'category', visible, for example, in the proliferation of new categories in childhood psychology and education.[143] This focus on approaching childhood as a transient state echoed work by Kidscape, studied in Chap. 4, in providing specific but interlinked support for children in infancy, childhood, adolescence, and as adults. Notions of survivorship therefore, and the sharing of lived experiences and emotions by survivors, came to the fore significantly later than the testimonies of children, but also challenged understandings of childhood.

Conclusion

Decades after children's voices were sought out by charities, social policymakers, and media in the 1970s and 1980s, in the late 1990s, and particularly from the 2000s, adults who had been abused in childhood—survivors—began to be heard. Survivor representatives themselves in part drove the process through which these individuals were increasingly sought out, listened to, and portrayed. Survivors took the lead in describing their experiences and emotions anew in literature, to agony aunts, and in newspaper interviews. Voluntary organisations were significant in providing a forum through which survivors could access peer support and contribute to political and media lobbying, and new groups emerged which cross-cut categories of self-help, identity politics, and 'professional' non-governmental organisations. The process through which survivors became visible was also, however, shaped by the interests and influences of, for example, publishing houses, journalism, academia, and social policy. Self-expression was also governed and narrated through the broader analytical categories of 'victim' and 'survivor', though these classifications were challenged, as well as adopted and changed, by voluntary groups.

Through these multiple fora, public and political attention turned to the long-term effects of child abuse for the first time in the 1990s and 2000s. The experiences and emotions of survivors became forms of expertise, consciously mobilised by survivors and sought out by media and policy. By the late 1990s, survivor representatives sat on consultative panels of select committees, large charities, and public inquiries, and also—at times in conflict with these formal roles—criticised social policy, political appointments, and judicial decisions through television and print media.

More than the parent organisations studied in Chap. 6, survivor groups became incorporated into a broad landscape of supportive statutory and voluntary services, and they provided significant levels of peer support by phone and through the new medium of the internet. Nonetheless, notable gaps in provision for survivor welfare remained, and the inclusion of survivor representatives in social policy was at times tokenistic, temporary, and not reflected in policy change.

This chapter—and this argument—raises a significant question: when experience and emotion developed as forms of expertise, whose experiences and emotions became powerful, and in which spaces, and why? Notably, women were the first and primary users of private spaces to discuss and disclose historic abuse: social surveys, agony aunt columns, and peer support phone lines. Both male and female survivor representatives became visible speaking publicly about their experiences through literature, public policy inquiries, and media. While the child was often addressed as genderless in the educational materials studied in Chap. 4, therefore, by the 1990s and 2000s the gender of survivors shaped how they responded to abuse on a personal level, but also whether this response was made in private or public spaces, and as a consumer, peer supporter, recipient of therapy, or prominent spokesperson. While experts by experience and emotion became prominent in the late twentieth century, researchers and policy-makers rarely made assessment of which demographic groups they were empowering—or disempowering, nor of the extent to which experiential experts were drawn from specific class, gender, ethnic, or age groups. The next chapter of this book, its conclusion, considers inclusion and diversity alongside other key issues for the future of child protection work, and discusses how looking to history can reframe present thinking.

Notes

1. Deborah Cohen, *Family Secrets: The Things We Tried To Hide* (London: Penguin, 2014), 75–76, 196; Martin Francis, 'Tears, Tantrums, and Bared Teeth: The Emotional Economy of Three Conservative Prime Ministers, 1951–1963', *Journal of British Studies*, 41 (2002): 354–387.
2. See on this: Paul Lerner, and Mark S. Micale, 'Trauma, Psychiatry, and History: A Conceptual and Historiographical Introduction' in Paul Lerner and Mark S. Micale (eds) *Traumatic Pasts: History, Psychiatry, and Trauma in the Modern Age, 1870–1930* (Cambridge: Cambridge University Press, 2009), 1–27, Edgar Jones and Simon Wessley, 'A Paradigm Shift in the Conceptualization of for the future of psychiatric

canon and practice', *Journal of Anxiety Disorders*, 21 (2007): 164–175. For a discussion of the history and limitations of the Diagnostic and Statistical Manual, please see: Shadia Kawa and James Giordano, 'A brief historicity of the Diagnostic and Statistical Manual of Mental Disorders: Issues and implications for the future of psychiatric canon and practice', *Philosophy, Ethics, and Humanities in Medicine*, 7, no. 2 (2012).

3. Andrew Stanway, 'Preface', Oralee Wachter and Dr Andrew Stanway, *No More Secrets for Me: Helping to Safeguard Your Child Against Sexual Abuse* (London: Penguin Books, 1986), 7; Robin Lenett with Bob Crane, *It's OK to Say No!: A Parent/Child Manual for the Protection of Children* (2nd edition, London: Thorsons Publishing Group, 1986), 7.
4. Deidre Sanders, *The Woman book of love and sex* (London: Sphere, 1985).
5. Elizabeth Butler-Sloss, *Report of the Inquiry into Child Abuse in Cleveland 1987* (London: Her Majesty's Stationery Office, 1988), 11.
6. Ibid., 11.
7. Ibid., 11.
8. Hilary Freeman, 'When the past won't go away', *Independent on Sunday*, 8 August 1999, 4; Kidscape Offices, London (hereafter KO), Kidscape Annual Report 1996–7, March 1997, 1; KO, Kidscape Annual Report 1991–2, 'About KIDSCAPE….', March 1992, 3; Michele Elliott, *Dealing with Child Abuse: The Kidscape Training Guide* (London: Kidscape, 1989), 84; Shy Keenan and Sara Payne, *Where Angels Fear: two courageous women bringing hope out of horror* (London: Hodder & Stoughton, 2009), 21. ChildLine discusses receiving calls from adults—both who were concerned about the welfare of a child but also who were seeking help—in the following annual reports: Bodleian Library (hereafter Bod), P.C06240, ChildLine Annual Reports 1991–1994, *Annual Report 1994*, 'How ChildLine works', 7; Bod, P.C06240, ChildLine Annual Reports 1991–1994, *Annual Report 1993*, 'How ChildLine works', 5.
9. House of Commons, Home Affairs Committee, *The Conduct of Investigations into Past Cases of Abuse in Children's Homes, Fourth Report of Session 2001–2, Volume II: Memoranda*, 51.
10. Lisa O'Kelly, 'Cries from a nation's troubled psyche', *The Observer*, 3 October 1993, 25; Janie Lawrence, 'Agony aunts have problems too', *Independent*, 10 December 1992; Ruth Fisher, 'Agony aunts aid child victims', *The Observer*, 26 September 1993, 25.
11. Statistic created by examination of Factiva, a database collating over 32,000 newspapers, journals, and newswires. See, for example: Deidre Sanders, 'Dear Deidre: How can I tell husband about sex abuse?', *The Sun*, 16 May 1999, 31; Deirdre Sanders, 'Bride won't make love: Dear Deidre', *The Sun*, 15 June 2002, 38; Deidre Sanders, 'Dear Deidre', *The Sun*, 12 June 2002, 33; Deidre Sanders, 'Dear Deidre', *The Sun*, 14 January 2001, 43; Deidre Sanders, 'Dear Deidre: Overcoming child

abuse', *The Sun*, 31 December 2002, 43; Deidre Sanders, 'Dear Deidre: Abuse agony', *The Sun*, 7 February 2003, 39; Deidre Sanders, 'Dear Deidre: Hurt by family secret', *The Sun*, 3 June 2003, 39.

12. 'So hurt by evil abuser', *The Sun*, 6 December 2006.
13. Deidre Sanders, 'Longing to share my abuse secret', *The Sun*, 7 November 2006.
14. 'Overcoming child abuse', *The Sun*, 31 December 2002.
15. O'Kelly, 'Cries from a nation's troubled psyche', 25.
16. Ibid., 25.
17. Virginia Ironside, *Problems! Problems! Confessions of an Agony Aunt* (London: Robson Books Ltd, 1991), 75–76.
18. Ironside, *Problems! Problems!*, 87; Lawrence, 'Agony aunts have problems too'. For a later account, see: Deidre Sanders, 'Parents abused sis as well as me', *The Sun*, 25 June 2007.
19. Lucy Cavendish, 'Agony Aunts interviewed', Lucy Cavendish Counselling, 21 July 2017 <http://www.lucycavendishcounselling.com/2017/07/21/agony-aunts-interviewed/> (29 January 2018).
20. O'Kelly, 'Cries from a nation's troubled psyche', 25.
21. Ironside, *Problems! Problems!*, 111.
22. Lawrence, 'Agony aunts have problems too'; O'Kelly, 'Cries from a nation's troubled psyche', 25.
23. Ironside, *Problems! Problems!*, 108–109; Lawrence, 'Agony aunts have problems too'; O'Kelly, 'Cries from a nation's troubled psyche', 25.
24. Cohen, *Family Secrets*, 179.
25. Romi Bowen and Angela Hamblin, 'Sexual Abuse of Children', *Spare Rib*, May 1981, Issue 106.
26. Louise Armstrong, *Kiss Daddy Goodnight: A Speak-Out on Incest* (New York: Simon & Schuster, 1978), back cover, 15, 264.
27. Ibid, back cover.
28. See for example: Julie Bindel, 'Louise Armstrong', *Guardian*, 24 September 2008.
29. Armstrong, *Kiss Daddy Goodnight*, 65, 67, 68, 69, 70, 116.
30. Ibid., 116.
31. Louise Armstrong, 'Incest: A feminist core issue that needs re-politizising' <http://www.arte-sana.com/articles/incest_feminist_core.htm> (1 May 2018).
32. Victoria Bates, '"Misery Loves Company": Sexual Trauma, Psychoanalysis and the Market for Misery', *Journal of Medical Humanities* (2012) 33, 61–81.
33. Ibid., 62.
34. Dave Pelzer, *A Child Called It: One Child's Courage to Survive* (Florida: Health Communications Inc., 1995); Dave Pelzer, *The Lost Boy: A Foster Child's Search for the Love of a Family* (Florida: Health Communications

Inc., 1997); Dave Pelzer, *A Man Named Dave: A Story of Triumph and Forgiveness* (New York: Plume, 2000).

35. Dave Pelzer, *A Child Called It* (London: Orion Books, 2009), 4–7.
36. Ibid., 41.
37. Brendan O'Neill, 'Misery lit ... read on', *BBC News*, 17 April 2007 <http://news.bbc.co.uk/1/hi/magazine/6563529.stm> (10 March 2014).
38. Reflecting on the reasons behind the declining popularity of misery lit, see: Bates, '"Misery Loves Company": 73–74. Contemporary journalists made challenges to—and reflections on—Pelzer's accounts, see, for example: Pat Jordon, 'Dysfunction For Dollars', *The New York Times Magazine*, 28 July 2002; Geraldine Bedell, 'Child abuse as entertainment', *The Observer*, 2 September 2001; 'A million-dollar industry called Dave', *Independent*, 10 February 2004.
39. Anne Rothe, *Popular Trauma Culture: Selling the Pain of Others in the Mass Media* (New Jersey, New Brunswick, 2011), 93.
40. Jordon, 'Dysfunction For Dollars'; Bedell, 'Child abuse as entertainment', 'A million dollar industry'.
41. See discussion in: Keenan and Payne, *Where Angels Fear*, 9. See also framing of Pelzer's books on their front covers, in terms of 'courage to survive' and 'triumph and forgiveness'—Pelzer, *A Child Called It*; Pelzer, *The Lost Boy*; Pelzer, *A Man Named Dave*. This framing is consistent across the American and British editions of these books. Contrastingly, for a set of contemporary newspaper accounts written by survivors who emphasised negative emotions and life outcomes, rather than narratives of resilience and survival, see: Madeline Bunting, 'Hush, hush, whisper who dares, 'I used to feel terribly angry with my mother but it's the abuser you should be angry with', *Guardian*, 22 March 1994, 9.
42. 'Can you get over child abuse?', *Daily Mail*, 29 April 1998, 59.
43. Jane Cousins Mills, '"Putting Ideas into Their Heads": Advising the Young', *Feminist Review*, 28 (1988), 164.
44. Bedell, 'Child abuse as entertainment'.
45. Ibid.
46. Mary Braid, 'Child abuse inquiry launched: Wide-ranging investigation to shape policy on preventing attacks', *The Independent*, 10 August 1994; Bodleian Law Library, KN 176.41 INQ 1996, Lord Williams, 'Foreword', National Commission of Inquiry into the Prevention of Child Abuse, *Childhood Matters: The Report of the National Commission of Inquiry into the Prevention of Child Abuse. Volume One: The Report*, (London: The Stationery Office, 1996), xi.
47. Sarah Boseley, 'Agony aunt on child abuse inquiry', *Guardian*, 10 August 1994, 6.

48. National Commission of Inquiry, *Childhood Matters*, xi–xii.
49. Corinne Wattam and Clare Woodward, '"And Do I Abuse My Children? No!": Learning About Prevention from People Who Have Experienced Child Abuse', *Childhood Matters. Volume Two*, 50–147.
50. Ibid., 50.
51. Ibid., 51.
52. In on online survey advertised and hosted by the BBC between November 2009 and April 2011, 47,869 individuals aged between 18 and 80 reported experiencing child sexual abuse and provided data about life satisfaction. Of these individuals, whose responses were analysed by three psychologists, 83.1 per cent identified as women (Claire F. Whitelock, Michael E. Lamb, and Peter J. Rentfrow, 'Overcoming Trauma: Psychological and Demographic Characteristics of Child Sexual Abuse Survivors in Adulthood', *Clinical Psychological Science*, 1, no. 4 (2013): 353–355).

    Other studies have managed to find equal numbers of male and female participants, for example, this study in American interviewed 64 women and 57 men. This gender-balanced sample was recruited through significant canvassing for participants in transport stations, shops, schools, libraries, churches, cafes, and social service agencies (Claire Burke Draucker, Donna S. Martsolf, Cynthia Roller, Gregory Knapik, Ratchneewan Ross, and Andrea Warner Stidham, 'Healing from Childhood Sexual Abuse: A Theoretical Model', *Journal of Child Sexual Abuse*, 20, no. 4 (2011): 435–466.
53. Wattam and Woodward, '"And Do I Abuse My Children? No!"', 56–147.
54. Ibid., 74.
55. Ibid., 115.
56. Ibid., 75–76.
57. Ibid., 80–81, 105, 137–139.
58. Ibid., 132–142.
59. Ibid., 132–142.
60. Christine Walby, Matthew Colton, and Maurice Vanstone, 'Victimization, Care and Justice: Reflections on the Experiences of Victims/Survivors Involved in Large-scale Historical Investigations of Child Sexual Abuse in Residential Institutions', *British Journal of Social Work*, 32 (2002), 546.
61. For an example of a parallel piece of work, looking to collect reflections from survivors, please see: Walby, Colton, and Vanstone, 'Victimization, Care and Justice', 546.
62. National Commission of Inquiry, *Childhood Matters*, p. 4.
63. *Hansard*, House of Lords, fifth series, vol. 578, col. 737; *Hansard*, House of Commons, sixth series, vol. 284, col. 267; *Hansard*, House of Commons, sixth series, vol. 291, col. 1036; *Hansard*, House of Lords,

fifth series, vol. 578, col. 742; David Brindle, 'Child abuse inquiry urges cabinet minister for children', *Guardian*, 22 October 1996, 10; Louise Jury, 'Child abuse inquiry launched by NSPCC', *Guardian*, 24 March 1994, 7; David Brindle, 'Public urged to act as abuse 'harms 1 million children a year"', *Guardian*, 23 October 1996, 2; C. J. Hobbs and P. L. Heywood, 'Doctors have a vital role in identifying children at risk of abuse', *British Medical Journal*, 1 March 1997, 314.

64. National Commission of Inquiry, *Childhood Matters*, 5–6.
65. Niall Dickson, 'For crying out loud: overleaf we outline new ways of helping parents and children', *Guardian*, 23 October 1996, 2–3.
66. Ibid., 547.
67. Ibid., 547.
68. Ibid., 547.
69. Home Affairs Committee, *The Conduct of Investigations into Past Cases of Abuse*, 50.
70. Ibid.
71. The sociologist Nancy Whittier has described the 'survivor movement' in America in *The Politics of Child Sexual Abuse: Emotions, Social Movements and the State* (Oxford: Oxford University Press, 2009). Her book is based on 40 interviews with activists from feminist and survivor groups, as well as 'counter-mobilisations' such as false memory groups. Groups which emerged in the American context include the Rape, Abuse and Incest National Network, established in 1994, Pandora's Project, established in 1999, and the National Association of Adult Survivors of Child Abuse, established in 2001. In Australia new groups included Adults Surviving Child Abuse, founded in 1995, and in Europe, Survivors Voice Europe, focused on abuse by the clergy, and isurvive, an online self-help community.
72. The Survivors Trust, 'About TST' <http://www.thesurvivorstrust.org/about-tst/> (22 April 2015).
73. 'CIS'ters—surviving rape & sexual abuse' <http://www.cisters.org.uk/> (6 May 2015); 'Male Survivors Trust' <http://malesurvivorstrust.org.uk/> (6 May 2015).
74. Keenan and Payne, *Where Angels Fear*, 27.
75. Sharon Hendry, We're the pervs' enemy … we will make THEIR lives a misery', *The Sun*, 10 April 2006.
76. Keenan and Payne, *Where Angels Fear*.
77. Heather Kirby, 'I was a child sex abuse victim', *The Times*, 22 November 1996, 16; Sophie Goodchild, 'Paedophilia in Britain: the victim's story', *Independent on Sunday*, 24 June 2007, 17.
78. Kirby, 'I was a child sex abuse victim', 16; Freeman, 'When the past won't go away', 4.

79. Kirby, 'I was a child sex abuse victim', 16.
80. Home Affairs Committee, *The Conduct of Investigations into Past Cases of Abuse*.
81. Keenan and Payne, *Where Angels Fear*, 25–6.
82. See for example: Freeman, 'When the past won't go away', 4.
83. Joanna Bourke, *The Story of Pain: From Prayer to Painkillers* (Oxford: Oxford University Press, 2014), 52.
84. See, for example, the variety of emotions within the artwork and poetry on the One in Four website, <http://www.oneinfour.org.uk/survivors-voices-uk/> (10 May 2018).
85. Companies House, National Association for People Abused in Childhood, Financial statements.
86. Alex Mold, 'Patient Groups and the Construction of the Patient-Consumer in Britain: An Historical Overview', *Journal of Social Policy*, 39 (2010): 509–528; Alex Mold and Virginia Berridge, *Voluntary Action and Illegal Drugs: Health and Society in Britain since the 1960s* (Basingstoke: Palgrave Macmillan, 2010), 22, 147; Crossley and Crossley, '"Patient' voices, social movements and the habitus': 1488.
87. Brief summaries of these measures and more are outlined in: 'The Government Policy Context', Catherine Itzin, *Tackling the Health and Mental Health Effects of Domestic and Sexual Violence and Abuse* (London: Department of Health, 2006), 19–29.
88. Ibid., 20.
89. See for example: Home Affairs Committee, *The Conduct of Investigations into Past Cases of Abuse*, 47–55.
90. Itzin, *Tackling the Health and Mental Health Effects of Domestic and Sexual Violence and Abuse*, 3, 4, 5, 7.
91. Ibid., 5.
92. Ibid., 60–61.
93. Ibid., 60–61.
94. Ibid., 60–61.
95. A Delphi Method consultation provides questionnaires to experts in a series of rounds (the Victims of Violence and Abuse Prevention Programme used three). The questionnaire responses are anonymised, and an analyst summarises the data found after each round and distributes this summary to all participants, with the hope that the experts will consider alternative viewpoints in the subsequent rounds and that the group will find a common answer. Catherine Itzin, Susan Bailey, and Arnon Bentovim, 'The effects of domestic violence and sexual abuse on mental health, *The Psychiatric Bulletin*, 32 (2008): 448–450.

96. Catherine Itzin, Ann Taket and Sarah Barter-Godfrey, *Domestic and sexual violence and abuse: tackling the health and mental health effects* (London: Routledge, 2010), 189–190.
97. Catherine Itzin, Ann Taket, and Sarah Barter-Godfrey, *Domestic and Sexual Violence and Abuse: Findings from a Delphi expert consultation on Therapeutic and Treatment Interventions with Victims, Survivors and Abusers, Children, Adolescents, and Adults* (Melbourne, Australia: Deakin University, 2010), vii.
98. Itzin, Taket and Barter-Godfrey, *Domestic and Sexual Violence and Abuse: Tackling the Health and Mental Health Effects*, 189–190.
99. Ibid., 189.
100. Itzin, Taket, and Barter-Godfrey, *Findings from a Delphi expert consultation*, v, 63–70.
101. Ibid., iv, v, 63–70.
102. Ibid., 95.
103. Ibid., 95.
104. Itzin, Taket and Barter-Godfrey, *Domestic and Sexual Violence and Abuse: Tackling the Health and Mental Health Effects*, 14.
105. Ibid., 1.
106. Itzin, *Tackling the Health and Mental Health Effects of Domestic and Sexual Violence and Abuse*, 1, 5, 13, 42.
107. Ibid., 11.
108. These limitations are echoed in concurrent literature about how patients have been involved in health policy reform. See, for example: Crossley and Crossley, "Patient' voices, social movements and the habitus': 1477–1489; Mold, 'Patient Groups and the Construction of the Patient-Consumer in Britain': 505–521.
109. Sara Payne, *Redefining justice: Addressing the needs of victims and witnesses* (London: Ministry of Justice, 2009), 5; Sandra Walklate, 'Courting Compassion: Victims, Policy, and the Question of Justice', *The Howard Journal of Criminal Justice*, 51 (2012): 109–121.
110. See, for example, the significance of using funds to improve statutory provisions for victims as documented in: *Cross Government Action Plan on Sexual Violence and Abuse* (London: Her Majesty's Stationery Office, 2007), 23–24.
111. 'NAPAC's Peter Saunders on "Big" Charities', *The Needle*, 24 October 2013 <https://theneedleblog.wordpress.com/2013/10/24/napacs-peter-saunders-on-big-charities/> (4 May 2015). For an academic analysis of the Jimmy Saville case, see: Chris Greer and Eugene McLaughin, 'The Sir Jimmy Savile scandal: Child sexual abuse and institutional denial at the BBC' *Crime, Media, and Culture* 9 (2013): 247–248, 252.

112. Joe Murphy and Humfrey Hunter, 'Attack by children's charities steps up the pressure on Hodge', *The Evening Standard*, 4 July 2003, 6; Peter Saunders, 'Letters to the editor', *The Times*, 23 September 2003; Matthew Norman, 'With a past like hers, Margaret needs a bit more humility', *Independent*, 10 March 2015; 'Rights of children and workers—Debate-The Register—Letter', *The Times*, 14 October 2002, 17; Geoffrey Lakeman, 'Paedo gets £5,500 for "stress', *Daily Mirror*, 3 March 2005, 1, 4.
113. 'Rights of children and workers', 17.
114. Murphy and Hunter, 'Attack by children's charities steps up the pressure on Hodge', 6; Saunders, 'Letters to the editor'; Matthew Norman, 'With a past like hers, Margaret needs a bit more humility', *Independent*, 10 March 2015 <http://www.independent.co.uk/voices/comment/with-a-past-like-hers-margaret-hodge-might-show-a-bit-more-humility-10098871.html> (15 June 2015).
115. Nick Speed, 'Hodge's care home blunders may have 'let in' paedophiles', *The Sunday Times*, 6 July 2003, 6.
116. Geoffrey Lakeman, 'Paedo gets £5,500 for "stress', *Daily Mirror*, 3 March 2005, 1, 4; James Slack, 'Human rights fiasco', *Daily Express*, 2 March 2005, 33; Chris Brooke, 'Euro Judges take pity on the paedophile who found it stressful waiting to face trial ... and award him £6,000', *Daily Mail*, 2 March 2005, 6.
117. Testimony from Worrall Thompson is at: 'Chef backs help for abuse victims', *Coventry Evening Telegraph*, 15 September 2003, 19; Emma Maier, 'Celebrity chef makers plea for child abuse helpline for adults', *Third Sector*, 17 September 2003, 1. Testimony from Hall is at: Alexa Baracaia, 'My tormet at hands of father, by Jerry Hall', *London Evening Standard*, 10 May 2006, 1; 'Jerry's agony', *The Sun*, 11 May 2006; 'Jerry: My abuse hell', *The Express*, 11 May 2006, 6.
118. Coverage is Ibid. Analysis from *Third Sector* is at: Penelope Gibbs, 'Communications—Press Celebrities can't do everything', *Third Sector*, 23 May 2007, 23.
119. Keenan, *Broken*, 255–269.
120. Clare Dwyer Hogg, 'To catch a child molester', *Independent on Sunday*, 10 February 2008, 47.
121. Louise Carpenter, 'I will survive', *The Observer*, 10 February 2008.
122. 'Wonder Woman: Shy Keenan', 6 September 2010 <http://www.youtube.com/watch?v=D4rEwituBus> (10 March 2014).
123. A Family Affair', *Newsnight*. Keenan further emphasised this critical position in subsequent newspaper coverage, telling the *Independent* in 2008 that when she was nine, she had told a social worker that her stepfather was sexually assaulting her on a regular basis. After talking to him, the

social worker wrote that Shy had forced herself upon him on her notes. This short statement, Keenan felt, 'influenced everyone else in authority I tried to tell.' (see Dwyer Hogg, 'To catch a child molester', 47).

124. Hendry, We're the pervs' enemy'.
125. 'A Family Affair', *Newsnight*.
126. Carpenter, 'I will survive'.
127. Description of programme and full transcript available at: Sarah Macdonald, 'Suing the Pope - Colm's story', *BBC News*, 29 January 2003.
128. Full transcript available at: Sarah Macdonald, 'Suing the Pope - Colm's story', *BBC News*, 29 January 2003.
129. Full transcript available at: Sarah Macdonald, 'Suing the Pope - Colm's story', *BBC News*, 29 January 2003.
130. 'Pope admits church lacked vigilance', *Al Jazeera English*, 16 September 2010, 2; 'Abuse victims call for Pope apology', *Daily Star*, 16 September 2010, 1.
131. Full transcript available at: Sarah Macdonald, 'Suing the Pope - Colm's story', *BBC News*, 29 January 2003.
132. Ibid.
133. 'Adver Comment ... Listen to those who know', *Swindon Advertiser*, 14 June 2007.
134. Ibid.
135. Home Affairs Committee, *The Conduct of Investigations into Past Cases of Abuse*, 52.
136. Nadia Khomami, 'Theresa May scraps panel for inquiry into child sex abuse, report says', *Guardian*, 21 December 2014 <http://www.theguardian.com/global/2014/dec/21/theresa-may-child-sex-abuse-inquiry-panel-scrapped> (16 May 2015).
137. Wattam and Woodward, 'And Do I Abuse My Children? No!', 1.
138. Home Affairs Committee, *The Conduct of Investigations into Past Cases of Abuse*, 51.
139. Williams, 'Foreword', *Childhood Matters. Volume Two*, p. vii; Meg Munn, 'Foreword', *Child Protection All Party Parliamentary Group: Seminar Series of Child Sexual Abuse* (London: Child Protection All Party Parliamentary Group, 2014), 3.
140. See, for example: One in Four, *Survivors' Voices: Breaking the silence on living with the impact of child sexual abuse in the family environment* (One in Four, November 2015).
141. Pennies versus Pounds, *Community Care*, 11 April 2007.
142. Armstrong, *Kiss Daddy Goodnight*, 116.

143. For a fascinating account of the emergence of one particular new category, autism, see: Bonnie Evans, *The metamorphosis of autism: A history of child development in Britain* (Manchester: Manchester University Press, 2017). In terms of the history of post-war education, see: David Crook, 'Local Authorities and Comprehensivisation in England and Wales, 1944–1974', *Oxford Review of Education*, 28, no. 2–3 (2002): 247–260; David Crook, 'Politics, politicians and English comprehensive schools', *Journal of the History of Education Society*, 42, no. 3 (2013): 365–380; A. H. Halsey, *Education, economy, and society: a reader in the sociology of education* (New York: Free Press; London: Collier-Macmillan, 1965); Richard Harris and Samuel Rose, 'Who benefits from grammar schools? A case study of Buckinghamshire, England', *Oxford Review of Education*, 39, no. 2 (2013): 151–171; Terry Haydn, 'The strange death of the comprehensive school in England and Wales, 1965–2002', *Research Papers in Education*, 19, no. 4 (2004): 415–432. For an account of 'staging and aging' in the early twentieth century, see: Clementine Beauvais, 'Ages and ages: the multiplication of children's 'ages' in early twentieth-century child psychology', *History of Education*, 45, no. 3 (2015): 304–318.

Open Access This chapter is licensed under the terms of the Creative Commons Attribution 4.0 International License (http://creativecommons.org/licenses/by/4.0/), which permits use, sharing, adaptation, distribution and reproduction in any medium or format, as long as you give appropriate credit to the original author(s) and the source, provide a link to the Creative Commons license and indicate if changes were made.

The images or other third party material in this chapter are included in the chapter's Creative Commons license, unless indicated otherwise in a credit line to the material. If material is not included in the chapter's Creative Commons license and your intended use is not permitted by statutory regulation or exceeds the permitted use, you will need to obtain permission directly from the copyright holder.

CHAPTER 8

Conclusion

Scholars of social policy, history, and media have outlined the ways in which prominent physicians, children's charities, and 'moral panics' have shifted the understandings of child abuse and guided child protection policy in the late twentieth century.[1] Yet, attention must also be paid to the activism and campaigning of people who were themselves personally affected by child abuse. This is a recent history. It was as recently as the 1960s that clinicians invented the battered child syndrome, hoping to draw public and political attention towards abused children. Discussions about this term between paediatric radiologists and the NSPCC were ingrained with concern about the emotional inner lives and lived experiences of children and parents. Nonetheless, children, parents, and survivors did not initially have public policy or media spaces in which to represent their own experiences in their own terms.

This began to change from the late 1960s and through the 1970s, as parents formed small self-help groups and made representations to Parliament, looking to make public the inner dynamics of family life. Likewise, sets of moral and media crises—notably about paedophilia and the death of Maria Colwell—brought to the fore questions of how parents, teachers, the state, and the voluntary sector should educate, protect, and empower children. The processes through which experience and emotion became forms of expertise, akin to and in tension with medical, legal, social work, and political forms of evidence, accelerated from the 1980s. It

© The Author(s) 2018

J. Crane, *Child Protection in England, 1960–2000*, Palgrave Studies in the History of Childhood,
https://doi.org/10.1007/978-3-319-94718-1_8

was in this decade that numerous new groups led by parents mobilised, alongside groups looking to represent children and to provide mechanisms for children's self-representation on the public stage and in everyday life. These new voluntary groups drew on and contributed to a reconfiguration of parents and children in professional discourse, whereby psychologists and social workers made new examination of the inner lives of families. Such organisations powerfully mobilised media interest in parent and child emotions and experiences—often representing their work in terms of tropes of ordinariness, respectability, and gendered emotion.

By exposing their experiences and emotions, parents found new levels of influence and shifted professional, media, and policy debates of the 1980s and 1990s. Many parent campaigners displayed professional and experiential forms of expertise, and clinicians and social workers, likewise, following pressure from parents, began to discuss their family, personal, and emotional lives in press. By the 1990s and 2000s, the processes through which experience and emotion became expertise shifted once again. Importantly, for the first time, survivor experiences became publicised through agony aunt columns, public policy research, and in memoirs. The fora through which survivor experience became visible, for the first time, extended earlier interests in, and mechanisms created to access, child and parent voices, and also reflected the development of trauma studies. While the experiential and emotional accounts offered by children, parents, and survivors were in part in tension with professional accounts, for example in the Cleveland case, from the 1990s new models of partnership also developed between statutory authorities, families, and media. In this context, and particularly under the New Labour governments, leaders of voluntary organisations were appointed on consultative panels and as tsars, exercised informal power in Tony Blair's extended 'sofa government', and made significant interventions through media collaboration.

By looking at this history, we see the extent to which experience and emotion have become specially valued, akin to and challenging ideas about professional expertise and evidence, and thus a growing influence in policy and upon broader social attitudes, in late twentieth-century Britain. This book thus traces the emergence of a politics of expertise, experience, and emotion, and builds a framework for later examinations of how, exactly, children, parents, and survivors navigated, used, rejected, and subverted new public and political spaces. Already from this book, it is clear that any types of experience and emotion which became significant were heavily mediated: by cultural narratives and structural hierarchies; by the work of campaign groups, press, policy, and psychological and sociological research; and by conversations between and among children, parents, and survivors. Moving into the twenty-first century, questions began to emerge about *whose* experiences and emotions were being disseminated publicly, and about the extent to which voluntary organisations were representative of broader identity-constituencies. Critical challenges were also raised in relation to survivor memoirs, with press asking whether the public sharing of experience was—and should be—therapeutic, mobilising, or entertaining.

The history of late twentieth-century Britain is incomplete without attention being paid to small-scale sites of family and voluntary activism, which transcend precise characterisation but which incorporated facets of self-help, identity politics, and non-governmental organisations. These forms of activism have blurred the lines between 'the public' and the long-standing sites of 'expertise' in medicine, law, and policy. Voluntary groups were often organised and led by people who themselves had personal experiences of the issues faced by their membership. Through the campaigning of these small organisations, some members of the public have themselves become 'expert'. This has, to some extent, always been characteristic of lay people drawn into the organisation of voluntary action, but status was now conferred as the result of personal experience and the description of emotion.

Voluntary organisations may have been characterised by their development of a form of experiential and emotional expertise, but the deployment of professional forms of knowledge was also important in establishing their influence. Nonetheless, the small size of these organisations, and their struggles for funding, enabled them to remain critical of government, media, and professions. The work of these groups thus adds nuance to theories in policy, sociology, and history that there was a 'gap' between 'the expert' and 'the public' in the post-war period, whereby 'experts' gained authority over 'the public' and the public felt less engaged in the processes of democracy.[2] Experiential and emotional forms of expertise have bridged gaps between expert and public thinking, and children, parents, and survivors have actively mobilised, deployed, and subverted these new forms of moral, social, and political authority.

Newness

The changes highlighted in this book have longer-term precedents. The historians Brian Harrison, Craig Calhoun, and Beth Breeze have all cautioned against seeing post-war trends in the voluntary sector as 'new', tracing older traditions in late nineteenth-century publicity campaigns, identity politics, and philanthropy.[3] Certainly, the small voluntary organisations traced in this book did not embody an unprecedented form of activism. The work of these groups echoed long-standing traditions of mutual aid and self-help. 'Figurehead leaders' have long been significant in the voluntary sector.[4] These groups sought to influence policy-makers and to seek funding from the state while also criticising contemporary governments, paralleling the long history of a 'moving frontier' between state, citizen, and voluntary organisations.[5] Concerns about child abuse likewise have faded in and out of concern through various historical periods, as has state and social work interest in identifying 'problem families'.[6] Even the idea that experience is a form of expertise has historical precedent: the belief in particular that mothering skills were derived from home life has functioned throughout the early and mid-twentieth century, for example.[7]

Nonetheless, some facets of the activisms traced in this book were peculiar to Britain in the late twentieth century. The successes of voluntary groups traced here were facilitated by growing political interest in public participation, which Alex Mold and Virginia Berridge have persuasively argued was distinctive to the post-war period and particularly to the 1990s and 2000s.[8] In the 1960s and 1970s, numerous activists mobilised to address issues of identity and inequality—a driving force behind the campaigning of many of these organisations.[9] The work of second-wave feminism in particular was significant in presenting the personal as political, and in encouraging multiple women to discuss and to challenge their experiences of violence. More broadly, the voluntary sector was flourishing in this period, also visible in the development of non-governmental organisations and new self-help groups, each presenting conflicting models of experience and expertise which underpinned the shifts explored by this book.[10]

Debates about child abuse and child protection also emerged in a renewed and distinct form from the 1960s. Importantly, new moral and political thinking about 'the family' inflected such debates—anxieties about an overt 'invasion' into family life and, by contrast, about the 'breakdown' of a former 'golden age'.[11] Notably, children, parents, and survivors themselves increasingly played a role in defining these concerns, in the contexts of newly emergent 'confessional cultures' and 'cultures of self-expression'.[12] Discussions about child abuse did not shift from a medical to a social problem over the late twentieth century, nor from concerns about physical to sexual to emotional violence. Rather, this book has demonstrated that these understandings were entwined. From the 1960s discussions, paediatricians immediately looked to assess the social and psychological causes of abuse and to make referrals to social agencies. Even by the mid-to-late 1980s, abuse had not solely become a social problem: paediatricians continued to discuss abuse as a 'preventable disease' or 'health problem'.[13] Discussions about child protection also interlinked thinking about the minds, bodies, and emotions of children, parents, and survivors, in terms of the physical effects of emotional turmoil, for example.

Another factor distinct to the late twentieth century, and which facilitated the influence of small voluntary groups, was changing communication technologies. Joining peer support meetings, telephone helplines became significant for children, parents, and survivors—a distinctly post-war medium first deployed by voluntary organisations including the Samaritans (established in 1953), Britain's Gay Switchboard (1974), and ChildLine (1986). Spokespeople for ChildLine spoke passionately about the 'value of voice' which, they contended, enabled children to further 'emotionally engage' with discussing their experiences.[14] In later years, groups seeking to connect with children, parents, and survivors also made substantial use of the internet, a new form of technology to the 1990s and 2000s which enabled people to make their experiences visible from their own homes, in private, and anonymously, if wanted. Survivor groups in particular created websites quickly and cheaply which were used to lobby and criticise political work, to bring people into contact with one another, and to share experiences and emotions expressed through art, poetry, and text.

Politically, the Premiership of Margaret Thatcher brought a distinct new set of contexts for the voluntary sector and for child protection. Attempts by government to 'tame' the voluntary sector, and to push large voluntary groups to meet centralised priorities, created new spaces for smaller organisations to flourish.[15] While popular individualism was a key ideological theme in this moment, new collective solutions also emerged in child protection, consciously forged by charities looking to promote group responses to family problems, and to counter a perceived 'breakdown' in community life.[16] The New Labour years likewise brought a distinct set of challenges and opportunities for voluntary groups. Individual figurehead leaders became the key focus of policy consultation. Nonetheless, Blair's governments also introduced new legislation, responding to the Sara Payne campaign, which looked to give parents more rights—and more responsibilities—in their own communities.

A set of entwined cultural, political, technological, and social shifts, therefore, made the narratives traced in this book distinct to the late twentieth century, and also revealing about the growing power of expertise, experience, and emotion in multiple public spaces. The narratives traced in this book were also distinct, in several ways, to modern *British* history. On the one hand, late twentieth-century North America and Western Europe also saw the development of child, parent, and survivor organisations.[17] Nonetheless, this book has also demonstrated how distinct cultural assumptions, political contexts, and modes of voluntary action shaped how family activism was realised in Britain, for example in terms of specific and historically grounded conceptions of public and private space, family life, confessional culture, respectability, and individuality. In the 1940s, 1950s, and 1960s, communities of clinicians—dermatologists, paediatric radiologists, and general practitioners—worked between Britain and America to conduct the initial pioneering research about the battered child syndrome. In subsequent decades, however, child, parent, and survivor groups only occasionally made direct contact with their American and European counterparts. The lack of contact reflected the limited resources held by these small groups but also, as this book has traced, a cultural assumption that child protection issues in Britain were 'unique', and that British people would discuss experience and emotion in a less explicit manner than those in America, for example.[18]

Contemporary Relevance

Today, it may seem obvious that politicians would declare their intentions to protect children from child abuse—as seen, for example, in the centrality of child protection to general election manifestos.[19] However, this book provides a timely reminder that it was only in recent years that child protection has featured so prominently on the political agenda. As demonstrated in the introduction, there was concern about 'cruelty to children' in the Victorian period and about child sexual abuse in the 1920s. Thereafter, awareness of, and concern about, child abuse was in part lost, particularly with the fracturing of the women's movement and as the NSPCC redirected its attentions elsewhere.[20]

Concerns about child abuse therefore may seem pervasive and powerful today but have faded in and out of social and political attention over time. In this context, policy-makers and professionals cannot afford to be complacent that continuing attention will be paid to the narratives of children, parents, and survivors. Indeed, another significant 'lesson' from this book is that while there has been a broad shift towards listening to explanations of experience since 1960, not all individuals have benefited. Looking to cases such as at Rotherham, where 1400 children were sexually abused for over 16 years between 1997 and 2013, demonstrates that further efforts must be made to enable children to describe their experiences, with particular attention paid to facilitating the testimonies of structurally disadvantaged children. Innovation may come from the voluntary sector, and historically small charities and campaign groups have made notable attempts to address structural inequalities, and to ensure that all children feel comfortable in reporting abuse. At the same time, voluntary groups and policy-makers have also shied away from analysing the relationships between child protection and power, and from confronting questions of *whose* experiences and emotions have become expertise over the late twentieth century.

In terms of future discussion, this book also demonstrates that political and public concerns about child protection have at once been deeply political but also framed as inherently non-political. With growing social and political concern about child abuse since 1960, interest groups have sought to delineate social changes—or even social groups—whom they dislike as threats to the protection of children. Historically, the New Right and Margaret Thatcher were significant in this regard. In 1974, Keith Joseph looked to tie the post-war settlement to a vision of Britain as a 'nation of hooligans and vandals, bullies and child-batterers, criminals and inadequates'.[21] A decade later as prime minister, Thatcher's famous speech in *Woman's Own*, which used the phrase 'no such thing as society', argued that the post-war welfare expansion had placed an increased financial burden on individual men, women, and families. This, Thatcher argued, had facilitated a *moral* decline whereby children who had 'the right to look to their parents for help, for comfort' were experiencing 'either neglect or worse than that, cruelty'.[22] These speeches sought to tie social concerns about child abuse to the post-war settlement; a critique which was remade by the *Daily Mail* in the 1970s and 1980s in terms of linking violence to the permissive society.[23]

Concerns about child protection have been deeply political—used to criticise the post-war settlement and permissive society, for example—but at the same time politicians and media have sought to present child protection as non-political and an 'all-party' concern.[24] While positioning child protection as non-political, politicians have also accused one another of using the topic politically, for 'cheap publicity stunts' or 'great public relations play'.[25] Recognising this politics, one survivor, testifying to the Home Affairs select committee in 2002, argued that he wanted his 'experiences to be used to inform' not 'as a weapon to score political points'.[26] A vision of child protection as non-political has enabled politicians to bypass questions about how different parties support statutory services and the voluntary sector. At the same time, this vision has also enabled small charities to offer relatively radical programmes, visible, for example, in terms of how Kidscape's educational materials bypassed concurrent New Right anxieties about sex education.

Overall, this book traces a politics of expertise, experience, and emotion which developed in the late twentieth century in Britain, and which was often mediated and represented by small voluntary organisations. These small groups collaborated with and criticised clinicians, social workers, and policy-makers, and in doing so carved out a new space in media and public policy in which the experiences and emotions of public groups would be sought out as 'expert'. These groups challenged conceptual and lived gaps between expert and public thinking and divisions between 'professional' and 'personal' forms of expertise. They reshaped ideas of child protection to include public consultation, though there were limits in the extent to which their work would be able to subvert long-standing power structures, with gender, race, ethnicity, class, and age continuing to inflect the ability of children, parents, and survivors to enforce change. Nonetheless, the development of an expertise and a politics grounded in experience and emotion was a significant phenomenon of late twentieth-century Britain, which must be explored, traced, and analysed across the fields of health, welfare, and social life.

Notes

1. Descriptions of the role of moral panic: Phillip Jenkins, *Intimate Enemies: Moral Panics in Contemporary Great Britain* (New York: Aldine de Gruyter, 1992); Ian Butler and Mark Drakeford, *Scandal, Social Policy and Social Welfare* (Bristol: Policy Press, 2006); Ian Butler and Mark Drakeford, *Social Work on Trial: The Colwell Inquiry and the State of Welfare* (Bristol: Policy Press, 2011); Beatrix Campbell, *Unofficial Secrets: Child Sexual Abuse: The Cleveland Case* (London: Virago, 1988), Stuart Bell, *When Salem Came to the Boro, the true story of the Cleveland Child Abuse Crisis* (London: Pan Books, 1988); Mica Nava, 'Cleveland and the Press: Outrage and Anxiety in the Reporting of Child Sexual Abuse', *Feminist Review*, 28 (1988): 103–121.

   Discussion of development of social policies around child protection and child welfare: Harry Hendrick, *Children, Childhood and English Society, 1880–1990* (Cambridge: Cambridge University Press, 1997), 60–65; Harry Hendrick, *Child Welfare: Historical Dimensions, Contemporary*

Debate (Bristol: Policy Press, 2003); Nigel Parton, *The Politics of Child Protection: Contemporary Developments and Future Directions* (Basingstoke: Palgrave Macmillan, 2014); Harry Ferguson, *Protecting Children in Time: Child Abuse, Child Protection and the Consequences of Modernity* (Basingstoke: Palgrave Macmillan, 2004).

Description of the role of large children's charities, provided by themselves, and by care-leavers: Terry Philpot, *NCH: Action for Children: The Story of Britain's Foremost Children's Charity* (Oxford: Lion Books, 1994); Winston Fletcher, *Keeping the Vision Alive: The Story of Barnardo's 1905–2005* (Essex: Barnardos, 2005); Dennis Burnier-Smith, *Thomas John Barnardo, His Life, Homes and Orphanages: A Short History* (Milton Keynes: AuthorHouseUK, 2010).

2. Yaron Ezrahi, *The Descent of Icarus: Science and the Transformation of Contemporary Democracy* (Massachusetts: Harvard University Press, 1990); Frank Fischer, *Democracy and Expertise: Reorienting Policy Inquiry* (Oxford: Oxford University Press, 2009); Anthony Giddens, *The Consequences of Modernity* (California: Stanford University Press, 1990); Matthew Hilton, James McKay, Nicholas Crowson and Jean-François Mouhot, *The Politics of Expertise: How NGOs Shaped Modern Britain* (Oxford: Oxford University Press, 2013), 7–8.
3. Brian Harrison, *Drink and the Victorians: The Temperance Question in England 1815–1872* (London, 1971), as cited in Justin Davis Smith, 'The voluntary tradition: Philanthropy and self-help in Britain 1500–1945', in (eds) Justin Davis Smith, Colin Rochester, and Rodney Hedley, *An Introduction to the Voluntary Sector* (London: Routledge, 1994), 15; Craig Calhoun, '"New Social Movements" of the Early Nineteenth Century', *Social Science History*, 17 (1993): 385–427; Beth Breeze, 'Is There a "New Philanthropy?", in Colin Rochester, George Campbell Gosling, Alison Penn and Meta Zimmeck (eds) *Understanding the Roots of Voluntary Action: Historical Perspectives on Current Social Policy* (Brighton: Sussex Academic Press, 2011): 182–195.
4. Clare Mulley, *The Woman Who Saved the Children: A Biography of Eglantyne Jebb the Founder of Save the Children* (London: OneWorld Publications, 2009); E. Moberly Bell, *Octavia Hill: A biography* (London: Constable, 1942); Nancy Boyd, *Josephine Butler, Octavia Hill, Florence Nightingale. Three Victorian women who changed their world* (Oxford: Oxford University Press, 1982). See also: Eve Colpus, *Female Philanthropy in the Interwar World: Between Self and Other* (London: Bloomsbury, 2018); Gareth Millward, 'How much importance should we put on "great (wo)men"?', Voluntary Action History Society Blog, 10 June 2013 <http://www.vahs.org.uk/2013/06/how-much-importance-should-we-put-on-great-women/> (1 April 2015).

5. See: Geoffrey Finlayson, 'A Moving Frontier: Voluntarism and the State in British Social Welfare', *Twentieth-Century British History*, 1 (1990): 183–206.
6. See: John Welshman, *Underclass: a history of the excluded since 1880* (2nd edition, London: Bloomsbury, 2013); John Welshman, 'Troubles and the family: changes and continuities since 1943', *Social Policy and Society*, 16, no. 1 (2017): 109–117; John Welshman, *From Transmitted Deprivation to Social Exclusion: Policy, Poverty, and Parenting* (Bristol: Policy Press, 2007); Michael Lambert, '*Problem families and the post-war welfare state in the North West of England, 1943–74* (PhD thesis, Lancaster University, 2017).
7. Angela Davis, 'Oh no, nothing, we didn't learn anything',: sex education and the preparation of girls for motherhood, c. 1930–1970', *History of Education*, 37, no. 5 (2008): 663.
8. Alex Mold, 'Patient Groups and the Construction of the Patient-Consumer in Britain: An Historical Overview', *Journal of Social Policy*, 39 (2010): 510; Alex Mold, 'Making the Patient-Consumer in Margaret Thatcher's Britain', *The Historical Journal* 54 (2011): 509–528; Alex Mold and Virginia Berridge, *Voluntary Action and Illegal Drugs: Health and Society in Britain since the 1960s* (Basingstoke: Palgrave Macmillan, 2010), 147–149.
9. See New Social Movement theory: Adam Lent, *British Social Movements since 1945: Sex, Colour, Peace and Power* (Basingstoke: Palgrave Macmillan, 2001); David Meyer and Sidney Tarrow (eds), *The Social Movement Society: Contentious Politics for a New Century* (Lanham, Maryland: Rowman & Littlefield, 1998); Sidney Tarrow, *Power in Movement: Social Movement and Contentious Politics* (Cambridge: Cambridge University Press, 1998); Nick Crossley, *Making Sense of Social Movements* (Buckingham, Philadelphia: Open University Press, 2002). See also historical works which discuss a variety of sites of activism related to inequality and identity: Pat Thane (ed.), *Unequal Britain. Equalities in Britain since 1945* (London: Bloomsbury, 2010); Rebecca Jennings, '"The most uninhibited party they'd ever been to": The Postwar Encounter between Psychiatry and the British Lesbian, 1945–1971'. *Journal of British Studies*, 47 (2008): 883–904; Lucy Robinson, *Gay men and the left in post-war Britain: How the personal got political* (Manchester: Manchester University Press, 2007); Matthew Waites, 'Lesbian, Gay and Bisexual NGOs in Britain: Past, Present and Future', in Nicholas Crowson, James McKay, and Matthew Hilton, (eds) *NGOs in Contemporary Britain: Non-state Actors in Society and Politics since 1945* (Basingstoke: Palgrave Macmillan, 2009), 95–112; Stephen Brooke, *Sexual politics: Sexuality, family planning and the British Left from the 1880s to the present day* (Oxford: Oxford University Press,

2011); Gareth Millward, 'Social Security Policy and the Early Disability Movement—Expertise, Disability and the Government, 1965–77', *Twentieth Century British History*, 26 (2015): 274–297; Sue Bruley, 'Consciousness-Raising in Clapham: Women's Liberation as "Lived Experience" in South London in the 1970s', *Women's History Review*, 22 (2013): 717–738; Bridget Lockyer, 'An Irregular Period? Participation in the Bradford Women's Liberation Movement', *Women's History Review*, 22 (2013): 643–657; Sarah Browne, 'A Veritable Hotbed of Feminism: Women's Liberation in St Andrews, Scotland, c. 1968–1979', *Twentieth Century British History*, 23 (2012): 100–123; Sarah Browne, *The women's liberation movement in Scotland* (Manchester: Manchester University Press, 2014); Jeska Rees, 'A Look Back At Anger: the Women's Liberation Movement in 1978', *Women's History Review*, 19 (2010): 337–356.

10. On non-governmental organisations, see: Hilton, McKay, Crowson and Mouhot, *The Politics of Expertise*; Matthew Hilton, Nick Crowson, Jean-Francois Mouhot and James McKay, *A Historical Guide to NGOs in Britain: Charities, Civil Society and the Voluntary Sector since 1945* (Basingstoke: Palgrave Macmillan, 2012); Matthew Hilton, 'Politics is Ordinary: Non-governmental Organizations and Political Participation in Contemporary Britain', *Twentieth Century British History*, 22 (2011): 230–268.

    There are many definitions of self-help, peer support, and mutual aid in the voluntary sector. See, for example, on therapeutic communities for drug users: Mold and Berridge, *Voluntary Action and Illegal Drugs*, 19–22, 26. On playgroups, please see: Angela Davis, *Pre-school childcare in England, 1939–2010* (Manchester: Manchester University Press, 2015), Chapter Four: Playgroups. Discussing self-help groups for multiple sclerosis patients, Malcolm Nicholas and George Lowis, 'The early history of the Multiple Sclerosis Society of Great Britain and Northern Ireland: A socio-historical study of lay/practitioner interaction in the context of a medical charity', *Medical History*, 46 (2002): 141–174.

11. Deborah Cohen, *Family Secrets: The Things We Tried To Hide* (London: Penguin, 2014); Pat Thane, 'Family Life and "Normality" in Postwar British Culture', in Richard Bessel and Dirk Schumann (eds) *Life After Death. Approaches to a Cultural and Social History of Europe during the 1940s and 1950s* (Cambridge: Cambridge University Press, 2003), 193–210.
12. Cohen, *Family Secrets*, 179; Adrian Bingham, *Sex. Private Life, and the British Popular Press 1918–1978* (Oxford: Oxford University Press, 2009), 75–76; Martin Francis, 'Tears, Tantrums, and Bared Teeth: The Emotional Economy of Three Conservative Prime Ministers, 1951–1963', *Journal of British Studies*, 41 (2002): 354–387.

13. David Nicholson-Lord, 'Study shows child abuse as health problem', *The Times*, 1 December 1984, 3; Roger Scott and John Woodcock, 'The Doctor in Child Abuse Storm', *Daily Mail*, 24 June 1987, 1.
14. John Cameron, in '30 Years of ChildLine (1986–2016)', Witness seminar, held 1 June 2016 at the BT Tower, London, held at Modern Records Centre, Coventry, 45.
15. See: Andrew Gamble, *The Free Economy and the Strong State: The Politics of Thatcherism* (Basingstoke: Palgrave Macmillan, 1994), 14; Martin Durham, *Sex and Politics: The Family and Morality in the Thatcher Years* (Basingstoke: Palgrave Macmillan, 1991). In terms of changes around the voluntary sector in the 1980s and under Thatcherism see: Nicholas Crowson, Matthew Hilton, James McKay and Herjeet Marway, 'Witness Seminar: The Voluntary Sector in 1980s Britain', *Contemporary British History*, 25, no. 4 (2011): 499–519.
16. For a fascinating discussion of the roots of popular individualism, and its realisation in 'telling stories', see: Emily Robinson, Camilla Schofield, Florence Sutcliffe-Braithwaite, and Natalie Thomlinson, 'Telling Stories about Post-war Britain: Popular Individualism and the 'Crisis' of the 1970s', *Twentieth Century British History*, 28:2 (2017): 268–304.
17. For discussion of parent advocacy groups against false accusations of abuse in the American context, see: Gary Alan Fine, 'Public Narration and Group Culture: Discerning Discourse in Social Movements', Hank Johnston and Bert Klandermans (eds) *Social Movements and Culture* (Minnesota: University of Minnesota Press, 1995), 138; Lela Costin, Howard Jacob Karger, and David Stoez, *The Politics of Child Abuse in America* (New York: Oxford University Press, 1996), 35. For discussion of survivor groups in the American context, and interviews with activists, see: Nancy Whittier, *The Politics of Child Sexual Abuse: Emotions, Social Movements and the State* (Oxford: Oxford University Press, 2009).
18. Idea of 'imported problem' raised by Michele Elliott, the leader of Kidscape, in a retrospective interview: Nancy Stewart Books, 'Interview with Michele Elliot, Founder of British Charity, Kidscape', 16 February 2011 <http://nancystewartbooks.blogspot.co.uk/2011/02/interview-with-michele-elliott-founder.html> (2 January 2015). Discussing how Dave Pelzer's book, an autobiographical account of abuse, was packaged and sold in Britain and America, see: Geraldine Bedell, 'Child abuse as entertainment', *The Observer*, 2 September 2001.
19. In terms of the 2015 election, see: *The Labour Party Manifesto 2015* <http://www.labour.org.uk/page/-/BritainCanBeBetter-TheLabourPartyManifesto2015.pdf> (24 April 2015), pp. 45, 51; *The Conservative Party Manifesto 2015* <https://www.conservatives.com/manifesto> (24 April 2015), p. 33; *Liberal Democrat Manifesto 2015* <http://www.

libdems.org.uk/read-the-full-manifesto> (24 April 2015), p. 1; *Scottish National Party Manifesto 2015* <http://www.snp.org/sites/default/files/page/file/04_16d_snp_election_manifesto_290x280x.pdf> (24 April 2015), p. 3; *The UKIP Manifesto 2015* <http://www.ukip.org/manifesto2015> (24 April 2015), p. 27.
20. Parton, *The Politics of Child Protection*, 21.
21. Vernon Bogdanor, 'Sir Keith Joseph and the Market Economy', Gresham College Lecture, 21 May 2013, <http://www.gresham.ac.uk/lectures-and-events/sir-keith-joseph-and-the-market-economy> (17 December 2013).
22. Margaret Thatcher Foundation Archives, 'Interview for Woman's Own ("no such thing as society")', 23 September 1987.
23. 'A giant stride on the road to disaster', *Daily Mail*, 24 August 1977, 6; Reginald Thomas. 'This evil trend', *Daily Mail*, 5 September 1977, 22; Dennis Stevens, 'Permissive perils', *Daily Mail*, 29 August 1983, 22.
24. Hansard, House of Commons, Sixth Series, 19 December 1988, vol. 144, col. 46; Hansard, House of Commons, Sixth Series, 15 May 1989, vol. 153, col. 142–148.
25. Hansard, House of Commons, sixth series, vol. 62, col. 975, 27 June 1984; Hansard, House of Commons, sixth series, vol. 125, col. 134, 12 January 1988.
26. House of Commons, Home Affairs Committee, *The Conduct of Investigations into Past Cases of Abuse in Children's Homes, Fourth Report of Session 2001–2, Volume II: Memoranda*, 53.

Open Access This chapter is licensed under the terms of the Creative Commons Attribution 4.0 International License (http://creativecommons.org/licenses/by/4.0/), which permits use, sharing, adaptation, distribution and reproduction in any medium or format, as long as you give appropriate credit to the original author(s) and the source, provide a link to the Creative Commons license and indicate if changes were made.

The images or other third party material in this chapter are included in the chapter's Creative Commons license, unless indicated otherwise in a credit line to the material. If material is not included in the chapter's Creative Commons license and your intended use is not permitted by statutory regulation or exceeds the permitted use, you will need to obtain permission directly from the copyright holder.

Index[1]

[1] Note: Page numbers followed by 'n' refer to notes.

© The Author(s) 2018

J. Crane, *Child Protection in England, 1960–2000*, Palgrave Studies in the History of Childhood,
https://doi.org/10.1007/978-3-319-94718-1

T

V

X